Private Planet

Private Planet

Corporate plunder and the fight back

David Cromwell

JON CARPENTER

Our books may be ordered from bookshops or (post free) from
Jon Carpenter Publishing, Alder House, Market Street, Charlbury,
England OX7 3PH

Credit card orders should be phoned or faxed to 01689 870437
or 01608 811969

First published in 2001 by
Jon Carpenter Publishing
Alder House, Market Street, Charlbury, Oxfordshire OX7 3PH
☎ 01608 811969

© 2001

ISBN 1 897766 62 9

Printed in England by J. W. Arrowsmith Ltd., Bristol

Contents

To Foske, Sean and Stuart,
and in loving memory of
Ruby Cromwell (1908-1984)

Acknowledgements

First and foremost, thank you to Foske for your love and support, and to our sons Sean and Stuart for endless challenges and inspiration. Grateful thanks also to my parents and 'wee' brother Kenneth for putting up with me all these years, and to my grandparents, especially Gran who was an early source of encouragement.

I am heartened that Jon Carpenter had the vision and, frankly, the nerve to take on this book – thank you.

A special thank you to David Edwards for his support above and beyond any feasible call of duty. I am indebted to those who not only waded through draft chapters, but provided helpful and encouraging comments: Katharine Ainger, Adrian Bebb, Amanda Brace, Peter Challenor, Barry Coates, Bryan Cromwell, Eileen Cromwell, Carl Davies, Jon Dunkley, Light-Fingered Fred, Steve Hall, Duncan McLaren, Rebecca McQuillan, Nick Milton, Doug Parr, Matt Phillips, Andrew Rowell, Matthew Spencer and John Spottiswoode. Helpful souls who provided additional information and support include John Ashton, Trevor Guymer, Caspar Henderson, Alison Hill, Mark Johnston, Chris Keene, Rob Lake, Peter Lang, Caroline Lucas, Aubrey Meyer, Jim Scott, Ian Taylor, Paul Vickers, John Walker and Anna White. Countless additional activists, campaigners, writers and others have inspired me and shaped my thinking; many of them are quoted in this book, though not all. I could not have written this book without them. The book's remaining errors, limitations and quirks remain my responsibility.

Finally, I hope that you, the reader, will be encouraged to learn more and, perhaps, to take action. The future depends on it.

Dark Heart

Preface by David Edwards

Defining globalisation

The corporate attempt to privatise the planet detailed in this book is often described using neutral-sounding words and phrases such as 'globalisation', 'neoliberal' and 'free trade'. Defining this corporate programme – as an attempt to reduce restrictions on foreign ownership, to reduce restrictions on direct foreign investment and to eliminate all restrictions on the movement of international capital – can similarly leave the reader with the impression that we are dealing here with a process that is ethically neutral, or perhaps even benign. It takes considerable effort to strip away the euphemism and jargon to reveal the reality.

Globalisation, in essence, involves the subordination of the well being of people and planet to maximised short-term corporate profit. To refine this further, we can say that it is a system intended to permit a small number of wealthy people to generate more wealth at the expense of the vast majority of poorer, powerless people now and far into the future.

Although media analysts like to present globalisation as shiny and new, it must realistically be seen as the latest expression of a long-standing and very ugly historical process. The Third World, to take the most obvious example, has long been perceived as a vulnerable source of cheap human and natural resources by the militarily and economically superior nations of the 'West'. No discussion was ever entered into, no Rousseauvian social contract was signed: military and economic power were employed to extract maximum profit at minimum cost. What began with Columbus as a crude quest for gold on Hispaniola in 1492, became a 'civilising mission' under Britain, a matter of 'manifest destiny' in the United States, and now, even more disingenuously, an attempt to raise the living standards of all citizens as part of a 'global village'.

Anthropologist John Bodley summed up the idea that tribal peoples have happily embraced progressive 'acculturation' by the West. In many cases, Bodley writes, the appearance of voluntary participation was in fact 'the direct outcome of the defeat of individual tribes in separate engagements in a very long war fought between all tribal peoples and industrial civilisation throughout the world.'[1]

This war has always been fuelled by greed and also a remarkably deluded sense of racial superiority. In the Northern Territory of Australia in 1901, 'It was notorious, that the blackfellows were shot down like crows and that no notice was taken.'[2] In Paraguay in 1903, settlers were killing Guayaki Indians and using their bodies to bait jaguar traps. In 1941 it was reported that local settlers still felt that killing Guayaki was not a crime, but rather 'a praiseworthy action, like killing a jaguar'.

Such prejudices are far more deeply-entrenched and long-lived than we would like to think, and globalisation is about far more than the greedy but decent pursuit of profit. Last year's media furore over the killing of white farmers and black workers by black 'war veterans' in Zimbabwe was a case study in racist reporting. While the killing of black workers was passed over in virtual silence, the media was filled with endless interviews with friends and families of white victims. It was almost as though the killing of whites by blacks violated some cosmic principle on which the very existence of the universe depends. The daily killing of fully 200 Iraqi children under five by Western sanctions, by contrast, was and is a matter of complete indifference. As Denis Halliday, former Assistant Secretary-General of the United Nations has noted bitterly, 'Iraqi kids don't count apparently. It is a racist problem, there really is no question about that. It's ugly.'[3]

George Kennan, head of the US State Department Policy Planning Staff, indicated the big picture, of which these examples constitute tiny fragments, in 1948. Kennan explained that the key post-war US foreign policy goal was to maintain the disparity in wealth between the United States and the rest of the world:

> Our real task in the coming period is to devise a pattern of relationships which will permit us to maintain this position of disparity without positive detriment to our national security. To do so, we will have to dispense with all sentimentality and day-dreaming... We need not deceive ourselves that we can afford today the luxury of altruism and world-benefaction... We should cease to talk about vague and unreal objectives such as human rights, the raising of living standards, and democratisation.[4]

Maintaining this 'pattern of relationships' has certain logical requirements. Prime among them is the fact that the exploited must be maintained in a position of weakness and despair to ensure that they do not entertain thoughts of bettering themselves. The real 'domino effect' that terrified Western planners during the Cold War, was not the threat of Communist expansion, but the threat of independent nationalism. Were the poor to throw off the dictatorship of the West and better themselves in one part of the world, then people elsewhere might be inspired to follow this 'threat of a good example'. Western and Western-backed 'Cold War interventions' in, for example, Vietnam, Nicaragua, Cuba, Guatemala, Iran and Chile, can best be understood in these terms. And as victims in Colombia, Haiti, East Timor, Chechnya and Iraq know, violence continues to be employed whenever and wherever Western control of resources is threatened.

The primary requirement is for a 'culture of terror' that 'domesticates the expectations of the majority' and undermines any aspiration towards 'alternatives that differ from those of the powerful', in the words of Salvadoran Jesuits who learned the lesson during the US-instigated holocaust of the 1980s.[5]

The point being, as journalist Penny Lernoux has noted, that the impoverished masses of the Third World 'will not stay quietly on the farms or in the slums unless they are terribly afraid'.[6]

Historian Mark Curtis's conclusions then, although unknown to the mainstream, are much as we would expect:

> Since 1945, rather than occasionally deviating from the promotion of peace, democracy human rights and economic development in the Third World, British (and US) foreign policy has been systematically opposed to them, whether the Conservatives or Labour (or Republicans or Democrats) have been in power. This has had grave consequences for those on the receiving end of Western policies abroad.[7]

It is in precisely this context that globalisation and, for example, the claims of biotechnology corporations that they are intent on feeding the poor of the world, need to be understood. As Susan George has noted:

> Food has become a means of insuring effective domination over the world at large and especially over the 'wretched of the earth'.[8]

There is no reason to expect this powerful weapon to be decommissioned any time soon. Above and beyond any 'humanitarian' corporate initiative, the fundamental needs remain: to maintain control, dependence and vulnerability.

All of this, of course, is a million miles from the picture of the world presented by the supposedly liberal-left media, with journalists like Andrew Marr of the *Observer* arguing that, 'In the end, the WTO is on the side of the angels. It is what the world's poor need most',[9] and with US commentators like *Time* magazine's Charles Krauthammer mocking the 'kooky crowd' at the April 2000 Washington DC protests against globalisation, as 'apolitical Luddites, who refuse to accept that growth, prosperity and upward living standards always entail some dislocation'.[10] An idea of the honesty, accuracy and neutrality of the corporate media can be gained by comparing and contrasting the murderous reality described above with Krauthammer's phrase 'some dislocation'.

It is significant that, in our time, there has not yet been a serious mainstream discussion of the implications for press freedom of the fact that the mass media is made up of profit-seeking corporations controlled by wealthy owners and giant parent companies, and dependent on corporate advertisers. In the United States, arms manufacturers General Electric and Westinghouse own NBC and CBS respectively. Oil companies such as Exxon, Texaco, and Mobil have representatives on the corporate boards of these media giants, as has Lockheed Martin, which builds the F-22 fighter. General Electric and Westinghouse make bomb parts and fighter planes that are used to bomb Iraq.

A small indication of the absurdity of the situation was provided by the *New York Times*, the day after Viacom – the movie, cable TV and publishing conglomerate – announced plans to purchase CBS, thereby becoming the third-largest media entity in the world. Although the *Times* devoted fully seven articles to the proposed takeover, not one quote from a single critic was printed about the threat to consumers or to democracy posed by this concentration of media power. In reporting opposition to globalisation, we should not expect the globalised corporate media to describe itself as part of the problem.

The silent society

It has long been recognised that industrial capitalism requires workers and managers performing specialised tasks. But if we are to understand the distortion and denial of basic reality that pervades our media and society, we need to understand that industrial capitalism also requires workers and managers thinking specialised *thoughts*. The 'big picture' described above is obscured with such success in part because many of us have been persuaded to focus our attention on isolated details and to reject all concern with wider issues deemed beyond our 'field of expertise'. A contributory factor is that, very often, absurdly, we allow our moral responsibilities to be defined by our job description.

When, on February 13, 2000, Hans von Sponeck, Assistant Secretary-General of the United Nations, resigned, asking, 'How long should the civilian population of Iraq be exposed to such punishment for something they have never done?', James Rubin, assistant to US Secretary of State Madeleine Albright, suggested that von Sponeck had spoken 'beyond the range of his competence or his authority'.[11]

This is the great lie that has deceived too many of us for too long: to be reasonable and competent, we must speak as specialists. As David Cromwell notes here, while 30 per cent of the natural world has been destroyed by human activity in the last twenty-five years, and a 60 per cent reduction in greenhouse gas emissions is required to stabilise the climate, currently a mere 5.2 per cent cut is being proposed through the Kyoto Climate Treaty. Our response? Vigorous attempts by big business to destroy the Kyoto Treaty, endless searching for new oil reserves, the creation of a 'jumbo jumbo' jet capable of delivering the anticipated 5 per cent annual increase in air travel. When asked their opinions on these developments, many climate scientists insist that it is not their job to speak on 'policy issues' or 'advocacy issues'. The destruction of the Earth, apparently, is always someone else's business.

This extraordinary cult of specialisation is all pervasive, even to the 'radical' extreme of society. There have been plenty of Greenpeace and Friends of the Earth campaigns on global warming, ozone depletion and species extinction, but not yet on the fact that, as an integral part of the wider corporate system, the corporate media has every reason to downplay (however unconsciously) globalisation and associated environmental threats that might lead to profit-sapping change. The point is obvious and vital and yet David Cromwell's *Private Planet* joins a tiny handful of books to have raised the issue.

When an interviewer challenged Noam Chomsky to explain what exactly qualified him, as a linguist, to speak out on domestic politics and foreign affairs, he replied, 'I'm a human being'.[12] In this book, David Cromwell – a specialist oceanographer by trade, but a human being by nature – powerfully continues the defence of our right to speak out as 'generalists' living in the real, and rapidly deteriorating, world against the inhumanity and irrationality of dumb specialisation.

Notes

1   Bodley, *Victims of Progress*, pp.43-4.
2   Quoted in Bodley, *Victims of Progress*, p.26.
3   Interview with the author, 30 April, 2000.
4   Quoted in Noam Chomsky, *Turning the Tide*, p.48.
5   Quoted in Noam Chomsky, 'Colombia – Part One of Two', *ZNet daily commentary* (www.zmag.org), 24 April, 2000.
6   Quoted in Herman, *The Real Terror Network*, p.3.
7   Curtis, *The Ambiguities of Power*, p.3.
8   Susan George, *How The Other Half Dies*, p.16.
9   Andrew Marr, 'Friend or foe?', *The Observer*, 5 December, 1999.
10   Quoted in Norman Soloman, 'Protests In Washington Clash With Media Spin', *Fairness and Accuracy In Reporting* (www.fair.org), April 2000.
11   Quoted, Anthony Arnove, 'Sanctions on Iraq: The 'Propaganda Campaign', *ZNet daily commentary* (www.zmag.org), 1 April, 2000.
12   Quote from Chomsky Archive at www.zmag.org.

INTRODUCTION

Reclaiming the commons

The rules set by the secretive WTO [World Trade Organisation] violate principles of human rights and ecological survival. They violate rules of justice and sustainability. They are rules of warfare against the people and the planet. Changing these rules is the most important democratic and human rights struggle of our times. It is a matter of survival.

Vandana Shiva, Indian activist[1]

Just a few years ago, powerful corporate and political elites seemed to be having things their own way. Economic globalisation was proceeding virtually unhindered. Anyone who questioned 'free trade' was one of the 'loony left', an 'eco-warrior', or an outdated 'protectionist'. But things are changing. There is now a mounting backlash from a broad alliance of overlapping public movements, and the battle lines are being drawn for the greatest ideological clash of the twenty-first century: the protection of people and nature from the forces of global capitalism that are attempting to privatise the planet.

Global capitalism, despite the rhetoric from politicians in power, is not as immutable as the laws of physics. The present system of conducting trade and investment, by which a few prosper and the many struggle or die, is surely not the end product of the human capacity for organising society. Nor is global capitalism an inevitable state of affairs, somehow mythically linked with economic efficiency, democracy and freedom. Economic globalisation is, in fact, being shaped with extreme vigour by powerful and wealthy corporate lobby groups in every international forum you have heard of – the World Trade Organisation, the World Bank, the International Monetary Fund, even the United Nations – as well as many more perhaps you never knew existed. Influential corporations and investors have governments bending over backwards in a desperate attempt to create a 'business-friendly environment' in order to attract and maintain capital from private interests.

So what *is* economic globalisation? Simply put, it is the increasing integration of national economies and transnational flows of investment around the world. Political leaders are continually exhorting us to play a part in helping our respective nations become 'internationally competitive' in the 'global market place'. They talk of the importance and benefits of 'free trade', of lowering 'barriers to trade' and sharing the benefits with the poor. Indeed, the solution to world poverty, we are told, is further 'liberalisation' of trade and investment. Opposing free trade, in the eyes of globalisation's proponents, is akin to opposing motherhood and apple pie; or worse, opposition condemns the poor to yet more poverty. How can anyone *not* wish to see greater trade between countries and greater transnational flows of capital?

However, the first thing we must grasp is that 'free trade' is anything but 'free'. It is an Orwellian term – akin to naming a national war machine the Ministry of Peace – of such monstrous proportions that until recently most people did not even question the term or the concept. Such acquiescence has been boosted by a largely uncritical and deceiving corporate mass media that is, in fact, an integral component of the elite interests that benefit from globalisation. One of this book's aims is to show that free trade is actually *forced* trade, depending as it does on the coercive efforts of powerful corporate and political groupings in the rich countries of the North to prise open the economies of the South in order to gain access to their plentiful natural resources, including cheap labour and even genetic material. There is also nothing 'free' about a system of trade which systematically degrades the environment and widens the gap between rich and poor, as we will see.

This is why some campaigners call for 'rewriting the global rules of trade' and advocate 'fair trade, not free trade'. Others go further and wish to see anything resembling state, or suprastate, hierarchies broken up so that communities can practise self-determination to the full – autarky. Personally, I do not argue against trade between nations – far from it. There is an argument in favour of allowing developing nations greater access to international markets as a stepping stone to poverty reduction, but it ought to be on terms which honour ecological and social values. Ironically, it has been the rich nations which have restricted access to their own markets, even as they have insisted on entering the fragile economies of the South, while at the same time trampling on human rights and the natural environment. One reason why international financiers and transnational corporations have been able to do this is because governments are desperate to attract capital in an uncertain global economy, and are therefore willing to suppress or even remove standards designed to protect employment conditions, reserves of natural resources or quality of life. Those are the real impacts of 'liberalisation'. As examples in this book will show – including climate change, GM foods and 'free trade' agreements – governments are constantly subjected to intense, secretive and well-funded corporate lobbying in order to adopt a business-friendly line; the threat of 'capital flight' – in other words, the withdrawal of investment – is ever present. Ironically and tragically, when governments dance to the tune of corporations, as they usually do on issues of real corporate concern, it is often performed courtesy of public funds. Our taxes directly subsidise the arms trade, the extraction of fossil fuels, the industrialisation of agriculture, road-building and other business activities that enrich the few, while impoverishing or threatening the many. As legal expert Richard Grossman warns, 'when corporations govern, democracy flies out the door'.[2]

Much of my basic argument, though not all the examples, may well be familiar territory to a few *cognoscenti*, and – to the extent that it registers at all in the mainstream – will no doubt be dismissed by sceptics as 'yet another anti-globalisation book'. There are at least two pre-emptive strikes that I feel compelled to make here. First, consider the reality of today's consumer society. Mainstream politicians, corporations and the mass media constantly broadcast the notion that, barring a few problems here and there, the present global economic system is fair, democratic and successful. Communism is a failed experiment and capitalism has won, goes the argument. Moreover, 'there is no alternative' in Margaret Thatcher's oft-repeated phrase; the possibility of organising society differently just does not appear on any serious agenda. The more often that this astonishing presumption is challenged, the better. Dissidents should try constantly to propagate their views, if only in an attempt to counter the constant barrage of mainstream propaganda.

Second, there is a pressing need for dissidents and activists to maintain and raise awareness of the links between their concerns, as well as their campaigning objectives, practical strategies, and political and corporate targets. There is a danger in separating, or even ignoring, issues that are fundamentally related. Environmentalists ultimately have the same goals as anti-poverty campaigners, for example. Opponents of the arms trade, as well as green activists, ought to be aware of the extent to which Western foreign policy has pursued a neocolonial agenda of domination over people and natural resources in the 'Third World'. Campaigners of various hues could usefully bring to public attention the degree to which government policy is skewed towards the interests of big business.

There is a tendency for campaigning groups to over-specialise, or to address the symptoms, rather than the underlying causes, of societal and environmental breakdown. This tendency, if left unaddressed, could scupper attempts to oppose and supplant the current system of economic globalisation. I have attempted to counter this in the book by tackling issues that at first sight may appear somewhat disparate, though they are, in fact, all interlinked. This simply reflects the deep-rooted nature of the economic, environmental and social problems that afflict us. Moreover, all the topics covered here impinge on the daily lives of each and every one of us – from our efforts (or lack of them) to combat global warming, to the food that ends up on our plates.

Let us begin by acknowledging that, for many of us living in the largely affluent countries of the North – in Europe, North America, Oceania – there is no denying that we enjoy a high standard of living as a result of post-WWII economic growth (although growth since the 1970s has rarely matched the preceding post-war decades). Comfortable homes, foreign holidays, a car (perhaps two or more), expensive consumer goods, cable television and so on, have become the norm. But at what price to the environment and to people elsewhere? And at what price to our own quality of life? Witness the daily media reports on suicide (especially among young males), divorce, stress, depression, inner city and rural poverty, asthma, crime and other symptoms of an unhealthy and divided society. At the same time, we are placing immense pressures on the world's resources and capacity to absorb our wastes – to the extent that even the Earth's climate system is at risk from human activities.

Private Planet is not intended to make you feel guilty or helpless about all of this, although some readers may well wonder if I am not being too critical. My answer to that charge is to quote George Orwell: 'If liberty means anything at all, it means the right to tell people what they do not want to hear'. But, despair not; my aim is not to make you feel miserable about the state of the world. On the contrary, my objective is to help you to counter the biased, confusing, self-serving – and often cynical – corporate and mainstream political depiction of society. Intellectual, emotional and spiritual energising is a necessary and powerful first step in creating communities based on social justice and environmental sustainability.

There is no single 'correct' set of demands that must be made by campaigners, nor 'true' path of sustainable development. And I certainly do not claim to have a blueprint for a better world or how to get there. But in building on the contributions of countless communities, activists, writers and dissidents, we can nonetheless identify the truth of what is happening around us and point to – indeed push for – any one of a number of fairer and more sensible ways of living. One simple but important example is the pressing need to stop the enormous public subsidies being spent by governments on supporting the destructive corporate activities mentioned above, when more sustainable, often smaller-scale, alternatives exist but languish for lack of support – strong local and regional economies, public transport, renewable energy, organic and low-impact farming.

This book should hopefully elucidate the links between aspects of your own life that you may hitherto have thought were unconnected. Why are our newspapers and television channels obsessed with sex, shopping and scandals? Why can't I find cheap, healthy organic food? Why are there so many poor people, despite decades of free trade and economic growth? Why are we losing countryside and species at horrifying rates? Why is so little being done to tackle climate change – the greatest environmental threat to humanity? Who is responsible for such inaction? Is it really the case that society is simply made up of lots of individuals, so that we all just have to do 'our bit for the environment', as some disingenuously claim? Or do a small number of actors on the world stage have much more power than the rest of us – the vast majority – and are able to stall or even stifle efforts which they perceive are a threat to 'profit margins', 'international competitiveness' and 'investment opportunities'?

I hope that in reading this you will become more aware of just how vulnerable centralised state and corporate power is to significant grassroots awareness and activism. This is ample cause for hope and cautious optimism. As described in Chapter 1, the defeat – temporary or otherwise – of the notorious Multilateral Agreement on Investment is a heartening example of what can be done by informed citizens working together. I hope that reading *Private Planet* will encourage you to question the status quo more deeply than ever before and possibly even motivate you to work towards developing a better alternative, whatever that may turn out to be. This book does not give a prescription for such a 'new way of life' – that has yet to be worked out, though there are plenty of examples discussed elsewhere.[3]

Perhaps the only topic on which I am remotely professionally 'qualified' to comment – as a physical oceanographer – is climate. However, while few of us are 'experts' in any one of the fields discussed here, and even fewer – if any – are experts in more than one, everybody is affected to a large degree by all of the topics. We are therefore – each and every one of us – qualified to comment on them if there is any grain of truth in the statement that we live in a free, democratic society.

One of the book's main arguments is that the continued liberalisation of global trade and investment, and government skewing of the odds in favour of big business, are tools which enable international investors and transnational corporations to 'enclose the commons'. This age-old process first arose as a means for the private control of land, forests, rivers and natural resources which had hitherto been public property in pre-industrial Britain. In England, the process first reached a peak in the fifteenth and sixteenth centuries, when landlords fenced in previously open land to which their tenants traditionally had access for grazing livestock. In Scotland, during the Highland Clearances of the eighteenth and nineteenth centuries, people were evicted from their traditional holdings and many were forced to emigrate to make way for the more profitable business of sheep farming. Between 1840 and 1889, around 35,000 people departed Skye alone, most of them unwillingly headed for the New World. To put this emigration in some perspective, fewer than 10,000 people live on the island today. But at least the population there is now relatively stable. In other parts of the Highlands, glens which were once the homes of thriving communities stand deserted. Moreover, the famed Highland scenery with its bare mountains and wild moors is largely an unnatural scene of man-made dereliction and dwindling biodiversity.

The new enclosure movement of recent decades – driven by powerful corporate and political forces around the globe – is a continuation of the same process, demanding access to land and people in the developing world; biodiversity, including the very genetic makeup of plants and people; the food chain; and even the global atmosphere and oceans for the dumping of industrial waste products. The most serious consequence is that humankind's ability to respond to the threat of catastrophic climate change has been compromised – perhaps even destroyed – by vested interests opposing the transformation to a society based on decentralised renewable energy. In such a society, ownership of power generation in local communities would be intimately tied up with strong, self-reliant local democracy. At the moment – notwithstanding limited devolution in the United Kingdom – political power in Britain is too concentrated in central government. Increasingly, such power is itself being lost to corporate groupings such as the World Trade Organisation, World Bank and International Monetary Fund, or to influential business lobby groups such as the European Roundtable of Industrialists, the World Economic Forum and the World Business Council for Sustainable Development, all of which have managed to rewrite the rules of international trade and investment for the benefit of transnational corporations and powerful investors. It is clearly important to comprehend, anticipate and oppose the corporate-driven mechanisms by which the transfer of public resources into private hands is taking place, if there is ever going to be a healthy, just and ecological future.

In *Private Planet*, I shine a spotlight on the mass media because this is the source of most people's information – or rather, misinformation – about politics, democracy, the environment – in fact, the state of the planet. Most media outlets promote the corporate drive for new 'growth opportunities', but under-report or ignore the corporate fuelling of global warming, environmental destruction and human rights abuses. The media generally ignore the hardship of farmers in developing countries who have no choice but to harvest cash crops for export to bale out their debt-ridden governments, or who are restricted to buying seed and herbicides from biotechnology giants like Monsanto. And the media largely fail to investigate why billions of people around the world are being left to languish under a system of global economic apartheid that has seen disparities between rich and poor escalate as controls on international flows in capital and trade drop by the wayside.

Business-as-usual apologists proclaim their freedom to operate in a deregulated global economy while at the same time they suppress the freedom of the communities they trample upon. The economic globalisers are unable to deliver 'consumer freedom' for you or I to choose fresh air, clean water and healthy soil; or food grown organically and untarnished by genetically modified organisms; the freedom to use energy generated by renewable sources, rather than global-warming, pollution-ridden fossil fuels; the freedom to live close to where we work, shop and relax; to walk and cycle in comfort and safety; and the freedom to live in a society devoid of big-monied political lobbying and stupefying media white-washing by powerful vested interests.

If deregulated international trade and capital flows could deliver even some of the above, then economic globalisation would have some merit. The truth is that the global players' much-vaunted pursuit of consumer freedom is as illusory as transnational company altruism. What evidence can there possibly be for such a deluded view after decades of neoliberal policies? When were private corporations *ever* motivated by the desire to reduce poverty or protect the environment? Is it even conceivable that big business can take the long view necessary to save the planet?

We have already come a long way since the damp squib that was the corporate-dominated 1992 United Nations Conference on the Environment and Development in Rio de Janeiro. As the writer Michael Goldman warned:

> If we are to learn anything from the 1992 Earth Summit in Rio – the Greatest Commons Show on Earth – it is that the objective of the Summit's major power brokers was not to constrain or restructure capitalist economies and practices to help save the rapidly deteriorating ecological commons, but rather to restructure the commons (e.g. privatize, 'develop', 'make more efficient', valorize, 'get the price right') to accommodate crisis-ridden capitalisms. The effect has not been to stop destructive practices but to normalize and further institutionalize them, putting commoners throughout the world at even greater risk.[4]

These are words we might well bear in mind during the media circus that will engulf 'Rio+10' to be hosted by South Africa in 2002. It is now up to us, the commoners, to wrest control back from the elite politicians, investors and industrialists who have presumed to know what is best for us.

Notes

1   *The Guardian*, 8 December, 1999.
2   Richard Grossman interviewed by David Barsamian, *Z Magazine*, January 2000, p. 44.
3   See, for example, *Living Lightly*, Walter and Dorothy Schwarz.
4   Goldman, *Privatizing Nature*, p. 23.

FIXING THE RULES OF THE GAME

Global corporate control at public expense

Globalization is not just the spread of the market into new countries and regions, penetrating deeper into areas of life that were previously governed by other systems of social rules. Globalization is also the replacement of diverse modes of human intercourse with the single mindset and values of universal commercialism.

Robin Hahnel[1]

Globalization is not a policy choice – it is a fact.

Bill Clinton[2]

The banana war

In the spring of 1999, the European public were bemused to learn that they were at war with the United States over bananas. Under an agreement called the Lomé Convention, former European colonies in Africa, the Caribbean and the Pacific are guaranteed access for their products into the European Union. This preferential treatment for poor countries in the South is intended to protect their fragile economies. Bananas from the Dominican Republic, for example, are grown mostly by family farm producers on small plantations. On the other hand, US-owned transnational corporations (TNCs) in Latin America produce bananas on huge, chemically-intensive plantations. 'Dollar bananas' can be produced more cheaply than those from the Lomé-protected farmers because of the superior economies of scale and also the poor working conditions of the dollar banana employees. Moreover, dollar bananas are produced cheaply at the expense of the environment and human health. In Chile around four million kilos of pesticides are dumped annually on the 220,000 hectares of land that are devoted to fruit production for export. Many of these chemicals are highly toxic. Among them are nine of the 12 most toxic pesticides in the world.[3]

The global banana market is dominated by just three US-owned TNCs: Chiquita, Dole and Del Monte. In 1992, this trio had 66 per cent of banana sales in Europe.[4] The companies complained for several years about the protectionism afforded by European Union nations to their former colonies. Then, on 11 April 1996, the United States government requested a ruling at the World Trade Organisation, the powerful successor to the General Agreement on Tariffs and Trade,[5] on the legality of EU policy. The case was brought on behalf of the Chiquita Banana Corporation. Two days after President Clinton's administration asked the WTO to rule against European banana trade rules, Chiquita paid $500,000 into the funds of Clinton's Democrat Party.[6]

A WTO panel found against the EU, a decision that was upheld in September 1997. The EU issued a proposal to address the ruling, while maintaining its quotas for Lomé-protected producers. While awaiting the WTO's final judgement, the US retaliated against the EU in March 1999, imposing huge increases in import duty on a diverse range of European goods worth more than $500 million, including Scottish cashmere knitwear, Italian cheeses and French handbags. Thousands of jobs were at stake. In an age when politicians and media commentators routinely speak of 'the increasing integration of the global economy', the US and EU were now engaged in a surreal trade war. The normally cosy Clinton-Blair relationship was brought 'to the verge of a diplomatic incident'.[7] In April 1999, the WTO gave the US the go-ahead to impose punitive tariffs on £120 million of European exports, effectively backing Washington's claim that the EU was wrong to limit imports of bananas. Europe was told it would have to revise its rules, and a deepening trade war appeared to be averted. The effect on farmers in former European colonies remains to be seen.

A remarkable feature of the above episode is that the United States does not actually produce bananas itself. The US government brought the case before the WTO at the behest of a US-owned company operating in Central America. The banana war is one of the most visible examples to date of trade disputes between large economies, involving underlying environmental and social tensions. A major trade row, also between Europe and the US, is now brewing over genetically modified foods. But what are the real issues at stake in such disputes? A growing number of campaigners – trade unionists, Third World development workers, environmentalists, church activists and others – claim that TNCs are hindering efforts to protect the environment and to promote social justice. Industry and investors are doing this by their aggressive bolstering – indeed hijacking – of intergovernmental 'free trade' bodies such as the WTO, and through trade agreements operating amongst blocs of countries, notably the North American Free Trade

Agreement (NAFTA) covering Canada, the US and Mexico, the Asia-Pacific Economic Co-operation forum, and even the European Union. Several environmental initiatives have fallen foul of these free trade conglomerates. These include the United States' efforts to protect dolphins killed during tuna fishing and turtles killed during shrimp fishing. Other examples include Indonesia's moves to ban exports of non-processed wood in an attempt to reduce the number of trees felled; Denmark's efforts to protect its refillable bottle system by requiring all beer and soft drinks to be sold in refillable bottles; and Sweden's attempts before joining the EU to introduce a ban on imports of products containing or produced with ozone-destroying chemicals.[8]

This list is not exhaustive. In 1998, for example, the Canadian government was forced into a humiliating retreat on its year-old ban of the gasoline additive methyl-cyclopentadienyl manganese tricarbonyl (MMT) which is an octane enhancer. The retreat occurred despite evidence that 'the manganese used in the octane enhancer can cause nervous-system problems'.[9] But the company manufacturing MMT, the US-based Ethyl Corporation, launched a $250 million law suit against the Canadian government, arguing that the ban was a restraint on free trade under the terms of NAFTA. The Canadian government agreed to lift the ban and pay limited costs to Ethyl Corp rather than enter into a costly and potentially precedent-setting legal battle. As trade researcher David Wood warned, this example highlights 'how NAFTA and similar agreements can be used to override national environmental health laws'.[10] In the same year, again under NAFTA, two Mexican local authorities were sued for preventing US companies from establishing toxic waste dumps in their jurisdictions. Given this backdrop in the run-up to the millennium round of global trade talks at Seattle in November 1999, the attention of activists, and to some extent the mainstream media, was increasingly focused on that most influential overseer of free trade – the World Trade Organisation.

The World Trade Organisation

Since its inception on 1 January, 1995, the World Trade Organisation has been the most powerful trade body in the global economy. It currently has 139 member states and over 30 more clamouring to join. One country keen to enter the WTO, having recently negotiated the support of both the US and the EU, is China, which represents a huge new pool of potential consumers and producers. The WTO's proponents, among which number the world's largest corporations, argue that the organisation is needed to administer legally binding rules for international trade. The creation of the WTO was, in fact, a great victory for the many corporations who had been relentlessly pressing governments to accelerate the transformation to a 'business-friendly' global economy. The key objective here is the 'liberalisation of trade': in other words, the removal of barriers to trade and foreign direct investment in order, the corporate argument goes, to generate increased prosperity for the world's population. As President Ronald Reagan said in 1985, 'Our task is to knock down barriers to trade and foreign investment and the free movement of capital'. His successor, George Bush, enthusiastically continued the process, offering his steadfast commitment to 'free markets and to the free flow of capital, central to achieving economic growth and lasting prosperity'. The principal tool for strengthening and expanding such free markets and free flows is the WTO, by enforcing trade rules which promote these aims. Any trade disputes between nations are settled by a panel of three unelected trade experts, meeting behind closed doors. Environmental lawyer Steven Shrybman describes the WTO as 'the most important element of an international corporate strategy to codify the rules upon which a global system of investment, production and trade depend'.[11] It is deeply ironic that 'free trade' can exist only because of decades-long, corporate-driven processes to shape the economy according to the needs of big business and investors.

Creating a corporate 'level playing field' for investment is high on the WTO agenda; the aim is for foreign companies and investors to be treated on a par with domestic companies and investors. But the ongoing liberalisation of trade and investment is clearly not helping the poor; in fact, it is deeply damaging, as we will see in more detail in Chapter 2. In 1997, the United Nations Conference on Trade and Development reported that mounting evidence showed 'that rising inequalities are becoming more permanent features of the world economy'. And at the WTO ministerial meeting in May 1998, 'many of the developing [countries] echoed the apprehension expressed by people's organisations concerning the impact of liberalisation and globalisation'.[12]

Critics of the WTO claim that it has weakened national – and even local – government sovereignty. In all but one case brought before its dispute resolutions panel, the WTO has come down on the side of corporate interest, rather than environmental protection or social justice. In January 1996, the WTO upheld complaints of discrimination made on behalf of polluting Venezuelan and Brazilian oil refineries, and thereby allowed their products to enter the US market, despite the US Clean Air Act which was designed to maintain high standards of air quality in the United States. In March 1998, the WTO began investigating a claim brought by the EU against India, which it accused of limiting the EU's access to raw hides and furs from India. In effect, the EU was attempting to force India to kill more animals for export.

In 1997, the WTO ruled against an EU ban imposed in 1989 on imports of American beef produced using artificial growth hormones that are linked to cancer 'unless the EU can prove that eating American beef is unsafe'. In 1999 the EU widened the embargo on American beef following scientific tests which showed that 12 per cent of 'hormone-free' US beef actually contained hormone residues. The WTO stated that the EU had no right to ban the importation of US beef containing growth hormones and authorised the US government to impose punitive trade sanctions worth US$116 million on European goods.

The threat of a similar WTO ruling hung over the 1993 EU ban on bovine somatotropin (BST) – also known as recombinant Bovine Growth Hormone (rBGH) – which boosts milk production, after the US government raised the case on behalf of the giant Monsanto corporation. The use of BST has actual and potential side-effects, both for cattle and human health.[13] The US wanted the WTO to outlaw any ban on hormone-treated cattle as an impediment to free trade. However, the Codex Alimentarius Commission, the UN Food Safety Agency representing 101 nations worldwide, ruled unanimously in favour of the 1993 European moratorium in August 1999. Following the Codex ruling, the US dropped its threats to pressure Europe on the issue of rBGH at the WTO later that year. Most campaigners believe that this is only a temporary reprieve.

Some governments use uncertainty over WTO regulations to prevent the incorporation of trade measures into new and existing environmental agreements. For example, trade officials at environmental negotiating meetings have argued that eco-labelling should not be encouraged by the Intergovernmental Panel on Forests. They have also tried to ensure that trade measures are not incorporated into the so-called Prior Informed Consent Convention on trade in toxic products or the Biosafety Protocol to the Convention on Biodiversity.[14] The World Wide Fund for Nature (WWF) has attacked WTO rules for threatening the Montreal Protocol on ozone depletion, the Basle convention banning the export of hazardous waste to countries where it cannot be properly managed, and even the UN Framework Convention on Climate Change.[15]

When government ministers met in Seattle in November 1999 to discuss a new round of trade liberalisation, the agenda included investment, agriculture, forest products and government procurement. There were warnings in Britain that the minimum wage was under threat and that the National Health Service could face anti-trade rulings by the WTO.[16] For some time prior to the meeting, the US had been continuing the Reagan-Bush agenda of the 1980s by leading calls for further liberalisation of investment, the accelerated opening up of Third World markets, and the easing of restrictions of, in the words of Bill Clinton, 'farm products'. This latter point was a pretext for boosting the sales of US biotech companies, particularly in the field of genetic engineering (see Chapter 7).

The WTO negotiations in Seattle were behind closed doors, as ever. The developed world – supported by powerful companies – attempted to dominate proceedings by, for example, barring delegates from developing nations from the exclusive 'green room' where important elite discussions were being held. As we will see in Chapter 8, the Seattle summit ended in disarray following largely peaceful street protests and the newly-found confidence exhibited by many developing country delegates inside the conference centre.

Private interests have been influential in attempting to use the WTO to liberalise financial services sectors, including banking and investment. The Financial Services Agreement, which came into force in March 1999, provided greater access to financial corporations wishing to move into 'emerging markets', where previously there had been measures in place to protect domestic sectors from overseas competition. A major lobby group which successfully pushed for financial services deregulation was the Financial Leaders Group (FLG), with business representatives mainly from the EU and the US. The FLG was responsible for identifying barriers to trade, after which the EU and US delegations would request that these obstacles be addressed during negotiations. When agreement was finally reached, EU trade commissioner Leon Brittan could say with some satisfaction that 'the close links established between EC[17] and US industry ... were an essential factor in obtaining the final deal'.[18]

There are other business fora besides the WTO where policies on economic globalisation are hatched. Even the United Nations is a party to such dealings. The UN and corporate bosses meet regularly through the Geneva Business Dialogue (a joint venture of the International Chamber of Commerce and the UN), and the Transatlantic Business Dialogue (heads of TNCs and top national and international officeholders) in 'consensus-building' exercises. The UN and the international business sector have pledged to 'forge a close global partnership to secure greater business input into the world's economic decision-making and boost the private sector in the least developed countries'.[19] Fearing the growing backlash against global capitalism, the buzzphrase of such powerful groupings is now 'managing globalisation'. At the same time as securing access to top-level UN officials, the International Chamber of Commerce is keen to counter the threat to business of human rights and environmental pressure groups working with the UN: 'We have to be careful that they [the activists] do not get too much influence ... Governments have to understand that business is not just another pressure group but a resource that will help them set the right rules'.[20]

Business has been winning the battle for the heart and mind of the UN. Until 1993, the UN had been working on a code of conduct for transnational corporations. This work was dropped as part of an internal reorganisation. The UN Conference on Trade and Development took over work related to transnational corporations but this does not extend to regulating their conduct. David Korten, author of *When Corporations Rule the World,* has warned that UN Secretary-General Kofi Annan is 'firmly committed to using UN and other public funds to subsidise the corporate buy-out of Third World economies'.[21]

Other corporate-packed groupings where the globalisation script is being written include the European Roundtable of Industrialists, the World Business Council for Sustainable Development (WBCSD), and the annual Bilderberg Summits. The WBCSD portrays itself as the leading business coalition striving for environmental sustainability. But behind the green-tinged rhetoric has been a successful twin-track approach of liberalisation and self-regulation, rather than government intervention, as the route to sustainability. Meanwhile, the Bilderberg talks, named after the Dutch hotel where the first meeting took place in 1954, provide conditions of exclusive luxury, vast armed security and secrecy for elite interests to get together. Prime Minister Tony Blair, when questioned in 1998 in the House of Commons, failed to disclose his attendance at the Bilderberg meeting in Athens in 1993. Attendees at the 1999 gathering in Sintra, Portugal, included Northern Ireland Secretary Peter Mandelson, former US Secretary of State Henry Kissinger, billionaire oil and banking tycoon David Rockefeller, Monsanto chief Robert Shapiro, and the head of the World Bank, James Wolfensohn.

Although policy is not decided at such meetings, they are part of the consensus building which directs the thinking of the world's most powerful political and corporate figures. Gibby Zobel, a journalist at *The Big Issue* who obtained leaked documents of the 1999 gathering, reported that although 14 media chiefs and journalists from eight countries attended, none of them chose to tell their readers of the meeting. 'It would not serve their interests to be cut out of the elite loop', said Zobel.[22] We return to the important issue of media reporting (or non-reporting) of issues related to economic globalisation in Chapter 3.

Whereas the Bilderberg group is an informal arrangement, yet another business forum, called the Trilateral Commission, is a more formal and focused affair. It combines top businesspeople, politicians and bankers from Japan, the US and the EU. Edicts from the Trilateral Commission are taken seriously by governments, such as the following: 'Europe must become more competitive by deregulating labour markets and streamlining burdensome welfare systems'.[23] Of all the business-dominated alliances, however, the WTO is the most powerful. Although it is nominally an intergovernmental body, as Tony Juniper of Friends of the Earth says, 'its aims and remit have been shaped by companies and industry bodies such as the International Chamber of Commerce'.[24] Even Arthur Dunkel, head of the ICC working group on trade and investment, and former director-general of GATT, has raised the question, 'Who is driving the process in trade policy – governments or the business community?'. Dunkel concedes that collusion between governments and TNCs lies behind the opposition of civil society to the WTO.[25] Not only is there such collusion, but any pretence of democracy or public interest is shattered by the secretive disputes resolution tribunal persistently overruling public health or environmental protection laws. It is no wonder that there is so much public pressure to reform, even dismantle, the WTO.

The very concept of democratically-elected governments acting on behalf of an electorate which can vote for change is being eroded by the sham of 'democracy' provided by free markets. There are some powerful figures, such as US investor David Rockefeller, who look with favour upon business as the 'logical entity' to take the place of governments.[26] The transfer of power from communities and governments to business is a dominant characteristic of the process of economic globalisation. This trend is neither accidental nor inevitable, but is largely a direct result of rewriting the rules of trade and investment to favour large-scale business enterprises.

Globalisation or globaloney?

If small is beautiful, as the title of the famous book by E. F. Schumacher goes, is big necessarily ugly? The unprecedented growth and power of transnational corporations now means that they are responsible for one-third of global production and two-thirds of world trade. The 10 largest companies together turn over more money than the 100 poorest countries combined.[27] The dominance of big corporations has been enabled by technological advances – for example, in telecommunications – and by the deregulation of trade and investment by the WTO (often at the behest of TNCs themselves). Corporations can and do threaten to relocate to locations in the world where labour is cheaper and environmental standards are lower. This fuels a 'race to the bottom' as governments bend over backwards to appease TNCs in order to attract much sought-after investment. Politicians everywhere are doing their utmost to promote economic growth in pursuit of 'international competitiveness', but at the expense of people and the environment.

This is a view which is rarely aired in the mainstream press and broadcasting, for reasons that we will explore in Chapter 3. Even when it is aired, the response, if any, from other sectors of the media is invariably dismissive. According to Diane Coyle, economics editor of *The Independent*, the concern amongst greens, the churches, Third World campaigners and others over the unregulated operations of big business is misplaced. 'It's a red herring', she claimed in December 1997 during a televised debate on how the world might look in the new millennium. Coyle dismissed fears over globalisation as 'globaloney'. The mainstream viewpoint – held by the majority of politicians, as well as academics and journalists working in this area – is that TNCs are, barring a few deviant examples, responsible global citizens, creating new wealth, and bringing capital, technology and expertise to developing nations. According to *The Shell Report – 1998,*

'Increased activity by large companies in developing countries can boost trade, create jobs and help to alleviate poverty'.[28]

But with the rise in public opposition to economic globalisation, the corporate world is now on the defensive. In April 1999, Federal Reserve Chairman Alan Greenspan retorted that free trade raises living standards, and deplored any action taken to protect domestic industries from foreign competition. 'The United States', said Greenspan, 'has been in the forefront of the postwar opening up of international markets, much to our, and the rest of the world's, benefit. It would be a great tragedy were that process reversed'.[29] C. Fred Bergsten, director of the Institute for International Economics, concurred and added a warning about the increasing influence of anti-free trade activism:

> Most trade types thought the merits of free trade were so obvious, the bene-
> fits were so clear, that you didn't have to worry about adjustments – you
> could just let the free market take care of it. The sheer political gains of the
> anti-globalization side in the last few years have made the free trade side
> realize that they have to do something to deal with the losers from free trade
> and the dislocations generated by globalization.[30]

More defensiveness sprung from Michael Moore, former prime minister of New Zealand and new head of the WTO, when he insisted that his organisation 'is not a rich man's club'.[31] Before the millennium round of talks in Seattle, Moore claimed that protesters 'will be marching against opportunities for poor people to sell their products and services'.[32] This is the message that the corporate community, which includes the mass media, is keen to propagate. According to William Daley, US commerce secretary: 'People must be able to see and understand that the global trade system works for them and the environment in which they live'.[33] President Clinton told Congress: 'I think trade has divided us and divided Americans outside this chamber for too long. Somehow we have to find a common ground ... We have got to put a human face on the global economy'.[34]

The Asian meltdown

Such remarks from politicians and the business sector deserve further scrutiny. Consider the now toothless 'tiger economies' of southeast Asia. In 1990, dereg-ulation in these economies opened the floodgates to a massive influx of short-term foreign investment, as rich investors sought new markets. The global economy was buoyant. In 1997, the *World Bank Report* stated that 'the world economy grew at 3 per cent a year in the 1980s and 2 per cent in the first half of the 1990s', and that 'low and middle income economies grew more rapidly, aver-aging 3.4 per cent growth in the 1980s and 5 per cent in the 1990s'. US economist Robin Hahnel remarked:

In the same report we were told that 'growth in trade from increased trade liberalization, increased private capital flows and financial integration, and internal privatization and progressive dismantling of regulations and controls' had produced a rising global economic tide that was lifting all but the most unseaworthy boats.[35]

There were signs, however, that the growth in the global economy was unsustainable. Worldwide, new borrowing increased twentyfold from 1983 to 1998, while production only tripled. Daily trading in currency markets grew from $0.2 trillion in 1986 to $1.5 trillion in 1998. Less than 2 per cent of that $1.5 trillion was used to finance international trade or investment in plant and capacity. In other words, an astonishing 98 per cent was for purely speculative activity. Trading in derivatives, perhaps the riskiest of all financial instruments, increased 215 per cent per year between 1987 and 1997.[36]

It could not last. By July 1997, Thai property companies were in dire straits following the collapse of an artificially-inflated real estate bubble. A third of the stock market value was wiped out and banks which had funded the expansion collapsed. Foreign investors lost confidence and backed out. A wave of devaluations ensued, enveloping the economies of Thailand, Indonesia, South Korea and the Philippines. In a corporate coup of staggering proportions, the International Monetary Fund and the US Treasury devised a $120 billion 'rescue plan' for the free-falling Asian economies. This opened up Asian markets yet further to foreign capital, enabling corporations and investors in the US, Europe and Japan to buy Asian companies at rock-bottom prices. In April 1998, even Japan slipped into recession and the yen went tumbling. The devaluation of Asian currencies, especially the yen, hit Brazil's economy hard, dependent as it on income earned from exports to Asia. Apart from the devastating effects on people's jobs and livelihoods in many countries, the knock-on effects around the globe caused severe discomfort to even the most liberal of free-trade exponents, with calls for greater regulation of international flows of currency. Meanwhile, in South Korea, 20,000 firms had gone bust, and jobless rates of around 10 per cent were predicted. The Thai government decided to expel up to a million migrant workers by the end of 1999, while South Korea planned to eject 146,000 and Malaysia 900,000.[37]

In 1998, the size of the Thai economy fell by 8 per cent, and more than 2 million people were out of work by November that year. The unemployment rate had climbed from 2.1 to 7.3 per cent and, according to the World Bank, about 1 million had been pushed below the poverty line. In Indonesia, the economy shrank by 14 per cent. Twenty million people lost their jobs in a year – the unemployment rate rose from under 5 per cent to over 13 per cent – and the number living in absolute poverty quadrupled to 100 million. The United Nations

Children's Fund (Unicef) predicted an increase in infant mortality of 30 per cent by the end of 1998. According to Oxfam International, in the Philippines alone IMF-imposed cuts in preventative health care programmes would result in 29,000 deaths from malaria and an increase of 90,000 in the number of untreated tuberculosis cases.[38] These are some of the people that *The Independent*'s economics correspondent Hamish McRae would later describe as 'inevitable victims' of the crash.[39] The southeast Asian economic 'miracle' was over. But this enabled global corporations to move in and snap up Asian businesses at knock-down prices. The *Washington Post* noted in late 1998 that, 'Hordes of foreign investors are flowing back into Thailand, boosting room rates at top Bangkok hotels despite the recession. Foreign investors have gone on a $6.7 billion shopping spree this year, snapping up bargain-basement steel mills, securities companies, supermarket chains, and other assets'. [40]

It is important to note that when the IMF moves in to 'bail out an ailing economy', as the politicians and media would have it, it does so with public money, donated by contributor governments. Despite recent talk of reform, the IMF remains essentially an agent providing insurance cover for private investors at public expense. It is a popular misconception, originated by elite interests and propagated by the mainstream media, that IMF bailouts are designed to help debtor countries. In fact, the bailouts help international investors: they are the ones who actually receive the money. As Robin Hahnel observes: 'it is just one more case of privatizing the benefits of an economic activity – in this case, international lending – and socializing the burdens associated with that activity: risk of international default'.[41]

The cancer of capitalism

In Chapter 2 we will examine more closely the persistence of poverty in both the North and the South despite – in fact, as a result of – the increasing liberalisation of international trade and capital flows. The evidence suggests strongly that ongoing economic globalisation will lead to yet more weakening of labour conditions and environmental protection, while at the same time increasing the transfer of powers of self-determination and economic control from local communities to corporate headquarters. These are the inevitable consequences of a global economic system that is dependent on the endless pursuit of profit and growth. Hahnel rightly points out that the current balance of power in society 'is extremely favorable to those who favor further *un*democratic, *in*equitable, environmentally *de*structive, and *in*efficient globalization, and extremely unfavorable to opponents of this unfolding disaster'.[42]

Writer David Korten likens the modern capitalist society to cancer in a healthy body. Survival and recovery depends on the speedy creation of diverse, interlocking, locally-based economies and societies. This, in turn, depends on allowing space for community-level experimentation in which economic and other resources are directed locally and democratically, rather than being 'controlled by distant corporate bureaucracies intent on appropriating wealth to enrich their shareholders'.[43] Korten calls for a transformation from global capitalism to what he calls a system of 'mindful markets'. This recalls the original depiction of the market economy provided by Adam Smith in *The Wealth of Nations*. Smith envisioned 'mindful ethical cultures' combined with economies rooted in a particular locality, with small, locally-owned companies satisfying the needs of the community in which they are based. [44] This is almost exactly the opposite of the current system of global economics whose architects frequently, and unwittingly, cite Smith as an icon.

Whilst global capitalism continues to hold sway, almost all politicians and economists are failing to recognise – far less quantify – the full costs incurred by society and the environment for spiralling consumerism, unrestricted transnational flow of capital and the globalisation of markets. According to Ed Mayo, director of the London-based New Economics Foundation, old-style economists have not caught up with the need to describe how a just and sustainable economy will work in practice:

> At present we have an economy which can only understand people and nature through the narrow prism of buying and selling. Conventional economics assumes that people's motives are selfish ('economic man'), that they are concerned with maximising their own satisfaction ('utility') and that their needs can be expressed in what they can pay for ('effective demand').[45]

Until a transformation from capitalist to sustainable economics takes place, society will continue to consume resources at unacceptably high levels, pursue the illusory fix of fossil fuels and nuclear power, and even endanger the climate system, as we will see in Chapter 4.

Financial turmoil in the late 1990s – in Russia, Latin America, southeast Asia and even Japan – demonstrated that no nation is immune to disturbances which ripple through the unstable pyramid of playing cards that is today's global system of capitalist economics. And, just as global warming is predicted to lead to a rise in the frequency and magnitude of severe climatic events, the occasional gust of wind through capitalist society is in danger of hitting us harder – and more often – than ever before. The underlying problem is that global capitalism is driven by a debt-based financial system which creates an inexorable need for the economy to grow. It is therefore instructive at this point to take a brief look at money, the bizarre way in which it is created, and the impact this has on the planet.

Money makes the world go down

Money is a cunning invention. The historical record shows that it was in use as early as 2400 BC in Mesopotamia and Egypt. There is also evidence of money changing hands in China and the Aegean in the seventh century BC, and in fourth century BC India. The reason for its emergence appears to be tied to the expansion of trade – encouraging two or more communities to settle on a common currency – but it has also been used within communities for payment of fines, taxes, levies and wages.[46]

The social and moral damage that can ensue from the accumulation of money and wealth has long been recognised. The Greek philosopher Aristotle (384-322 BC) wrote:

> Where some people are wealthy and others have nothing, the result will be either extreme democracy or absolute oligarchy, or despotism will come from either of those excesses.[47]

Both the prophet Mohammed and Jesus of Nazareth warned against the love of money. Usury – earning interest by lending money – was prohibited in both Islam and Christianity, but by the late Middle Ages pecuniary interest, international trade and banking all flourished. In the late fifteenth century, Europe actually went into an inflationary spiral with wages lagging behind prices. The reason was the massive inflow of gold and silver from the Americas, first looted from the natives by the Spanish conquistadors, then subsequently mined by the First World using mainly indigenous slave labour working under appalling conditions. Entrepreneurs found they could make easy money and the poor were exploited.

During the European Renaissance, port cities such as Antwerp, Amsterdam, Venice and Genoa stimulated the rise of banking. But modern banking, in which bank notes were issued, only started later when a Scots gambler named John Law fled from England to France to escape a murder charge. Ingratiating himself with the French regent, Philippe Duc d'Orléans, he obtained permission to issue bank notes in the form of loans against the security of the land of France. Soon the notes were trusted more than hard coin, and they were readily exchanged. But too many notes were issued and Law fled France in 1720 leaving collapsed fortunes, falling prices, a depressed economy and an enduring suspicion of banking.

Two of the most important thinkers on the relationship between money and society were Adam Smith (1723-90) and Karl Marx (1818-1883). Smith's view was that the wealth of a nation ought not to be measured in terms of money but in terms of its useful labour force. Moreover, Smith was well aware of the vulgarity associated with the accumulation of money:

With the greater part of rich people, the chief enjoyment of riches consists in the parade of riches, which in their eyes is never so complete as when they appear to possess those decisive marks of opulence which nobody can possess but themselves.[48]

Marx too argued that 'value' resided in labour but that cash often triumphed. He also went further in attacking the unequal distribution of wealth between worker, capitalist and landlord, arguing that it was a consequence of the capitalist system of production.

In 1876, Western nations adopted the gold standard. This linked the issuing of money to gold reserves and provided a relatively fixed exchange-rate system. But it collapsed with the outbreak of the First World War. Afterwards, the victors imposed massive reparations on Germany which responded by over-issuing money. Catastrophic inflation ensued. Conditions in Germany were ripe for the rise of fascism. Meanwhile, the 1929 Wall Street Crash caused economic depression, poverty and unemployment around the world.

The fragility of capitalist economics motivated delegates from 44 countries to meet at Bretton Woods in the United States in 1944. They agreed a new international money system of fixed but adjustable exchange rates, with the International Monetary Fund as its custodian. It led to a period of comparative stability in which liberal trade, capital controls and fixed exchange rates created, as journalist Will Hutton put it, 'prosperity and full employment for a generation'. The US dollar, backed by gold, was a *de facto* world currency operating 'within an orderly international framework; a unique and possibly unrepeatable set of circumstances'.[49]

But this golden age – if that is indeed what it was – came to an abrupt end in 1971 when President Nixon terminated the guarantee to exchange one ounce of gold for $35. This ended what some saw as the over-valuation of the US dollar against the German mark and led to a boost in US export volumes. Many countries had pegged their currencies to the dollar or other 'strong' currencies, while other countries floated their exchange rates independently. With a volatile devaluing dollar the result was international monetary instability, which has in part contributed to the present Third World debt crisis. In short, as the world's economy has become increasingly globalised, the international monetary system has become increasingly fragile.

Let us examine the monetary system in a little more detail. One of the major services provided by banks and building societies (or credit unions in North America) is, of course, the lending of money. Indeed, many of us are bombarded with pleas from financial institutions to take out more loans on 'easy terms'. The fact is, they do not so much lend money, as *invent* it. Michael Rowbotham explains it thus in his 1998 book, *The Grip of Death*. Consider two individuals, A and B. A deposits one pound in a bank. On the back of this, the bank is allowed to create a pound (or more) to lend to B, charging B interest. But the bank does not lend A's pound to B. A's bank account remains intact. Now for the really clever part. When B repays the pound loan – the pound which the bank brought into existence out of nothing – the bank keeps it, plus whatever interest B had to pay! Money has been created out of the debt which B incurred.

The same thing happens when a bank or building society grants a mortgage. Rowbotham's latest figures reveal that, in the UK, mortgages account for over 60 per cent (£420 billion) of the money stock and, in the US, over 70 per cent ($4.2 trillion). As well as money arising out of personal debt related to mortgages, credit cards and so on, money is created out of industrial and commercial debt; for example, loans granted to companies by banks. In fact, in the last 30 years or so, the share of UK money which exists as 'legal tender' – the notes and coins in your purse or wallet – has dropped from 20 per cent to 3 per cent. The rest has been created out of debt, literally borrowed into existence. Rowbotham shows how this debt-based financial system drives the need for unsustainable economic growth by identifying three ingredients: competition for money, lack of purchasing power and wage dependence. We consider each one briefly in turn.

With so much debt sloshing around the financial system, there is intense competition for the limited money in circulation. Nobody – whether an individual or a company – wants to have to go into debt in order to buy what they need or to get their products into the market place. But debt – and the money supply – is escalating and the effect is a push towards an ever bigger economy. Although politicians and corporate bosses often deploy rhetoric about succeeding in a competitive business environment, the hard reality according to Rowbotham is that 'the economy has become an arena of cut-throat, all out, undisguised financial warfare for jobs, money and sales, and for personal and industrial survival'.[50]

In this hothouse of financial turmoil, mounting industrial debt requires that companies set sufficiently high prices on their goods and services to help pay off their debts. Salaries distributed amongst employees must be sufficiently high to enable people to buy these products. But there is insufficient money to do this. Money required to pay salaries is in competition with money required to pay off company debts. As Rowbotham says, 'industrial debt elevates the prices of goods and services above distributed incomes'. People simply do not earn enough to buy the products made by industry. The result is a chronic shortage of purchasing power. People are forced to borrow money to buy the goods and services they want – or simply need – generating more debt-based money, thus compounding the problem.

In addition to competition for money and the lack of purchasing power, there is the problem of wage dependence. Society's dependence on work to provide income locks all of us into forced economic growth. This is made worse by society's seeming reluctance to share out the work available to all those who wish to work. Practical solutions such as job-sharing and reduced working hours are dreadfully underutilised. As a result, each labour-saving advance in technology throws workers onto the scrapheap of unemployment. Those people fortunate enough to have a job are supporting – by means of taxes on their salaries – those who are out of work. But unemployment support is meagre and the unemployed are excluded from much of the economy, unable to afford goods and services which companies are desperate to sell (to repay their own debts). The pressure on the employed to produce and earn more increases inexorably, locking them into a pathological pattern of forced economic growth. This is why, as we saw above, the present system is analogous to cancer.

In simple terms, debt fuels the 'need to grow'. In *The Grip of Death*, Rowbotham demonstrates carefully and powerfully how this has transformed national and global networks in transport, agriculture and food production, wreaking havoc amongst local communities, producers and markets, while increasing waste, pollution and poverty around the globe; how 'Third World debt' was created and is perpetuated by the developed nations as a mechanism of neocolonialism; how transnational corporations gain increasing dominance in the global economy; and why 'debt-money' is inherently undemocratic and a threat to human rights. This is clearly unsustainable. However, there are alternatives such as Local Exchange Trading Systems (LETS) which allow goods and services to be marketed without the need for money. The most successful LETS scheme operates in the small American town of Ithaca, New York, where hundreds of thousands of 'Ithaca Hours' have been traded by more than 3,000 participants. The currency is accepted by more than 250 local businesses. In the UK there are already more than 400 LETS schemes in operation. Local money systems promote economic self-reliance by enabling communities to reduce their reliance on inherently unstable national and global economies.[51]

To sum up, rather than making the world go round, money – as it is presently created and used – makes the world fall down. Following the Asian meltdown of the late 1990s, Paul Volcker, former chairman of the Federal Reserve Board, conceded the precarious nature of the financial system:

> Suddenly, it all seems in jeopardy. All that real growth – all the trillions in paper wealth creation – is at risk. What started as a blip on the radar screen in Thailand – about as far away from Washington or New York as you can get – has somehow turned into something of a financial contagion.[52]

It is interesting to note that Volcker equates 'real growth' with 'trillions in paper wealth creation'.

In short, the capitalist imperative to continually generate more profit derives from the debt-based financial system. This system underlies the corporate need to find new investment opportunities around the globe. From the perspective of big business, this requires that developing countries and previously 'underexploited' business sectors – such as insurance services, education, forestry and agriculture – have to be prised open to allow wealthy companies and investors to move in. The case of the stalled Multilateral Agreement on Investment is an archetypal example – both in terms of the stacking of the odds in favour of global capitalism and the growing public opposition to such corporate protectionism.

Case study: the Multilateral Agreement on Investment

Consider the following news stories from around the world. Toronto's education authorities have been threatened with lawsuits by a multinational agribusiness company, following the refusal of Toronto schools to serve hormone-treated beef to pupils. Glasgow City Council's decision that its fleet of vehicles should switch from petrol to clean electricity has been challenged in the courts by a consortium of oil companies which could have provided cheaper fuel. And a housing authority in Delhi, which terminated a contract with one of its suppliers because of the firm's long record of employee exploitation, has been fined tens of thousands of pounds. An international insurance company with shares in the firm declared that awarding of the fine was a satisfactory result.

OK. I admit it – these are not real items from today's news, but some critics argued they could have been if the far-reaching Multilateral Agreement on Investment (MAI) had been adopted by the Organisation for Economic Co-operation and Development, the Paris-based club of 29 rich nations which accounts for 92 per cent of the world's flow of corporate capital. The MAI was a clarion call to activists the world over. The agreement would have actually overridden the laws of many nations, and would have granted transnational corporations and investors the new right to sue governments for alleged breach of the pact. Conversely, however, governments, communities or individuals would not have been able to sue companies or investors for any breach of environmental or social law.

Many citizens were unaware of this dangerous and far-reaching proposed treaty, at least until after the talks collapsed in October 1998 when the French walked out. Although the MAI was ultimately defeated by an unprecedented alliance of public interest groups, as we describe below, there are clones of the treaty which threaten to emerge at any of a number of nexuses of power in the global economy, such as the World Trade Organisation. The MAI's designers and defenders are still beavering away behind the scenes, lobbying, bartering and devising similar measures to extend their hold over governments. This is the motivation for presenting below a brief history of how the investment agreement originated, and how it would have operated if it had been agreed to by signatory nations.

Like the WTO which preceded it, the aim of the MAI and similar agreements now being considered in its place is to promote economic growth. Whereas the WTO was set up to lower trade barriers, the MAI was intended 'to provide high standards of investment protection and liberalisation of investment regimes'. Renato Ruggerio, WTO director-general between 1995 and 1999, reportedly proclaimed: 'We are writing the constitution of a single global economy.'[53] In the early days of MAI, discussions took place behind closed doors at the OECD. Multinational companies played a crucial role behind the scenes, with corporate lobby groups consulted right from the preparatory phase of an MAI feasibility study and continuing throughout the negotiations. The Business and Industry Advisory Council, which is an umbrella group of various business associations, was involved early on in the development of the MAI. The International Chamber of Commerce was able to transfer almost all the proposals in its April 1996 report, *Multilateral Rules for Investment*, into the first MAI draft just nine months later.[54] 'Trade and investment are two sides of the same coin. We trade to invest and we invest to trade', said Stephen Canner, vice-president of investment policy for the United States Council for International Business (USCIB), a group of large US multinationals.[55] The USCIB had regular meetings with US negotiators immediately before and after each MAI negotiating session. A model for the MAI was the North American Free Trade Agreement (NAFTA) between Canada, the United States and Mexico. But because of the newer treaty's more powerful provisions it was described by some opponents as 'NAFTA on steroids'.

Preparations for a new agreement on international investment began as early as 1991, just after the US and a few allied countries had halted moves at the UN to draft a code of conduct to be applied to transnational corporations. MAI negotiations began in May 1995, but details of the proposed pact only became publicly available in 1997 after an earlier draft was leaked and posted on the internet by the Washington-based pressure group Public Citizen.[56] The leak confirmed the worst fears of environmentalists, Third World campaigners and trade unions, because the MAI opened up the possibility of giving transnational corporations and international investors a way to bypass the court system of any country. Disputes under the MAI were to be dealt with by an international panel consisting of industry experts that would interpret the treaty and issue binding rulings. Fortunately, disagreements between the European Union and the United States meant that the first deadline for signing the MAI in May 1997 was missed.

The key principle of the MAI was non-discrimination against foreign investors; in other words, foreign and domestic investors would enjoy a 'level playing field'.

However, the draft MAI's wording was that foreign investors must be treated 'at least as well' as domestic investors. This would promote the continued spending of public funds to attract foreign investors but would not allow domestic companies any form of preferential treatment, to promote local enterprise for example, even if this happened unintentionally. Rather than the 'equal treatment' described by the MAI's proponents, this would have created a structural advantage for foreign investors, primarily the large transnational corporations. Xanthe Bevis, a Green Party councillor in Oxford, expressed fear that 'local authorities may be liable to pay costs if a transnational company takes them to the MAI's International Tribunal to seek compensation for loss of earnings'. Bevis cited a possible example 'of a local authority discriminating in favour of companies with higher environmental and employment standards'.[57] Stung by mounting criticism of this kind, the British government, an ardent supporter of the MAI, attempted to reassure local authorities that they would not, in fact, be liable to court claims under the new pact.[58] Presumably, citizens were to be content with the prospect of only national governments being taken to court by disgruntled investors!

The responsibility for the UK's role in MAI negotiations lay with officials at the Department of Trade and Industry. Margaret Beckett, then head of the DTI, wrote in response to the many hundreds of letters sent to her department: 'We do not want an MAI which might threaten our commitment to sustainable development, core labour standards and the proper regulation of business. I do not believe that the MAI will be an obstacle to those objectives'.[59] Whitehall officials subsequently claimed that the UK had persuaded the OECD into accepting an environmental review of the MAI which was making 'good progress'.[60] But according to Barry Coates, director of the London-based World Development Movement, the review did 'not begin to address the fundamental concerns that non-governmental organisations have raised'.[61] Developing countries were to be invited to sign up to the MAI when completed on a 'take it or leave it' basis. As WDM warned, they 'will be unable to resist the pressure. The MAI is unfair and potentially devastating for the poorest countries'.[62]

Campaigners regarded the DTI's support for the MAI as inconsistent with the OECD's ambitious programme – announced in November 1997 – to halve world poverty by 2015. But when questioned about the MAI at a public meeting, Clare Short, the UK Secretary of State for International Development, simply brushed aside concerns: 'There have to be structures in poor countries for economic growth to be realised for them.'[63] The fundamental problem is that these structures are being designed and implemented for the benefit of transnational corporations and investors, not the world's poor.

The UK government seemed content to steamroller the impending agreement through with little or no public consultation. On 23 July, 1997, a sparsely attended

House of Commons heard Alan Simpson, Labour MP for Nottingham South, lambast the MAI as 'a crook's charter of an agreement'. It would, 'for the first time place the rights of companies above those of countries and the rights of shareholders above those of citizens'.[64] WDM added a significant detail: 'The United States has applied to exempt all its existing state and local government laws, policies and programmes from [the MAI's] provisions. This reveals that the country that has been pushing hardest for the MAI refuses to apply it at home'. Negotiators from the United States also took the highly unusual step of seeking exemption from a so-called 'standstill' provision that would prevent governments from enacting new laws that might violate the agreement. This meant that the US could pass future laws on issues such as government subsidies and procurement of services that did not conform to the MAI. It is worth noting that the United Kingdom government proposed no such protective measures for its own civil society.[65]

In Scotland, fears were expressed that the MAI would restrict the powers of the newly established Scottish Parliament. According to Kevin Dunion, director of Friends of the Earth Scotland, 'The MAI is anti-democratic. Just as the Scottish people have won a hard-fought battle for devolution, the MAI will squeeze out local decision-making and hinder the proper strategic development of the Scottish economy'.[66] Anne McKechnie of the Glasgow branch of WDM warned, 'Donald Dewar [the late Secretary of State for Scotland] has promised to end our feudal system of land ownership. MAI could scupper that'.[67] By insisting that foreign investors were to be treated to a level playing field with home investors, land use reform that favoured community ownership might actually have contravened MAI rules.

Apart from a few honourable exceptions, notably in *The Guardian,* mainstream journalists in the UK ignored the MAI or actually spoke up in its favour. Diane Coyle, economics editor of *The Independent,* accused campaigners of adopting the rhetoric of the 1960s and 1970s in portraying multinationals 'as the evil agents of western imperialism' and retorted 'in fact, multinationals are the goodies on the international investment scene'. Of the MAI itself she wrote: 'Obviously, the agreement is designed to make foreign investment easier, and this means striking a balance between corporate and other interests.'[68] These 'other interests' include those related to the environment, public health, secure employment and poverty reduction.

Throughout 1997, worldwide opposition to the MAI among non-governmental organisations mounted. At the MAI meeting held in Paris in October that year, a coalition of more than 50 groups from 25 countries – including Oxfam, Friends of the Earth, the World Development Movement and the World Wide Fund for Nature – demanded that the OECD suspend negotiations and commit to public assessment of the social, environmental and development impacts of the MAI. Unsurprisingly, the OECD refused. In some quarters, there was downright hostility to such demands: 'We will oppose any and all measures to create or even imply binding obligations for governments or business related to environment or labour', stated Abraham Katz, president of the United States Council for International Business.

But the international public opposition was gaining momentum. By the time negotiators assembled in Paris for the February 1998 meeting, vigorous campaigns were taking place in each OECD country. Action was focused on informing the public and mobilising parliaments. Some media coverage belatedly appeared, and the first street demonstrations highlighted the growing public protest. In what amounted to a partial victory for campaigners, rather than sign the treaty in April 1998, as had been anticipated, the OECD announced that negotiations had been suspended for six months. Ministers agreed on 'a period of assessment and further consultation between the negotiating parties and with interested parts of their societies'. Subsequently, there was scant evidence of any such consultation. Indeed, the Labour government in the UK refused calls for a government-sponsored parliamentary debate or an independent assessment of the MAI's impact on sustainable development, the EU, Labour's 'ethical' foreign policy, local democracy, Scottish and Welsh devolution and existing multilateral agreements related to the environment, labour standards and human rights.

Apparently undeterred by opposition, the DTI maintained a gung-ho approach to the pact, stating that, 'The UK strongly feel[s] that all levels of government should be bound by the disciplines of the MAI'. This was a strong statement indeed; the loss of sovereignty involved would dwarf the impact of the EU's Maastricht Treaty (which *had* aroused considerable debate in the mainstream media and political domains). Once a country had signed up to the MAI it would not be able to withdraw for five years, and even then it would still be bound by the agreement for a further fifteen years.

Behind the scenes, the negotiators were becoming less optimistic that the MAI would ever be signed. The NGO campaign coincided with a withdrawal of support from the business lobby. Even the right-wing press took to referring to the MAI as 'the treaty that no-one wants'. When negotiators got together again in October 1998 the MAI was dead in the water, at least within the forum of the OECD. The French had declined to rejoin the talks, leading to their collapse – any treaty required unanimity amongst all EU countries. The *Financial Times* spoke of an 'embarrassing halt' and cast the US attempts to foist an agreement on developing countries as 'neo-imperialism'.[69] However, French Prime Minister Lionel Jospin did not rule out the concept of MAI to regulate foreign direct investment, saying that a more appropriate forum would be the World Trade Organisation in which, unlike the OECD, developing nations have a voice. Sadly, the reality is that the views of developing countries carry much less weight at the WTO than those of the rich countries of the North, who are more often than not liable to do the bidding of TNCs. The WTO is fundamentally flawed because it is representative only of the interests of corporations and money; in other words, only the richest one-tenth of 1 per cent of people. As David Korten observed, that 'is contrary to life, the principles of life and everything we need to get a world that works both for people and planet'.[70]

Following a British government reshuffle in 1998, Brian Wilson, the new junior trade minister with responsibility for MAI negotiations, quickly conceded that the failed agreement was no longer an OECD issue but also 'stressed Britain's continuing commitment to clear international rules for companies investing overseas'.[71] He also spoke of starting afresh with 'a blank sheet of paper'.[72] This was a curiously disingenuous phrase; it is hardly plausible that the interests of investors would not be hard-wired into any starting point for negotiations in other corporate institutions, whether it be at the World Bank, the International Monetary Fund or the WTO. Barry Coates rightly warned that 'we obviously need to stay vigilant to stop MAI-like provisions being pushed in other agreements'. [73]

Just before the MAI talks collapsed at the OECD, a coalition of activists in Scotland was attempting to raise the profile of this unprecedented treaty which had slipped past most mainstream media outlets.[74] The Scottish Campaign Against the MAI comprised campaigners from Reforesting Scotland, Friends of the Earth Scotland, WDM, and the Green, Labour and Scottish National Parties. After attracting expressions of interest from several MPs, the trade union UNISON, the Glasgow Human Rights Centre, Oxfam and the Quakers, the Campaign set out to reach a wider audience by publishing a citizen's charter in June 1998.

The *Scottish Charter Against the MAI* began by pointing out that the United Nations International Covenant on Economic, Social and Cultural Rights states, 'All peoples have the right of self-determination. By virtue of that right, they freely determine their political status and freely pursue their economic, social and cultural development'. According to a coalition spokesperson, 'The MAI, currently being negotiated, challenges this [self-determination] by removing the rights of states and communities, at a local, regional, national and international level, to regulate foreign investors. It would transfer power from democratically elected governments to unaccountable companies'. In an echo of the 1320 Declaration of Arbroath, in which Scotland asserted its independence, the Charter went on to declare, 'We, the people of Scotland, demand the right to: control development in our own communities; promote Scottish initiatives; regulate the activities of all companies operating in Scotland, in co-operation with international agreements; protect our people, culture and environment'. And, in a show of solidarity with the poor around the world, 'We support the rights of all peoples to fair trade and sustainable development'.[75] The coalition called on all candidates for the first Scottish parliamentary election in May 1999 to reject moves towards the MAI.

The Council of Canadians (CoC), a public movement opposing the destructive forces of globalisation, has been vigilant in monitoring any reappearance of the MAI. In March 1999, Murray Dobbin of CoC issued a warning via the internet that 'the bureaucrats who helped bring us the MAI are beavering away on another chapter in the neo-liberal assault on government'.[76] The powerful economic tool being proposed this time was a multinational Agreement on Government Procurement (AGP) intended to regulate the way that governments use their purchasing power. Current purchasing policy delegated to Canadian municipalities (local authorities) allows preference to be granted to local firms, and thereby promotes secure local employment, supports local systems of production and distribution (so keeping down the environmental costs associated with transport), retains money within local communities, and generally stabilises and strengthens the local economy. It was the threat to this economic tool of self-determination that engendered so much opposition to the MAI. The Agreement on Government Procurement is a WTO-based initiative, involving 26 other nations, all of them also members of the OECD.

The shock of the MAI spurred other coalitions of public movements. Realising that an effective weapon of campaigning *against* something is to campaign *for* a sustainable alternative, an international grouping developed a citizen-based alternative. Dubbed the Citizens' Public Trust Treaty, it 'calls upon the nations of the world to ensure the rights of present and future generations to genuine peace, social justice and ecological integrity'. Taking the form of a proposed United Nations General Assembly Resolution, the Citizens' Treaty was launched on 1 January, 1999, immediately following the fiftieth anniversary of the Universal Declaration of Human Rights. The treaty's proposers noted that the economy is becoming increasingly centralised under the influence of TNCs and financial institutions, at the expense of ordinary people. Deregulation of financial markets has produced an unstable 'global casino' vulnerable to massive speculative capital flows. Moreover, 'International trade agreements such as NAFTA, GATT, and now the proposed Multilateral Agreement on Investment have diminished the power of governments and elevated the rights of corporations above those of nations and their citizens.'[77]

It remains to be seen whether it will take another fifty years for the resolution to be adopted. Nevertheless, the initiative demonstrates the growing strength of citizen coalitions spanning environmental, social justice, church and human rights groups, and their refusal to accept that the globalisation being dumped upon us by transnational corporations and investors is either 'inevitable' or 'desirable', as they and their political and media allies would have us believe. With such a growing grassroots coalition lined up against the might of the OECD, the World Bank, the IMF and the WTO, there is at least a spark of hope for a fairer society in the future.[78]

Regulate or die

A fierce battle is unfolding between the proponents of globalisation who talk of the need for 'international competitiveness' and 'streamlining public services', and those voices on the other side who are calling for greater regulation of international trade and finance in order to uphold standards of health, labour and environmental protection. Occasionally, mainstream politicians will acknowledge public fears about the impact of globalisation, but then claim that integration of the global economy must continue yet further in order to share the benefits and thus tackle society's problems (often caused or exacerbated by earlier economic growth). Thus, Clare Short wrote in *The Guardian* in the approach to the WTO meeting in Seattle: 'The developing world cannot escape from poverty unless its economic growth increases year on year. Attracting foreign investment is crucial and so is the ability to gain access to world trade markets.'[79] US Commerce Secretary William Daley maintained the media offensive, saying that the WTO should intensify existing cooperation with the International Labour Organisation to tackle the problem of rising unemployment and job insecurity. The WTO should also, he said, review the environmental impact of a new round of trade talks to help counteract the 'tremendous distrust and fear' among the general public about trade and a 'lack of understanding about its broader economic benefits'. Daley concluded, 'people must be able to see and understand that the global trade system works for them and the environment in which they live'.[80]

This book aims to show that the growing public opposition to such rhetoric is both valid and heartening. Many are beginning to realise that economic globalisation is a toxic phenomenon – sometimes literally. Many developing countries are struggling to achieve a toe-hold in the global economy, even to the extent of sacrificing public and ecological health to attract inward investment. Consider the following case study from Cambodia, devastated by heavy US bombing and a civil war sustained by the United States between 1969 and 1975, then subjected to the genocidal rule of the Khmer Rouge for the following three years.[81] In the 1990s, the country found itself on the receiving end of a poisonous get-rich scheme involving the importing of several thousand tonnes of toxic waste from a Taiwanese petrochemical company, Formosa Plastics Group. In November 1998, the toxic waste was quietly transported to the coastal Cambodian city of

Sihanoukville, following the agreement of the Cambodian government to receive it: such is the desperation of some countries not to miss out on the 'benefits' of globalisation. Formosa Plastics, unable to dump the waste at home in Taiwan because of the fear of civil protests there, initially denied that the material was dangerous. However, a World Health Organisation official in Cambodia declared that tests had found extremely high levels of inorganic mercury in the waste.[82] Four people died during riots when word got out about the waste, and a dock worker died after cleaning out the hold of the ship which had brought the material. A senior Formosa Plastics official was later reported as saying, 'We plan to ship the waste out of Cambodia to either the United States or Europe, where disposal technology is sophisticated'.[83] In fact, plans to dump the waste in California fell through after environmentalists lobbied the US Environmental Protection Agency to revoke the dumping permit. Undeterred, Formosa's president said that the waste would be returned temporarily to Taiwan while they sought another dumping location in 'an advanced country, preferably the US'.[84] In March 2000, it was reported that the Dutch government had accepted a secret shipment of the toxic waste three months earlier.[85]

That dirty word: 'protectionism'

Calls for higher standards of environmental integrity, human health or social justice are all too often brushed aside by corporations and mainstream politicians as 'protectionism' and 'impediments to free trade'. Proponents of trade and capital liberalisation lampoon protectionism as 'uncompetitive' and 'backwards'. But, as Tim Lang and Colin Hines reminded us in their 1993 book, *The New Protectionism*, if one thinks about those aspects of life which matter to us, such as a clean environment and secure employment, to protect is surely good. They distinguish between *old* protectionism and *new* protectionism. Under old protectionism countries protected their national industries by, for example, imposing tariffs on goods entering the country to make them more expensive than domestic goods. The state also worked with the private sector to guide investment where it was needed. Once the industry had been established nationally it could then, in theory, expand into exports and compete in world markets. This 'import substitution model' has been responsible for the growth of such trumpeted economies as Brazil and South Korea, but with appalling social inequalities and at considerable environmental cost.[85]

Moreover, old protectionism has actually been used by big and powerful interests to pursue their own private goals. In that sense, it is comparable to free trade, notwithstanding attempts by proponents of liberalisation to portray free trade and protectionism as diametrically opposed. In contrast, *new* protectionism 'seeks to protect *public* interests such as health, the environment, safety standards and reduction of poverty, against the interests of unrestrained trade'.[87] New protectionism offers a route to meet the global challenge of the three 'Es' of a healthy environment, a sane economy and social equity. Both old-style protectionism and free trade have failed to provide any of these.

New protectionism aims to promote social justice and environmental protection by strengthening and diversifying economies and communities so that as many needs as possible are met locally or nationally. Other needs could be catered for by looking to the surrounding region of neighbouring countries, and only as a last option to global trade. There are already enough resources to pay for this transition to a sustainable future by tackling the massive destabilising flows in the international financial system. A powerful and fair means of curbing movements in transnational capital, and redirecting funds to secure regional economies, would be to impose an international transfer tax on investment. This would be analogous to the proposed Tobin tax on currency transactions, named after the American economist who suggested it in the 1970s.

Can global markets be 'reformed'?

Despite the shockwaves which cascaded around global financial markets in 1998, mainstream politicians have restricted themselves to cautious and tentative statements about improving the 'transparency' of transnational capital flows. Gordon Brown, the UK Chancellor of the Exchequer and an influential figure in the International Monetary Fund, dipped his toe in a little further. Speaking at a summit of Commonwealth finance ministers in September 1998, he called for the setting up of a committee for global financial regulation. But rather than being a democratically elected or directly accountable body, Brown's global regulator would consist of the very institutions that support and promote the unsustainable global economy: the IMF, the World Bank, the Basle Committee for Banking Supervision, as well as 'other international regulatory groupings'. The committee would establish 'new codes of fiscal and monetary conduct, improve information flows to the private sector and find better ways of identifying risk to the world's financial system'. Although Brown made a weak and vague reference to 'the need for greater attention to the human costs of the global financial crisis', true to form the answer to the global crisis was 'not less globalisation, but more'.[88]

Similar principles were outlined by Lawrence Summers, then Deputy Secretary of the US Treasury, following the World Economic Forum in Davos, Switzerland, in January 1999. He called for improved transparency in the international 'financial architecture' and alleged that world markets were too reliant on the buoyant American economy – 'the only significant engine of growth at present'. In an echo of Brown's call to consider the human costs of the financial system, Summers admitted that policymakers had to combat inequality – 'the

Achilles heel of the remarkable success of the American economy'.[89] Like Brown, Summers failed to provide any convincing explanation as to how more globalisation would or could reduce inequality.

The consensus amongst the rich and powerful G7 nations on regulatory reform of markets masks the underlying need for root-and-branch reform. Jeremy Warner, a business journalist, takes an anthropomorphic view of financial markets which 'after a severe shock ... are always repentant and risk averse'. Markets 'don't need to be told not to invest in high-risk regions' but 'like the compulsive gambler, they always return to the gaming table'. Putting regulation in place is futile because 'markets generally find a way round it'. In what, ironically, ought to be regarded as a damning indictment of capitalism by a business journalist, Warner adds that 'markets have always been largely driven by greed and fear – no code of conduct, however robust, would be sufficient to stop these extremes of behaviour'.[90] Such a cynical viewpoint may appear worldly-wise, but it is still rooted in the mindset that globalisation is inevitable and regulation counterproductive.

Some NGOs, such as the World Development Movement, have called for a regulatory framework to ensure that foreign direct investment and the operation of TNCs work for the maximum benefit of all stakeholders, in particular the poor. In a consultation paper for their *People Before Profits* campaign, WDM proposed a new international investment agreement (IIA) to 'enable governments to attract high quality investment as part of a sustainable development strategy' and to 'protect basic rights through global standards for the operations of foreign investors'.[91] As well as an IIA, multinational enterprises would have to adhere to core principles based on already agreed international standards: for example, under conventions and declarations of the International Labour Organisation, 'multinational conventions should uphold the rights of workers to form and join trades unions and bargain collectively and to a safe working environment'. Moreover, they 'should offer the best possible wages, benefits and conditions ... [and] should maintain the highest health and safety standards'.[92] Under international environmental agreements such as the Montreal Protocol, the Rotterdam Convention and declarations made at the 1992 Rio Earth Summit, 'multinational companies have responsibilities to undertake environmental impact assessments, to prevent and clean up pollution and meet their responsibilities on climate change, biodiversity, the sea, and ozone-depleting substances'.[93] The concept of regulating corporate activity is an old one. It is taken for granted that there should be rules governing the operation of corporations domestically. For example, in the UK, the Factories Act on Child Labour was passed as early as 1833. Similar international rules are, as WDM put it, 'a practical response to the internationalisation of economic activity'.[94]

Making investment work for people, argues WDM, also requires 'making space' for national strategies of sustainable development. For developing countries, this means cancelling 'unpayable foreign debt' and removing destructive IMF-imposed 'structural adjustment programmes' (see the next chapter). Corporations should also be held responsible in their home countries in the North for actions carried out by their often less well regulated subsidiaries in the South. For example, legal action against the oil company Unocal was taken in the United States for alleged human rights violations arising from its operations in Burma. In addition to an international regulatory framework for investment, WDM also sees a role for self-regulation by TNCs promoting best practice, although the group concedes that 'voluntary or "civil society" regulation will only ever be adopted by a few companies – and these will tend to be the ones already operating high standards'.[95]

All the above measures, if universally adopted, monitored and maintained, would certainly have a benign effect on economic globalisation, particularly for the vulnerable economies of the South. The new framework could thereby make a positive difference to the lives of hundreds of millions of citizens around the globe. At the core of this new framework would be a people-friendly international investment agreement, described above, and not a corporate-promoted MAI. WDM's proposal is that the IIA would still 'include basic protection of investors in order to ensure the continued expansion of investment flows globally'.[96] One might question, however, to what extent a continued expansion of investment is sustainable in a finite world. Moreover, would the proposed measures in effect maintain a continued dependence of developing countries on foreign direct investment from the rich North, albeit of a more benign nature? If so, the global economic infrastructure, comprising the multinational companies and financial institutions which have no democratic mandate and which have inflicted much of the social, economic and environmental damage around the world, particularly in the South, would likely remain largely in place. Those who had profited at public expense would retain their hands on the helm of the global economy.

There are others who argue that, in addition to the above important proposals for a new international regulatory framework, more radical measures are required for truly long-term sustainable development. Such a combined and strengthened package would be more likely to kickstart a genuine transformation to a citizen-based democracy. Without such a package, any societal gains achieved would likely be subsequently lost, with locally-determined paths of development being eroded once again by powerful companies and investors. The US writer and activist Michael Albert has worked hard to set out a practical economic vision based on decentralised and participatory decision-making.[97] The well-known linguist and social commentator Noam Chomsky says that Albert's ideas 'should be considered very seriously by those who are dedicated to making the world more just and more free'.[98]

From globalisation to localisation

In his book *Localization*, Colin Hines criticises development NGOs for adhering to the 'flawed paradigm that exports from the South to the North are a major route for the poor's development'.[99] Hines points out how the majority of social-needs activists have failed to take into account the pressures of globalization on government expenditure which is subservient to the mantra of 'international competitiveness' by which social and environmental priorities fall by the wayside. Hines warns eloquently that unless NGO 'demands are put within the context of overarching change that prioritizes protecting and rebuilding local economies, then campaign gains will be very limited in their scope'.[100]

Hines proposes a two-step reform of world markets. First, tackle the threat of capital flight. To some extent, this mirrors the apparent concerns professed by the G7's Brown and Summers above, but it goes much further by calling for the taxing of speculation and the introduction of purchase taxes on stocks, bonds and derivatives. These constraints on destabilising capital flows should be introduced over a stated period, to prevent the threat of financial withdrawal, and should be augmented by stringent laws to allow the confiscation of assets of anyone who tried to evade the legislative constraints prior to their implementation.

The second step of reform would be to keep capital local; in other words, an 'invest here, to prosper here' policy. This would entail restructuring the taxation system to serve people and the environment – by taxing 'bads' like pollution and depletion of natural resources, instead of 'goods' like employment; tackling corporate tax evasion; and, after due warning, closing offshore banking centres to prevent capital escaping banking and securities laws and national taxes. Local economies should be strengthened by retaining capital within the community. To facilitate this, central banks at national level would assist the rebuilding of local economies via smaller locally-based banks, credit unions and other local enterprises. Financial institutions – such as insurance, pension and endowment funds – should be encouraged, through legislative measures and tax breaks, to invest in the local community.[101]

The present unsustainable economic balance would be redressed in favour of local economies – including, as far as possible, local production for local consumption – as part of a reformed economy. But there would still be a place for responsible foreign direct investment in countries which needed help to become self-reliant, as WDM and other NGOs have argued, including 'tax penalties ... for foreign investment which does not directly help the Third World or eastern Europe to protect and diversify their own sustainable local economies'.[102]

Development campaigners have occasionally expressed scepticism of the Green – and progressive left – view that local economies should be strengthened, considering this to be a pretext for the blocking of imports from developing countries. This is perhaps based on a mutual misunderstanding of each others' position. Certainly, environmentalists must be aware that there can be incredible pressure on poor people in developing countries, arising from the urgent need for land or income, to exploit – perhaps even damage – their local environment. On the other hand, development campaigners pushing for a massive expansion of fairly-traded coffee, tea and other commodities, 'need to accept paradoxical goals: In the short term they [should] do all they can, but in the long term they should ideally work for less global and long distance trade and more local trade'. Long-distance trade has high environmental costs associated with fossil-fuel driven international transport. There are also social costs because such trade does not tend to benefit the local people, but instead benefits companies and investors holding the purse strings many hundreds or thousands of miles away. Therefore, environmentalists 'want all trade to be fair and to make the final price of all products reflect the full cost of production to both producers and the environment'.[103] In the short and medium term, then, developing countries need to have greater access to international markets – but in the longer term the balance for all countries should be a shift from long distance trade to local trade.

How will such a radical transition be funded? Ecological taxes on energy, other resource use and pollution will all help. But how will corporate obstructionism be overcome? By a broad-based citizen movement demanding action at the level of powerful regional groupings of countries, especially Europe and North America. Instead of the corporate-led World Trade Organisation, a shift from economic globalisation to localisation would be facilitated, argues Hines, by a World Localisation Organisation administering a General Agreement on Sustainable Trade. For example, Hines envisions an ecologically-reformed EU as being one major economic forum which would provide enough political clout to transform today's globalisation. A mutually-reinforcing package of new protectionist measures adopted in Europe could initiate a revolution on a global scale: import and export tariffs; controls on transnational corporations; keeping capital local; improving the efficiency of local competitiveness to maintain strong local economies; optimising the devolution of political power and democratic accountability; encouraging trade and aid which boosts self-reliance; and the promotion of environmental protection.[104]

Protecting the environment will mean accounting for the environmental costs of human activities, such as the pollution and energy use associated with long-distance transport. Resource taxes – on the consumption of the Earth's capital of wood, metals, minerals and so on – would also help pay for the economic transition outlined above. 'Protecting the local, globally', as Hines puts it, sums up the radical yet pragmatic worldview that is taking root in diverse communities around the world: the Scottish island of Eigg, where the locals now share land ownership; Bangkok, where several hundred Thai farmers have been protesting against the threat to traditional varieties of rice from genetically modified US imports; and the resistance of Indian villagers to the destructive large-scale development of the Narmada dam. These are just some of the people who do not accept the 'inevitability' of the globalisation process that is being foisted upon us by corporations and their political allies. There *is* an alternative to globalisation – a process of localisation in which communities, sustainable economies and the environment are safeguarded.

Notes

1   Robin Hahnel, 'Fighting Globalization', ZNet daily commentary (www.zmag.org), 22 September, 1999.
2   Bill Clinton, WTO ministerial meeting, 18 May 1998. Quoted in Madeley, *Big Business, Poor Peoples*, p. 17.
3   Lang and Hines, *The New Protectionism*, p. 122.
4   *Ibid.*, p. 121.
5   GATT emerged from the 1944 Bretton Woods conference in the United States, with the aim of devising mutually agreed rules between sovereign states to increase volumes of world trade by reducing tariffs imposed by one country on another country's goods. There have been many rounds of GATT negotiations since the first series in 1948. The eighth – the Uruguay Round – culminated in the establishment of the World Trade Organisation in 1995, a powerful body with the authority to adjudicate on trade disputes between signatories. For the first time, agreements were reached on insurance services, agriculture and intellectual property rights. The latter has caused tremendous disquiet amongst environmentalists because the provision for Trade-Related Intellectual Property Rights enables, for example, the exploitation of tropical genetic diversity by transnational corporations, or, as Vandana Shiva, the Indian activist, puts it: 'the monopolistic control of life forms' (see Chapter 7).
6   Recounted in Hines, *Localization,* pp.189-190.
7   *The Independent*, 5 March, 1999.
8   Hines, *Act local, act global*, p. 7.
9   *The Globe and Mail* (Toronto-based newspaper), 20 July, 1998.
10 David Wood, 'The international campaign against the Multilateral Agreement on Investment: a test case for the future of globalisation?', *Ethics, Place and Environment*, Vol. 3, No.1, pp. 25-45.
11 Steven Shrybman, *The Ecologist*, Vol. 29, No. 4, p. 270.
12 Quoted in Madeley, *Big Business, Poor Peoples*, p. 18.
13 See Paul Kingsnorth, *The Ecologist,* Vol 28, No 5, pp. 266-269.
14 Hines, *Act local, act global*, p. 8.
15 *The Guardian*, 6 October, 1999.
16 *Ibid.*
17 The European Community: precursor of the European Union.
18 Quoted in Balanyá *et al., Europe, Inc.*, p. 132.

19   *Ibid.,* quoted, p. 167.
20   *Ibid.,* quoted, p. 171.
21   *Ibid.,* quoted, p. 152.
22   Gibby Zobel, *The Big Issue*, 15-21 November, 1999.
23   Quoted in Belenyá *et al., Europe, Inc.,* p. 148.
24   Tony Juniper, *The Guardian,* 17 November, 1999.
25   *Ibid.,* quoted.
26   David Rockefeller, *Newsweek,* 1 February , 1999.
27   Hines, *Act local, act global,* p. 1.
28   Shell International, *Profits and Principles,* p. 36.
29   Quoted in Hahnel, *Panic Rules!,* p. 13.
30   *Ibid.,* p. 100.
31   *The Independent,* 27 September, 1999.
32   *Financial Times,* 3 September, 1999.
33   *Financial Times,* 30 September, 1999.
34   Quoted in Hahnel, *Panic Rules!,* pp. 98-99.
35   *Ibid.,* p. 3.
36   *Ibid.,* p. viii.
37   Diary of events and figures taken from *New Internationalist,* October 1998, p. 23.
38   Hahnel, *Panic Rules!,* p. viii, p. ix, p. 29.
39   *The Independent,* 18 February, 2000.
40   Hahnel, *Panic Rules!,* p. ix.
41   *Ibid.,* p. 58.
42   *Ibid.,* p. 101.
43   David Korten, 'Positive Futures Network', article based on Korten's 1999 book *The Post-Corporate World: Life After Capitalism,* distributed on uk-anti-maif e-mail list, 4 October, 1999.
44   *Ibid.*
45   *New Economics Magazine,* Winter 1996, p.2.
46   Parts of this section have been adapted from *New Internationalist,* October 1998, pp. 14-16.
47   Aristotle, *Politics,* 4. 1296a.
48   Smith, *Wealth of Nations,* p. 277.
49   Hutton, *The State We're In,* p. 313.
50   Rowbotham, *The Grip of Death.*, p. 39.
51   For more on alternatives to the present system of money creation, such as social credit, see Rowbotham, *The Grip of Death,* and Hutchinson, *What Everybody Really Wants to Know About Money.* Discussion of local exchange trading systems appears in many books dealing with new economics, such as Douthwaite, *Short Circuit* and Boyle, *Funny Money.*
52   Cited in Hahnel, *Panic Rules!,* p. 27.
53   Quoted in Scott Nova and Michelle Sforza-Roderick, *The Ecologist,* Vol. 27, No. 1, p.5.
54   Balanyá *et al., Europe, Inc.,* p. 112.
55   Lorraine Woellert, *Washington Times,* 15 December, 1997.
56   Charlotte Denny, *The Guardian,* 16 April, 1998.
57   Personal communication, February 1998.
58   Fax from Department of Trade and Industry to Southampton City Council, 11 February 1998.
59   Quoted in World Development Movement press release, 29 October, 1997.
60   Letter from the DTI to the author, 11 December, 1997.
61   Personal communication, 15 January, 1998.

62　'A Dangerous Leap in the Dark', World Development Movement briefing, November 1997.

63　Personal communication with Dr Jim Scott, Director of Save Our World campaign, regarding the UNED-UK Conference, London on Tuesday, 18 November, 1997.

64　Hansard parliamentary debates, 23 July, 1997, column 880.

65　*A Dangerous Leap in the Dark*, World Development Movement briefing, November 1997.

66　Personal communication, February 1998.

67　Personal communication, February 1998.

68　*The Independent*, 22 January, 1998.

69　*Financial Times*, 20 October, 1998.

70　Quoted in *The Guardian,* 6 October, 1999.

71　Press release from Department of Trade and Industry, 21 October, 1998.

72　E-mail message from WDM's Barry Coates to uk-anti-maif internet conference list, 26 November, 1998.

73　*Ibid.*

74　See Chapter 3 for an analysis of the media, with further examples of reporting which is biased, or silent, on environmental and human rights issues.

75　E-mail from Reforesting Scotland to uk-anti-maif internet conference, 9 June, 1998.

76　E-mail from Council of Canadians distributed on mai-not@essential.org internet conference, 2 March, 1999.

77　See website www.gn.apc.org/negreens/cptt.htm

78　For more on such developments, see Chapter 8.

79　*The Guardian*, 22 November, 1999.

80　*Financial Times,* 30 September, 1999.

81　Herman and Chomsky, *Manufacturing Consent*, pp. 260–296.

82　*The Independent*, 6 January, 1999.

83　*Ibid.*

84　*The Independent,* 2 April, 1999.

85　http://ens.lycos.com/ens/mar2000/2000L-03-20-05.html

86　Lang and Hines, *The New Protectionism*, pp. 135-136.

87　*Ibid.,* p. 7.

88　*The Independent*, 1 October, 1998.

89　*The Independent*, 4 February, 1999.

90　*The Independent*, 5 February, 1999.

91　'Making Investment Work for People: An International Framework for Regulating Corporations', World Development Movement, consultation paper, February 1999.

92　*Ibid.*

93　*Ibid.*

94　*Ibid.*

95　*Ibid.*

96　*Ibid.*

97　Albert, *Thinking Forward,* and internet resources at www.zmag.org on 'parecon' (participatory economics).

98　Albert, *Thinking Forward*, back cover.

99　Hines, *Localization*, p. 262.

100　*Ibid.*, pp. 198–199

101　Colin Hines, *The Guardian,* 17 November, 1997.

102　*Ibid.*

103　Lang and Hines, *The New Protectionism*, p. 119.

104　Hines, *Localization*, Chapters 6-12.

2

FORGOTTEN VOICES

Trampled underfoot by globalisation

There is no organization on earth that is doing more for the poor than we do.

James Wolfensohn, president of the World Bank[1]

The IMF, World Bank and WTO are forcing poor countries to pay foreign banks rather than invest in human needs.

Njoki Njehu from Kenya, director of 50 Years Is Enough[2]

Remnants of the technological revolution

In the first chapter, we critically examined the corporate and political rhetoric behind 'free trade' and 'international competitiveness'. We exposed the threats to environmental sustainability and social justice posed by private interests operating through powerful institutions such as the World Trade Organisation. We saw that big business protestations that free trade is simply about 'protecting investment' and 'creating a level playing field' obscure the reality that international trade and investment favour large transnational corporations at the expense of locally-based enterprises and communities. But this picture is not yet complete. We now turn our attention to how it is that the poor, both in developed and developing countries, are not simply missing out on the 'benefits' of economic globalisation, but are being systematically trampled upon. Not only is yet more liberalisation of trade and investment not the answer to assisting the poor, it will make things worse.

In 1999, the BBC Reith Lectures were given by Professor Anthony Giddens of the London School of Economics on the subject of globalisation. His take on the topic was rather optimistic. Rather than addressing head on the phenomenon of 'Coca Cola-isation' which has seen an Americanised version of consumerism sweep the globe, Giddens preferred to talk about what he termed 'reverse colonisation'. By this he meant such developments as Spanish becoming the dominant language in parts of the United States (for example, in Los Angeles) and the export of Brazilian soap operas to Portugal. Such a phenomenon, Giddens argued, demonstrates the strength, diversity and cross-fertilisation of cultures in today's world. He is correct, of course. The generic term 'globalisation' means more than just an increasingly integrated global economy. It also encapsulates the rise of the internet, increasing international travel, the meeting and mingling of different heritages; in short, the development of something akin to that oft-heralded and anticipated 'global village'. Giddens' enthusiasm for the cultural aspects of globalisation appeared to be offered as a counterbalance to the severe problems raised by the increasing integration of markets in goods, services and investment – economic globalisation. But his analysis gives little comfort to the poor. Yasmin Alibhai-Brown, writing in *The Independent*, lambasted Giddens for his sanguine view and self-styled persona as 'the God of Globalisation'. His 'optimism is enchanting but can only be sustained if you are part of the privileged global elite'.[3]

The United Nations estimates that the income gap between the richest fifth of the world's people and the poorest fifth, measured by average national income per head, increased from 30 to 1 in 1960 to 74 to 1 in 1997.[4] According to the UN Human Development Report 1998, over a billion people are deprived of basic consumption needs.[5] Three-fifths of the 4.4 billion people in developing countries lack basic sanitation. Almost a third have no access to clean water. A quarter do not have adequate housing. A fifth have no access to modern health services. Only a privileged few have access to motorised transport, telecommunications and electricity. Patterns of consumption display stark inequalities: the richest 20 per cent of the world's population consume 45 per cent of the meat and fish, while the poorest 20 per cent consume just 5 per cent. The richest 20 per cent consume 84 per cent of all paper, and the poorest 20 per cent just 1.1 per cent. But even among the rich, increasing consumption has not increased happiness – quite the reverse. According to a survey cited in economist Richard Douthwaite's 1996 book *Short Circuit,* the percentage of Americans who feel themselves to be 'happy' peaked in 1957, even though consumption has more than doubled since.

In *The Growth Illusion*, another ground-breaking book, Douthwaite carefully distinguishes between the phrases 'the standard of living' and 'the quality of life'. The former means 'the per capita rate of consumption of purchased goods and services' or, as Douthwaite puts it, 'the rate at which we will use up the earth's limited resources'. On the other hand, 'the quality of life' has a multiplicity of meanings, varying from person to person, but which could include such factors as family and home life, general contentment, income, levels of consumption, social values, home, employment, holidays, enjoyment of the natural environment, and so on. In a detailed British survey of 1,500 people carried out in the

1970s, of the replies that could be categorised 71 per cent were about factors that had little or nothing to do with money.[6]

It is not only in the 'developing' countries of the South that increasing numbers of communities have become disconnected from the global economy, but in isolated pockets of the 'developed' North as well. These are the dispossessed people whom Alibhai-Brown called 'the human debris in our runaway world'.[7] The 'human debris', of course, are the world's growing numbers of poor. How is this apparently irremediable problem to be tackled? The dominant view in society – that is to say, the view held by those in powerful positions – is that economic growth is the solution to poverty. Ross Clark, writing in The *Sunday Telegraph*, argues:

> The reason Western nations are richer than Third World ones is that their populations have been more effective in their efforts to create wealth. If the United Nations wishes to eradicate poverty, it ought to encourage poor nations to emulate rich ones, not pretend that the poor are having their human rights violated.[8]

There is no recognition, in such a view, that at least part of the reason why the West is rich is because it has plundered the resources and peoples of the developing world. On the other hand, Douthwaite's *The Growth Illusion* powerfully and precisely demonstrates 'how economic growth has enriched the few, impoverished the many and endangered the planet'. In any case, what *is* economic growth? Economists still tend to use an outdated measure called 'gross national product' (GNP). In the meantime, the British and US economies are actually running in reverse, as measured by the Index of Sustainable Economic Welfare (ISEW), introduced by economist Clifford Cobb. The ISEW, which ought to replace GNP as the measure of the health of an economy, takes account of such negative impacts as the costs of commuting, pollution, crime, ill health, and the loss of farmland and non-renewable resources. Looked at in this way, the US economy actually peaked in 1976 and has been on a downward trend ever since.[9]

An important aspect of economic growth in today's globalised markets is the drive towards export-led development, resulting in increasing volumes of trade between different countries. Although global trade has increased elevenfold in the past fifty years, poverty and unemployment are not even close to being eliminated. Like Douthwaite, the environmentalist and writer Tom Athanasiou is scathing of the notion that a growing economy will reduce poverty, calling it 'the hoariest of economic myths'.[10]

As we saw in Chapter 1, the British government, along with the other industrialised nations of the OECD, has declared its aim of halving world poverty by 2015. When it made this declaration it was supporting the discredited free-trader's dream, the Multilateral Agreement on Investment. The solution to global poverty, the public are being told by corporations and their political allies, is for the resources of the developing South – human and non-human – to be made increasingly available to the North and its ever-expanding consumerism. Thus, goes the argument, can the South enter the global marketplace and enjoy raised living standards – there is no feasible alternative path of development.

But the present path of development in the South, marked by economic globalisation and the so-called green revolution, is devastating traditional agriculture and communities in Third World countries. The original Western colonialists started the destruction of indigenous self-sufficiency, and transnational corporations and politicians have continued it, resulting in the loss of land rights for poor people in the South. As many as 20 million people have been driven from their land because of trade liberalisation.[11] Large areas used to have a low enough value that billions could afford to live there, producing food primarily for their own needs, even though their 'efficiency' was quite low by modern standards. Then came the spread of 'advanced' agricultural techniques, the dominance of transnational agribusinesses and the growth of global markets in agriculture. Land values went up and many peasant renters were evicted by land owners who wanted to plant more valuable export crops. Family plots were easy prey to local economic and political elites. Aggressive acquisition of land, through legal and extralegal means, has caused immense hardship for families forced to move away from their homes. At the same time, Third World governments have relaxed restrictions on foreign ownership of land, letting in multinational agribusinesses, thus adding to the human exodus. As economist Robin Hahnel has pointed out, globalisation has thrown peasants off land where they certainly made a poor living, 'but they were nonetheless better off than they now are, living in disease-infested slums surrounding swollen third world cities where productive employment is even less likely than it was in their rural villages, and where traditional social safety nets are nonexistent'.[12]

There are, however, promising signs of a backlash against this neocolonialism of the South by the North, based on the issue of crippling debt payments. Third World debt is an intrinsic component of economic globalisation which saw a rapid escalation in the 1970s when an excess of dollar profits arose amongst OPEC countries. Investors, with bags of spare petro-dollars, were keen to invest where they could, and many large loans at low rates of interest were offered to developing countries desperate for foreign exchange. Douthwaite describes a meeting of the Inter-American Development Bank in Madrid in 1981 during which 'senior bank officers queued up to offer funds to the man in charge of Mexico's borrowing as he lounged in an armchair at his hotel'.[13]

Corrupt regimes often creamed off much of the money for themselves, leaving their downtrodden populations to suffer. As world interest rates rose again, many poor countries struggled, and failed, to meet their debt commitments. Aid flows from North to South were exceeded by debt servicing payments from the South to governments, international institutions such as the World Bank, and commercial banks in the North. The United Nations Development Programme reported that 'debt repayments often absorb a quarter to a third of developing countries' limited government revenue, crowding out critical public investment in human development'.[14]

In 1997, the debt stood at over 2 trillion US dollars and was still rising. This represented $400 for every man, woman and child in the South. In the very poorest countries, the average income is less than a dollar a day. As strict conditions of debt relief, 'Structural Adjustment Programmes' (SAPs) imposed by the International Monetary Fund on the world's poorest countries, meant government cut-backs on healthcare and education; in other words, the basic services upon which people depend. In 1997, the IMF collected $643 million more in repayments than it provided in new loans to sub-Saharan Africa – the world's poorest and most hopelessly indebted region.[15]

The IMF and World Bank finally admitted in 1997 that the most poor and indebted nations of the South may never be able to pay off their debts and spoke grandly instead of 'debt forgiveness'. However, rather than heralding a new dawn of unconditional debt cancellation, the IMF and World Bank were merely proposing to reduce debt to a 'sustainable' level. These institutions were to dictate how much each country could afford to pay, and the poorest countries would remain locked into severe SAPs. The campaign for an unconditional cancellation of debt in 52 of the world's poorest countries was therefore launched by the Jubilee 2000 Coalition. Around 70,000 anti-debt activists attended the G7 summit in Birmingham, England, in June 1998 to press home their message, and the pressure has been growing steadily ever since.

'Can we afford it?' asked David Ransom, writing in *New Internationalist*: 'Well, if several hundreds of billions of dollars could be found within months to fend off the crisis in Southeast Asia, a mere $200 billion to cancel the illegitimate debts of the world's poorest people is clearly not beyond our means'.[16] Whether such a cancellation will be granted is doubtful. At the G8 (G7 + Russia) summit in Cologne in 1999, world leaders agreed to approve a 'relief plan' of around $70 billion, a move which aid and development agencies immediately criticised as inadequate and grossly oversold. Oxfam estimated that the plan would translate to no more than $50 billion of actual debt relief, less than one-tenth of the cost – $530 billion – of unifying East and West Germany after the fall of the Berlin Wall. The G8 package would mean that countries including Mali, Burkina Faso, Bolivia and Mozambique would still be caught in the debt trap – paying more for debt servicing than on essential health care and education.[17]

Aid agencies called for the number of countries eligible for debt relief to be doubled. Meanwhile, they questioned the very nature of the offered package. Christian Aid referred scathingly to the IMF as the 'unchallenged judge and jury over the economic development prospects of the world's poorest countries'.[18] The World Development Movement did not mince its words either, saying that 'debt relief is being used as a sugar lump to force countries to swallow poisonous IMF programmes'.[19] When the IMF and the World Bank held meetings in Washington DC in April 2000, they were targeted Seattle-style by 'anti-capitalism' protesters. An editorial in *The Independent* summed up the mainstream press reaction – that such protesters, if they had their way, 'would keep the poor in poverty'.[20] This echoed the sentiments of WTO head Michael Moore, expressed a few months earlier: 'The people who march in Seattle will be marching against opportunities for poor countries to sell their products and services'.[21] But Joseph Stiglitz, the former chief economist of the World Bank, disagreed, saying that such protesters 'were trying to bring to the fore a set of values that a large number of people … feel strongly about – issues that go beyond just making a living and materialism – that they care about the environment and about the poor in developing countries, and that they care about democratic processes'.[22]

Sustainable development campaigners point to the role of undemocratic institutions of globalisation – in particular, the triumvirate of the IMF, the WTO and the World Bank – in benefiting big business and investors while the poor remain poor. With aid flows falling in real terms, private capital flows are growing fast. An increasing amount of North-South financial flows is going direct to companies – often the same transnationals that have benefited from aid programmes – rather than to Southern governments. When finance is sent to governments in the South, it is transferred via institutions which lack transparency and accountability, such as the British Commonwealth Development Corporation and the International Finance Corporation – a part of the World Bank dedicated to supporting private sector investment in developing countries.[23]

The World Bank has now admitted that the poor bear the brunt of shocks in the global economic system. Following the economic crisis of 1997/98 (see Chapter 1), the World Bank reported that more than a quarter of the population of developing countries (over a billion people) would suffer falling living standards.[24] They would suffer the most because the crisis had reduced demand in countries of the North for basic commodities, of which there is already systemic overproduction, and upon which the South depends for income. Another damaging factor was that international capital had been withdrawn from 'emerging' markets in the South. But having correctly identified two fundamental flaws in the global economy, the World Bank drew back from calling for a radical restructuring of the rules governing trade and investment, a restructuring that should be built upon ecological principles honouring social justice and environmental protection.

Even in the so-called affluent countries of the North, there is a growing divide between the rich and the poor. In 1998, the UN stated that underconsumption and human deprivation are not just the lot of the poor in the South, but also of more than 100 million people in the rich North. Nearly 200 million people are not expected to survive to age 60 and more than 100 million are homeless. At least 37 million are unemployed, often experiencing a state of social exclusion. 'Many conclusions about deprivation apply to them with equal force'.[25] We will return to this point later in the chapter.

Sapping the poor

We referred above to Structural Adjustment Programmes (SAPs). These are the packages of policies aimed at securing the 'economic stability' of nations indebted to the IMF. It is a bitter irony that poor countries must accept SAPs as a condition of debt relief since, in practice, SAPs have punished the people debt relief is supposed to help – the poor. OECD targets to halve the incidence of extreme poverty and cut the child death rate by three-quarters by 2015 look ever more elusive. The British government's white paper on globalisation, published in December 2000, praised inward investment by transnational corporations as a means of poverty reduction. But as the British Green MEP Caroline Lucas pointed out: 'The expansion of these companies in the developing world is destroying indigenous traders and manufacturers who find they can't gain the economies of scale the large companies can achieve.' Ironically, and deceivingly, Minister for International Development Clare Short praised the countries of East Asia that 'have benefited from globalisation', while ignoring their current plight following the crash of 1997-1998; not to mention the inconvenient fact that, as Dr Lucas points out, 'East Asia's economy expanded at a time when they were allowed to protect their own industries – something which is now not allowed under World Trade Organisation rules.'[26] The white paper fits neatly into a context of promoting an unjust system of economics, leaving poor countries at the mercy of powerful companies and institutions, just as Structural Adjustment Programmes do. So, what are SAPs and why are they so destructive to the most vulnerable people in the Third World?

The philosophy underlying SAPs is the traditional notion that economic growth is the 'engine' that will generate wealth and development, the benefits of which will ultimately 'trickle down' through the economy to the poor at the bottom of society. Driven by the US-led vision of global free markets, the packages impose liberalisation, privatisation and deregulation of Third World economies: the people, land and environmental resources are thereby forcibly opened up to outside investment, annexation and exploitation. Laws and standards which safeguard employment, human health, animal welfare and environmental integrity are put under immense pressure or simply collapse in order that barriers to free trade are reduced or removed. As we saw in the previous chapter, the World Trade Organisation is the major institution behind such a 'race to the bottom'.

IMF-imposed SAPs are characterised by the reduction of government expenditure, the privatisation of state-run industries 'to increase efficiency', currency devaluation and export promotion, the raising of interest rates and the removal of price controls. These typically hit the poor the hardest. For example, the intended result of reducing government expenditure is to release government funds for debt servicing. But it is often government services to the poor which are easiest to cut. The introduction of user-fees puts health care and education beyond the reach of many people. Public sector workers are made redundant or have their salaries frozen. The number of teachers and doctors drops off. In Ghana, according to figures provided by the World Development Movement, the primary school drop-out rate reached 40 per cent following the introduction of school fees.[27] Hospital outpatient attendance fell by a third. In Mozambique, where half the population already lack access to formal health care, patients visiting Maputo Central Hospital now have to pay 50,000 MT (US$4) to see a doctor – the equivalent for the average Briton would be a payment of £160 to see his or her GP.

Privatisation of industries typically leads to lay-offs and increased unemployment. Since social welfare provision has been simultaneously reduced or removed under SAPs, the effect on low-income families can be devastating. Under the IMF's programme of reforms, the Zambian GNP fell by 16 per cent between 1991 and 1996. Privatisation of the Zambian Consolidated Copper Mines led to the lay-off of over 60,000 workers in just two years. In Bangladesh, privatisation of the jute industry, a major sector of the country's economy, had a devastating effect on production and workers with major knock-on effects throughout the entire population. In Uganda, touted by SAP supporters as a star economic performer, rushed privatisation led to the loss of 350,000 jobs with many workers receiving just one week's pay as compensation.[28]

The aim of currency devaluation and export promotion is to increase export revenues, thus generating extra foreign exchange which can be used to repay debts. But the impact on the poor is crippling: currency devaluation means that imports become more expensive, including vital resources such as imported medicines. Land is converted to growing huge monocultural swaths of 'cash crops' such as coffee – again to boost foreign exchange reserves – rather than being used to grow food for the local population. The cruel irony is that export prices often fall because many poor countries are simultaneously trying to sell the same commodities under SAPs, so that the countries are no better off than before. In Tanzania, currency devaluation has reduced the purchasing power of most people, just when they are expected to pay for health care. According to Christopher Mwakasenge, of the Tanzania Social and Economic Trust, the message is clear: 'SAPS ... have failed to help our country.'[29]

Raising interest rates is supposed to tackle inflation. But farmers and small companies, for example, can then no longer afford to borrow money and are often forced to cut production or end up bankrupt. As we saw in Chapter 1, this is an endemic problem in the present debt-based financial system. Removing price controls should supposedly lead to increased efficiency in food production, but more expensive basic commodities, such as bread, place even more pressure on already stretched household budgets. In Malawi, huge price rises have effectively halved the wages of agricultural workers, already a vulnerable group.

Years of crippling SAPs have shown in country after country in the South that such reforms do not work; indeed, they have exacerbated the plight of those they are supposedly designed to help – the poor. Politicians in the rich North, backed by the generally uncritical mass media, make grand statements about restructuring packages being explicitly designed to reduce global poverty. Free market reforms, we are told, are about 'providing a climate of stable investment', 'generating wealth and sustainable development' and 'tackling poverty'. The truth is rather different: free market reforms have the effect of extending the domain of influence of North-based corporations into the South while maximising their profit margins at the expense of the most vulnerable people and environments around the globe.

Poverty in the UK

While globalisation has widened the gap between the rich North and the poor South, it has done nothing to alleviate, never mind eradicate, the very real levels of poverty in the developed nations. 'The most striking effect of the process by which society has been "marketised"', wrote Will Hutton, author of *The State We're In*, 'is the growth of inequality.' Key factors have been the reduction in employment regulation, such as the curbing of trade union powers, the abolition of wages councils and a host of measures taken to make the labour market more 'flexible'.[30]

This corporate drive towards a 'flexible' labour market has impacted heavily on the unskilled and those with weak or no union representation. Hutton argued that the demand for high returns has put increasing pressure on companies to maintain the growth of profits and dividends, a view which is reminiscent of Rowbotham's analysis of the debt-based financial system (see previous chapter). A sure-fire solution for businesses under pressure is to cut wage bills and weaken job security, so that employment levels can be adjusted to accommodate changes in demand.[31] But then globalisation really begins to bite. The influx of low-wage, high-labour exports from the developing world forces manufacturers of high-labour products in the developed world to react, particularly in countries such as the UK 'which are very open to imports'.[32]

As a result, struggling British companies in industries such as textiles, shoes, toys and consumer electronics stop production in the UK and 'surrender the market to cheaper imports' or they relocate to other countries where costs, principally labour, are lower. The 'successful' companies which remain are the ones which move upmarket, and increase their 'efficiency' by installing labour-saving machinery and shedding unskilled and semi-skilled employees. It is estimated that 8 million jobs have been lost in the North through this 'quiet trade war'. Hutton reported that at least 400,000 and probably as many as half a million of these job losses were in Britain.[33]

For the most vulnerable sectors of society, the fall-out from globalisation's impact on employment patterns can be devastating. In the autumn of 1998, a British government inquiry into 'health inequality' revealed that the country's poor are literally going hungry.[34] Sir Donald Acheson, the inquiry chairman, spoke of 'food deserts' where it is almost impossible for many of the poorest people to obtain cheap, varied food. The poor cannot afford to get to out-of-town supermarkets, many of which have prospered at the expense of local shops. Hunger is particularly prevalent among single mothers who often struggle to ensure their own children are well-fed. In the past 20 years, the death rate of those at the top of the social scale has fallen by as much as 40 per cent, while at the bottom of the scale it has fallen by only 10 per cent. The health gap between rich and poor is therefore widening. In fact, the Acheson report stated that in terms of the divide between rich and poor, Britain is now the most unequal country in the world after the United States. The Labour government responded to Acheson by speaking grandly of tackling 'social exclusion' (which used to be called 'poverty') and declaring its intention to create a more equal, healthy society.

In August 1999, the media reported the launch of yet another government 'anti-poverty drive'. Alistair Darling, the Secretary of State for Social Security, was supposedly under pressure, ahead of the party's autumn conference, to assuage Labour Party activists over the government's continued failure to alleviate poverty. Darling responded by claiming that 1.25 million people would be lifted out of poverty as a result of the introduction of the national minimum wage, increases in child benefit, extra winter fuel payments for pensioners and the working families' tax credit. Critics reacted strongly stating that, welcome though these measures were, they were insufficient: the numbers being helped would be too small, and those at the bottom would remain in the 'poverty trap'.[35]

Recognising that poverty and unemployment are interlinked, one of Acheson's proposals to cut poverty was to increase benefit payments to those out of work. Paradoxically, this could make things worse by making it more difficult to escape from the poverty trap: the current taxation and benefit system discourages people from seeking employment and penalises employers from taking on new staff. Richard Lawson, the Green Party health spokesperson, called for a wage subsidy act which would identify 'private and public enterprises whose product is beneficial to society and the environment – including the remediation of bad housing and health damaging pollution'.[36] Lawson estimates that the potential jobs in such fields matches the number of unemployed. He also emphasises that poverty is detrimental to the individual's health and the well-being of the community and nation as a whole. Lawson, a general practitioner, estimates that as much as one-fifth of the National Health Service's resources is consumed in combating the ill-effects of poverty, such as poor housing and hunger.

Disturbing findings continued to trickle through into the public arena, albeit briefly. According to a report released in September 2000 by the Joseph Rowntree Foundation, around one-sixth of Britain's children live in poverty. The researchers said they were 'shocked' by their findings. It was noted that the government's much-heralded working families' tax credit, aimed at helping single parents go back to work, was 'set too low to meet basic health and food needs'.[37] Later in the same month, the Joseph Rowntree Foundation released another new report revealing that 11,500 lives are lost every year in Britain because of the 'health gap' between the rich and the poor. According to Dr Mary Shaw of the University of Bristol, one of the report's authors, 'Even a modest redistribution of income and wealth, through taxation and by enforcing the minimum wage, would greatly reduce the premature death rate among those under 65 in the country's poorest [areas]'. Dr Shaw added that the research showed that the number of 'lives that would be saved' by reducing the health gap was much higher than previously estimated. 'Improving conditions for today's children will improve the life chances of successive generations. In that sense, the estimates we have made of the number of lives that could be saved are conservative.'[38]

Another factor which impacts most heavily on the poor tends to be overlooked – pollution. Research performed by Friends of the Earth (FoE) reveals just how hard the poor are hit by industrial pollution: there are 662 polluting factories in the UK in areas with average household income of less than £15,000, and only five in areas where average household income is £30,000 or more. The overall trend is that the more factories there are in a given locality, the lower the average income. Following its survey, FoE called for an 80 per cent reduction in the amount of hazardous material released to air, water and land by 2005.[39] In general, in both the developed and developing worlds, it is the poorest who suffer most when the environment is damaged; the rich can either afford to develop coping strategies – for example, relying on bottled water instead of a polluted tap supply – or simply move away.

As a signatory to the World Health Organisation's European Charter on Public Health, the UK has already accepted that 'the health of every individual, especially those in vulnerable and high-risk groups, must be protected. Special attention should be given to disadvantaged groups'. In a shrewd campaigning move, FoE even quoted public health minister Tessa Jowell who had admitted in 1998 that 'more people suffer from poor health in the most deprived areas due to a range of factors including ... pollution'. Campaigners demanded that the environment be given a higher priority in government policies designed to tackle poverty and urban deprivation:

> The Government has yet to put forward any plans to tackle pollution injustice. Until they do, the poorer members of our society will continue to suffer from dangerous levels of pollution. Social exclusion can't be properly tackled unless the environment is put right at the top of the agenda.[40]

Unfortunately, as this book will demonstrate, Labour has backtracked on its 1997 election campaign pledges to 'place the environment at the heart of all policy' and 'to form this country's first truly green government'. Notwithstanding a belated and token speech on the environment by Tony Blair in October 2000, and a more robust one in March 2001 (followed the next day by a business-as-usual budget delivered by Gordon Brown), the prospects of Labour embracing the link between reducing poverty and protecting the environment appear dismal.

Removing the safety net

Linked to poverty, health inequality and pollution is another scandal which pervades the affluent countries of the North – homelessness. Shelter, a UK campaigning organisation, estimates that in 1997 there were around 400,000 homeless people in England alone.[41] During 1996-7, the total gross cost of providing temporary accommodation for homeless families was over £185 million. Over £51 million of this was spent on providing bed and breakfast accommodation. It is obvious – and Shelter and others have performed research to back this up – that homelessness has a negative effect on children's education, on employees or would-be employees, and on the national economy as a whole. Shelter estimates that the detrimental impact on the NHS of homelessness and poor housing is around £2 billion every year.[42] Clearly this represents a dreadful cost, both to those individuals caught up in the misery of homelessness, and to society as a whole. As with so many environmental and social problems endemic in modern society, reducing homelessness is a win-win strategy. Tackling the problem, and thereby helping individuals and the communities to which they belong, will actually create economic opportunities. A £2 billion investment programme to renovate old homes and build 150,000 new homes every year for the next 10 years would not only meet housing needs, but would generate an extra 30,000 jobs.[43]

The safety net for the homeless in Britain is woefully thin and, sadly, a short-term approach is taken where a long-term one is required. For example, local authorities are currently required to provide accommodation to homeless people for only 24 months. This is often not long enough for people to establish links with the local community, find settled employment, and build a new life, especially if additional assistance is required from social services and other agencies to deal with mental and physical problems brought on by long-term homelessness. However, in April 2000, the government published a housing green paper reaffirming two manifesto commitments. First, private landlords letting out shared properties would have to be licensed in order to improve safety and quality. Second, local authorities would have to provide long-term accommodation for homeless families. Chris Holmes, Shelter's director, welcomed the paper, saying that 'the proposals herald the most significant opportunity there has been for a generation to reform the current crisis-driven approach'.[44]

The challenge to government is not just to introduce new legislation to extend help to the homeless, welcome though that would be, but to introduce a phased transition to a new economic life which would, for example, see the granting of a 'citizen's income' to every man, woman and child. A citizen's income on its own would be insufficient to solve poverty, but should be part of an integrated raft of measures, such as land ownership reform and ecological taxation, to reverse the flow of wealth from poor to rich.[45] Instead, the Labour government embarked on an unpopular package of welfare and pensions reform. The package was touted by ministers as the way to 'get people off benefits and into work'. In 1999, when the Blair administration contributed to Nato's bombing of the former Yugoslavia (see Chapter 3), at least one Labour MP publicly questioned the government's spending priorities: 'I will vote against the Government [on its welfare reform package] because if there is money for Tomahawk missiles, I am sure there is money for the disabled.'[46]

In its continuation of the Tory policies of the Thatcher and Major years, we find the Labour government keen to reduce 'spiralling welfare costs' by encouraging more 'self-reliance' among taxpayers. Proposed measures include encouraging citizens to take out second and/or private retirement pensions (thereby reducing national pension costs), private health plans, and personal financial schemes to cover the costs of being looked after in a home for the elderly. In some cases, elderly or infirm people who can no longer cope with living on their own have had to sell their property to move into a nursing home, thereby losing out on the opportunity to bequeath their former family residence.

In order to hone the country into a lean, fit machine to 'compete in the international marketplace', the poor, disabled, elderly, 'unskilled' and other vulnerable groups are increasingly suffering under the demands imposed by economic globalisation. Even the safety-net measure of a national minimum wage (originally set at the pitiful rate of £3.60 an hour, since raised to £3.70) is under threat, simply because there will not be enough inspectors employed nationwide to enforce it. According to a document prepared by officials at the Department of Social Security, the Inland Revenue and the Contributions Agency, the national minimum wage (NMW) scheme was set up in April 1999 with just 63 inspectors covering the whole country. The document, *NMW Business Case Final Version*, estimates that only 200,000 workers are currently paid less than the minimum wage, in contrast to the government's inflated official claim that 2 million workers would benefit from its new legislation.[47]

And while official efforts are being expended on reducing fraudulent claims at one end of the tax spectrum (the poor end, naturally), the greater crime of business fraud, including corporate scams to reduce tax deductions, is not being tackled seriously. Indeed, it is deliberately overlooked. According to a report in *Red Pepper* magazine, minimum wage inspectors were warned to ignore evidence of corporate tax fraud uncovered in the course of their work, with the threat of dismissal hanging over their heads for 'unauthorised disclosure of official information'. Tax fraudsters will therefore be immune from the better internal cross-referencing within the Inland Revenue which is necessary to police the minimum wage. Robin Harris of the Public and Commercial Services Union, representing the NMW inspectors, called the ruling 'a nonsense' and added 'it is inefficient, contrary to official government policy and so we are campaigning as hard as we can for it to be changed. The [Trades Union Congress] is supporting us and we expect to be successful'. Meanwhile, the government is removing safety-net measures affecting the employment rights of workers in small firms; in other words, those most at risk from minimum-wage-defying employers. Such rights include the European Union working times directive, compensation payments, access to employment tribunals, and minimum wage protection itself.[48]

American pie in the sky

In the United States, an early failure of the Clinton tenure to address the needs of the vulnerable in that most unequal of rich Northern nations was the collapse of moves to overhaul its divisive, complex and costly system of health care. A task given to Bill Clinton's wife Hillary, it was always going to be an uphill struggle against powerful conservative lobbies in both Congress and the health insurance industry. She failed, and the most vulnerable members of American society are being left behind in the national drive to become economically competitive. For those rising numbers of people unfortunate enough not to have secure, satisfying employment, the consequences can be devastating, as author Richard Wilkinson described:

> To feel depressed, cheated, bitter, desperate, vulnerable, frightened, angry, worried about debts or job and housing insecurity; to feel devalued, useless, helpless, uncared for, hopeless, isolated, anxious and a failure: these feelings can dominate people's whole experience of life, colouring their experience of everything else. It is the chronic stress arising from feelings like these which does the damage.[49]

In *The End of Work,* Jeremy Rifkin warned that the technological revolution at the turn of the millennium was fuelling tensions between the rich and the poor, and further dividing the United States into 'two incompatible and increasingly warring camps. The signs of social disintegration are everywhere'.[50]

One such sign is the number of Americans living in poverty in 1992 – 37 million, which was greater than at any time in the preceding 30 years. More than 40 per cent of these were children. By 1997, the US Census Bureau reported that poverty rates had dropped to '1989 pre-recession levels'. But this still leaves the rate of poverty in the United States at 13.3 per cent. In other words, there are around 35 million people living in poverty in the world's richest nation. Amongst white Americans, the poverty rate is 11 per cent, for Afro-Americans, 26.5 per cent, and for Hispanics it is 27.1 per cent.[51] Edward Nathan Wolff noted that the share of income of the richest 20 per cent of US households rose from 43.6 per cent of all income in 1973 to 49.1 per cent in 1994. The share of the poorest 20 per cent fell from 4.2 per cent to 3.5 per cent. The average income of the poorest 20 per cent fell by 2.7 per cent between 1973 and 1994, and that of the second poorest 20 per cent fell by 3.8 per cent, while that of the top 20 per cent rose by 27.2 per cent and that of the top 5 per cent rose by a dramatic 44.2 per cent.[52]

The reform of the US welfare system which President Clinton signed into law in 1996, and which had been praised by Democrats and Republicans alike, has actually made the poor worse off. According to a study by the Center on Budget and Policy Priority, an independent Washington think-tank, the reforms have 'made impoverished families still poorer and deprived children in such families of benefits they once received'.[53] According to the study, the reforms hit poor single mothers the hardest; they were supposed to have been the main beneficiaries of the reforms. A decline in disposable income of the poorest 20 per cent was attributed to cuts in allowances as single mothers took low-paying jobs. There was also confusion about eligibility for state health benefits and food stamps. The new system 'couples incentives with penalties, provides job preparation and training for benefit recipients, but also sets a period beyond which assistance will cease, whether or not the recipient has found work'. In five years, the number on welfare dropped from 14 million to 7 million. While this is welcome in itself, voluntary groups have reported an increase in the doling out of charity, such as soup kitchens and food banks.[54]

Late in 1999, Los Angeles-based author Marta Russell took a critical look at the hopes raised by Republican presidential candidate George W. Bush that he would tackle the huge social problems facing the United States. Bush promised a 'new' fight against poverty, a stance mirrored by the Labour government in the UK, and that he would call upon America's 'armies of compassion' to donate to charity, thereby ending poverty, hunger, welfare and crime.[55] Now that he is President, even if Bush were to fulfil his promise to launch such an initiative, he would be doing nothing to address the fundamental problems which give rise to the continued need for such charity. As Russell explained:

> At best, charities postpone societal questions about economic equality. At worst, charities serve as self-serving tax shields and allow right-wing ideo-logues to assault the 'socialist' safety net while disingenuously claiming that private charities will pick up the pieces ... Charity is nothing less than an attempt to justify capitalism's inherent injustices which makes it a euphemism for economic oppression.[56]

Such economic oppression – including the income inequity we examined above – has grown together with economic globalisation, with jobs being shed as a result of pressure on companies to shave costs in the quest for increased 'efficiency'. As Rifkin reported, 'the nation's poor are concentrated in rural areas and in inner-city cores, the two regions hardest hit by technology displacement [of workers]'. He continued: 'A growing number of industry analysts fix the blame for the escalating poverty on intense global competition and changes in technology'. Rifkin quoted the editors of *Business Week*: 'For urban workers who counted on steady factory jobs that required little education, the losses have been devastating.'[57]

But even educated workers are not immune from devastating job losses. Cast an eye over the business pages of the newspapers almost every day and observe that company mergers – whether in the banking, oil, electrical, pharmaceutical, or any other industrial sector – frequently result in massive unemployment, while company directors earn handsome share pay-outs and bonuses. Although transnational corporations account for 70 per cent of global trade and 80 per cent of foreign direct investment, they directly employ only 3 per cent of the world's workforce.[58] Meanwhile, around a billion people remain un- or under-employed. The evidence therefore strongly suggests that, contrary to corporate propaganda,

TNCs will contribute little to solving unemployment and, by extension, to the alleviation of poverty.

Siding with the poor

If poverty which surrounds us in our own neighbourhoods is not sufficiently appalling to spur all of us onto a change of course which 'helps the poor without trashing the environment', as FoE's director Charles Secrett puts it, how much less likely is it when the poor are thousands of miles away? But more people in the rich North are recognising that their relatively comfortable lifestyles have been won at the expense of the poor elsewhere; the North's 'ecological footprint' encroaches onto the land, resources and peoples of the developing South. International trade and investment brings wealth to an elite few, but only because there is a net flow of resources from the South to the North.[59]

FoE have performed much admirable work pursuing an agenda which links environmental protection with social justice and an ecologically-based economics. *Tomorrow's World,* published by the group in 1997, reclaimed to some extent the radical nature of the overused – and abused – term 'sustainable development'. The book's authors did this by focusing on the concept of 'environmental space'. Simply put, this is the share of the earth's resources – such as energy, timber and land – which can be consumed without endangering environmental limits or depriving future generations of the materials they will need. The authors illustrate this by imagining a city covered by a huge impenetrable dome. No material can get in or out of the dome. Before long, the resources within the dome would be running low and waste material would be piling up. Life would become difficult or even impossible. In other words, every community needs resources to supply its needs and to absorb its waste. An expanding wealthy society needs more and more space to perform these functions. Ultimately, we should regard the entire planet as being enclosed within such a 'glass bubble'.[60]

By examining Britain's current consumption of various resources, one can esti-mate the 'number of planets needed to sustain current global consumption in 2050 if all countries consumed as Britain does now'. The results range from around 1.5 planets in terms of land usage, through to almost 4 planets for wood, and over 8 planets in terms of both aluminium consumption and energy use. Another way of looking at the environmental space limit associated with current energy consumption in Britain is to examine its equivalent in carbon dioxide emissions. Consider an environmental limit on climate change of 0.1°C per decade, as recommended by the UN Advisory Group on Greenhouse Gases.[61] It turns out that the atmospheric carbon dioxide would have to be stabilised at no more than 350-400 parts per million by volume (ppmv) in order to satisfy this condition (the current figure stands at 367 ppmv). If all the world's countries produced carbon dioxide emissions on a par with Britain, we would need more than 8 Earth atmospheres to contain the emissions and thus avoid dangerous climate change. As later chapters in this book argue, reversing the fossil fuel course of the developed North is an urgent necessity as well as an exciting opportunity for gains in employment, community self-reliance and social justice.

There are other ways in which awareness is growing among consumers in the North that the way we lead our lives impinges on people thousands of miles away. Take our spending habits, for example. Most people now buy their weekly groceries in one of the major supermarkets, either in the high street or in giant out-of-town parks. But how are the goods produced that end up in the supermarkets, and how much do the workers in exporting countries benefit from the trade? In 1996, Christian Aid in Britain launched a campaign to exert consumer pressure on the supermarkets 'to stop Third World exploitation'. Supermarkets were called upon to take three crucial steps:

- Adopt a set of ethical principles for doing business with poor countries.
- Put into action a code of conduct for all overseas suppliers used by supermarkets for their own brand products.
- Agree to have their codes of conduct independently monitored.[62]

Clare Short, then Shadow Minister for Overseas Development, took to the campaign with great gusto, appearing at many a photo opportunity. As the supermarkets got involved, most responding favourably, the campaign became the Ethical Trading Initiative. The biggest stumbling block to success so far is not so much drawing up a common code of practice, but the reluctance of the businesses involved to undergo independent monitoring. And if the code is found to have been violated – what then? The day when independent monitors or 'stakeholders' can significantly alter a company's business practices seems a long way off. NGOs in the UK tried to ensure that a review of company law, steered by business representatives and civil servants, would be a major step forward. But the proposals, published in March 2000, made it clear that company directors still had to act in the best interests of their shareholders only – rather than a broader group of stakeholders in the community at large – and that social and environmental issues did not have to be included in company annual reports unless directors considered them 'material'. The review was described by campaigners as a 'lost opportunity'.[63]

At root, the whole pattern of international trade is inherently unecological. As we saw in Chapter 1, Greens and other progressives argue that in a sustainable society, trading needs should be satisfied locally first, then nationally, and as a last resort, internationally. The Ethical Trading Initiative may well assist significant numbers of poor people in the short and medium term, and for that alone it is to be welcomed. But, in the longer term, it does little to reform the underlying trading and investment structures of globalisation which are eroding community self-sufficiency, labour standards and ecological health around the planet.

Investing for the future

It is not only how we spend our money that impacts on the poor, but how we save and invest it. Ethical and 'green' funds are a small, but growing, component of investment with the success of Friends Provident's Stewardship Fund, Triodos Bank, NPI, Shared Interest and many others. These various enterprises all have one thing in common: achieving profitable returns on ventures that attempt to honour social, environmental and cultural values. One of the most successful examples in recent years has been the Triodos Bank, which originated in the Netherlands and now also operates in Belgium and the UK. The bank had a total balance sheet of 800 million guilders (then around £250 million) in 1998, a rise of 23 per cent on the previous year. Peter Blom, the managing director, welcomed Triodos's success as a small bank, while recognising the dilemma of continued growth in a finite environment: 'We do not believe in expansion for its own sake … we want to be 'invited' – to be pulled to growth … we prefer to grow with our projects.' The mission of such enterprises in ethical investment is, of course, to provide dividends for investors, but to be simultaneously a positive influence in society. There is more to ethical investment than simply 'negative' screening. As Blom says, 'It is one thing not to invest in nuclear power and the arms industry. It is quite another to invest positively in activities you want to see happening. That is why Triodos Bank invests, for example, in solar and wind energy and organic agriculture'.[64]

Unfortunately, virtually all the major high street banks are still lagging far behind on sustainability and ethics. The Bank of Scotland ended up with egg on its face in 1999 when a planned deal with the American TV evangelist and right-wing politician Pat Robertson was scuppered in the wake of public outrage at Robertson's description of Scotland as a 'dark land overrun by homosexuals'. Two years earlier, I had already discovered just how little this bank was prepared to divulge about what they were doing with the money in my own account…

Whose money is it anyway?

On 11 September 1997, the Scottish electorate voted convincingly for a home parliament with tax-varying powers. The people chose to ignore those such as Sir Bruce Patullo, then Governor of the Bank of Scotland, who had warned that the possibility of higher Scottish taxes would scare away future investment. Patullo, however, was admonished during the devolution campaign by the Deputy Prime Minister, John Prescott, who told him to 'play around' with his money and leave the politics of devolution to ministers.

A week before the devolution referendum, *The Guardian* highlighted the bank's murky role in the financing of Indonesia's largest paper and pulp mill.[65] The project, involving the clearing of land and the enforced removal of thousands of villagers, had dubious environmental and ethical aspects. Suddenly, the bank – proud of its credit card which supported green projects at home – was not looking so eco-friendly. I was not surprised. The previous year, as a long-standing Bank of Scotland customer, I had moved my current account over to the Co-operative Bank. The Co-op was having quite a success with their advertising campaign promoting their 'ethical' stance, promising 'not to supply financial services to any regime which oppresses the human spirit' and aiming to 'encourage business customers to take a pro-active stance on the environmental impact of their own activities'. It may sound like a small step, but it's one which the major high street banks have yet to take.

I made the move after challenging the Bank of Scotland to provide details of how it was using the money in its customer accounts. My enquiries began at branch level before being passed up the chain of command to the 'Manager of Branch Operations'. The three main questions I directed at the bank were:

- Does the bank attempt to reduce the crushing effect of Third World debt on the poorest countries?
- Does the bank provide financial services to repressive regimes or companies which manufacture instruments of torture?
- Does the bank help to finance arms sales to repressive regimes?

I received a prompt reply saying that my points would be 'given due consideration by the Bank'; it sounded as though people back at head office were scurrying around indulging in a damage-limitation exercise. Two weeks later, I received a reply which frankly raised more questions than it answered. It was riddled with phrases like, 'The Bank's exposure to governments of Third World countries is very small'. There were no figures, and no details.

I wrote back to the bank, pressing for clarification – what did they mean by 'very small'; *did* the bank finance arms sales?; how much money were we talking about? Within days, I had a reply on behalf of Governor Patullo himself: 'I acknowledge that the statements made to date [by the bank] have been of a general nature ... however, on the grounds of commercial confidentiality, we really cannot give you more specific answers.' Translated into plain English, the response was: 'It's none of your business what we do with your money!'

Coda: Forgotten voices

As far as I am aware, it was the historian Mark Curtis who coined the Orwellian term 'Unpeople' in his powerful 1995 book, *The Ambiguities of Power*. These are the oppressed people around the globe, in rich and poor countries, whose impoverished lives (and deaths) he directly links to the postwar neocolonial foreign and economic policies of the West – in particular, the United States and Britain. These links are rarely discussed in depth, if at all, in the mass media. Unpeople include more than one million Iraqi people, over half of them children under 5, who have died as a result of sanctions imposed by the West since the end of the Gulf War.[66] Unpeople also include people of courage who are prepared to resist the mantra of 'international competitiveness', such as the 500 Liverpool dockers who were sacked in 1996 and replaced by a 'flexible workforce' of casual and part-time workers. The sacked Liverpool dockers won incredible solidarity from workers around the world and even attracted massive support from environmentalists and veterans of anti-road and other campaigns – a sign of the kind of coalition that anti-globalisation direct protest has come to signify.[67]

Unpeople are the people – the majority of the world's population – who do *not* enjoy the 'benefits' of globalisation – often women, as the UN Human Development Report noted in 1999.[68] Unpeople are also those who suffer most when natural disasters strike. Hurricane Mitch cut a devastating swath through Central America in 1998, with poor people bearing the brunt. Some of those who died – or who lost their land and livelihoods – were the *campesinos* (peasant farmers) who make little contribution to export earnings in Nicaragua, for example, but who provide up to 70 per cent of that country's staple foods – rice, maize and beans. The Nicaraguan monthly magazine *Envio* reported that 'the rains were simply the straw that broke the camel's back'. Many now had nothing but the muddy clothing they were wearing when they fled their flimsy shacks. As *Envio* said: 'The difference between what they had before and what they have now is not much. What has changed is that the cameras of the world's media are temporarily focused on them, so they can't be easily disguised behind figures of economic growth or stability.'[69] The media's focus has since shifted away from the plight of the hurricane-ravaged peasants of Central America – away from their poverty, their vulnerability to increasing incidences of climate disaster, and their struggle for land reform and social justice.

The public backlash against globalisation and the development of sustainable alternatives may build gradually, year by year, as people perceive control of their own lives slipping out of their hands, or it may take a huge leap forward in response to a catastrophic collapse of the global economic system – a prospect on which Richard Douthwaite has put even odds.[70] Under the seemingly relentless march of globalising economic and political forces, the quality of life for many people is stalling, falling or plummeting. We now turn to the question of why such a view of economic globalisation is not the mainstream view in the world around us. Understanding this is a necessary step to countering the globalising forces that are propelling us onwards to ever greater levels of inequality, environmental degradation and loss of democracy.

Notes

1   Quoted by Mark Weisbrot, ZNet daily commentary (www.zmag.org), 22 April, 2000.
2   Institute for Public Accuracy, Washington DC, email bulletin, 2 December, 1999.
3   *The Independent*, 6 May, 1999.
4   www.undp.org/hdro/index2.html
5   UN Development Programme, *Human Development Report 1998*.
6   Douthwaite, *The Growth Illusion*, pp. 9-10.
7   *The Independent*, 6 May, 1999.
8   Quoted in Curtis, *The Great Deception*, p.111.
9   Douthwaite, *The Growth Illusion*, p. 21.
10 Athanasiou, *Slow Reckoning,* p. 186.
11 John Madeley, *New Statesman*, 22 November, 1999.
12 Hahnel, *Panic Rules!,* p. 19.
13 Douthwaite, *The Growth Illusion*, p. 71.
14 Quoted in McLaren, Bullock and Yousuf, *Tomorrow's World*, p. 29.
15 Hahnel, *Panic Rules!,* p. 107.
16 David Ransom, *New Internationalist,* May 1999, p. 10.
17 Cited in *The Independent,* 19 June, 1999.
18 *The Independent*, 23 June, 1999.
19 *Independent on Sunday,* 20 June, 1999.
20 *The Independent*, 14 April, 2000.
21 *Financial Times*, 3 September, 1999.
22 Quoted in Marc Weisbrot, ZNet daily commentary (www.zmag.org), 22 April, 2000.
23 McLaren *et al., Tomorrow's World,* p. 36.
24 *The Guardian,* 3 December, 1998.
25 UN Development Programme, *Human Development Report 1998*.
26 Press release, Green Party of England and Wales, 11 December, 2000.
27 World Development Movement, debt campaign briefing, May 1999.
28 *Ibid.*
29 Quoted in *ibid.*
30 Hutton, *The State We're In.,* p. 170.
31 *Ibid.,* p. 171.
32 *Ibid.,* p. 171.
33 *Ibid.,* p. 172.
34 *The Independent,* 15 October, 1998.
35 *The Independent*, 23 August, 1999.
36 Letter sent to *The Guardian*, 28 November, 1998.
37 *The Independent*, 11 September, 2000.
38 *The Independent*, 26 September, 2000.
39 Friends of the Earth website: www.foe.co.uk/factorywatch
40 Friends of the Earth press release, 26 April, 1999.
41 www.shelter.org.uk
42 *Ibid.*
43 *Ibid.*
44 *Shelter update*, newsletter, August 2000, p. 1.
45 See the excellent Schumacher Briefing by Robertson, *Transforming Economic Life.*
46 Tam Dalyell MP, quoted in *The Independent*, 14 May, 1999.
47 *Red Pepper*, April 1999, p. 7.
48 *Red Pepper*, May 1999, p. 9.
49 Quoted in McLaren *et al., Tomorrow's World*, p. 285.

50   Rifkin, *The End of Work,* p. 177.

51   Figures from the US 1997 Census Bureau, available at www.census.gov

52   Cited in Hahnel, *Panic Rules!,* p. 8.

53   Quoted in *The Independent,* 23 August 1999.

54   *Ibid.*

55   Marta Russell, ZNet daily commentary (www.zmag.org), 1 October, 1999.

56   *Ibid.*

57   Rifkin, *The End of Work,* p. 180.

58   Hilary, *Globalisation and Employment.*

59   Once again, the terms 'North' and 'South' are being used conceptually, rather than strictly geographically. There are capitalists living in developing countries who have benefited enormously from globalisation, just as there are ghetto communities in developed countries – for example, the United States and Britain – which have seen a rise in ill-health, unemployment and hunger.

60   McLaren *et al., Tomorrow's World,* p. 6.

61   Cited in Hare, *Fossil Fuels and Climate Protection,* p. vi.

62   *Christian Aid News,* February/March 1997, pp. 6-7.

63   World Development Movement, 'WDM in Action', Summer 2000, p. 5.

64   *Triodos Bank Annual Review 1998,* p. 1.

65   *The Guardian,* 4 September, 1997.

66   John Pilger, *Paying the Price: Killing the Children of Iraq,* broadcast on ITV, 6 March 2000.

67   For a much fuller account of the Liverpool dockers, see Pilger's excellent *Hidden Agendas,* pp. 334-358.

68   www.undp.org/hdro/index2.html

69   Quoted in *New Internationalist,* May 1999, p. 12.

70   Richard Douthwaite, Schumacher Lectures, Bristol, October 1998.

3

SPOTLIGHT ON THE MEDIA

How the truth is hidden from view

What is being reported blandly on the front pages would elicit ridicule and horror in a society with a genuinely free and democratic intellectual culture.   Noam Chomsky[1]

I became a journalist to help spotlight the problems of the world. It is now clear that global media is one of them.   Danny Schechter[2]

The freedom of the press

The first two chapters of this book have argued that free trade primarily bene-fits transnational corporations and wealthy investors. Of course, it cannot be denied that many people, especially in the rich North, live a relatively affluent lifestyle. But this high-consumption way of life has been largely at the expense of the environment and less fortunate communities, particularly in developing coun-tries. Also, if we look at the statistics on crime, ill health and divorce, for example, one might reasonably conclude that such affluence has damaged our personal well-being and society at large. However, the hardest hit have been – and remain – the poor, hundreds of millions, perhaps billions, of people around the world, whom politicians admit have generally 'lost out' on the 'benefits of free trade'. The solution to poverty, we are told, is for these benefits to be spread more evenly throughout society by continuing the process of economic globalisation which has already caused so much harm. We have seen that, on the contrary, the current headlong rush to further liberalise transnational trade and investment has to be stopped. If this is so, why is it that the majority of people in the affluent North who live a reasonably comfortable life, and who therefore might have the time and energy to contemplate such matters, are not sufficiently concerned to demand of our elected representatives that society is reorganised? To help answer this, we must examine the role of the mainstream media in the modern world.

It is an unquestioned assumption, for the most part, that we enjoy the benefits of a free press in the West (the same applies to the broadcast media). Unlike in totalitarian or oppressive regimes, such as the communist dictatorships of the former Soviet Union and East European countries, or present-day Iraq, Iran, Libya and China, Western journalists are reputedly free to write about whatever they wish, holding politicians to account for their policies, scandals, misdemeanours or plain arrogance. Journalists constantly strive to seek out the truth in their media investigations of the world around us – so we are led to believe.

Press freedom is generally considered one of the defining features of libertarian Western democracies. The pre-independence American journalist John Peter Zenger was able to challenge the British Crown with critical articles which drew strength from the fact that he was a printer and publisher. Zenger declared in 1733: 'The loss of liberty in general would soon follow the suppression of the liberty of the press; for it is an essential branch of liberty, so perhaps it is the best preservative of the whole'.[3] According to historian David Chaney, 'the British press is generally agreed to have attained its freedom around the middle of the nineteenth century'.[4] Presumably it has never been lost since. In the 1970s, the presiding judge in the Pentagon Papers case (concerning secret US military planning documents on Vietnam) declared that the United States had a 'cantankerous press, an obstinate press, a ubiquitous press', and that this 'must be suffered by those in authority in order to preserve the even greater values of freedom of expression and the right of people to know'.[5] Mainstream journalists typically regard their profession as a 'crusading craft' full of 'disputatious, stroppy, difficult people' keen to get to the heart of the matter, even to the extent of bringing down a president, as in the Watergate affair.[6] As for media bias, it is merely a 'sharp reflection of the public mood at any given time', according to *Independent* journalist Anne McElvoy.[7] If the mass media devote extensive coverage to genetically modified crops, a royal wedding, or a drugs scandal involving a famous personality, it is simply an indication of where the public's interest lies. That, at least, is McElvoy's contention.

Perhaps most people have a healthy degree of scepticism about the media's priorities. It is common currency, for example, that sections of the tabloid press are not averse to the invention of salacious gossip about pop stars in an attempt to boost circulation figures. There is also, for example, a tendency for Rupert Murdoch's News International-owned *Times* newspapers to tread softly where his own interests may be under threat. One very notable case was the rejection of former Hong Kong governor Chris Patten's memoirs by publishers HarperCollins – part of Murdoch's media empire – when it became clear that Patten's criticisms of the Chinese government could upset Murdoch's empire-building in the region. Similar tensions were at the root of the removal of Andrew Neil,

Murdoch's editor at the helm of the *Sunday Times,* following that newspaper's revelations of the linkage of British aid for the Pergau dam in Malaysia to a £1.3 billion contract to buy British arms. Because of his satellite broadcast media interests in the region, Murdoch was wary of upsetting the Malaysian government. He told Neil: 'you're boring people. You are doing too much on Malaysia... They're all corrupt in that part of the world'.[8] As a result of such blatant owner-intervention in editorial matters, non-Murdoch journalists have been known to express their scathing antipathy to Murdoch and his media empire – with the implication that at least *they* work for a newspaper free from such pressures. The observation of Charles Arthur, technology correspondent of *The Independent*, is perhaps not unusual amongst non-Murdoch journalists: namely, that the Murdoch press 'has a noxious commercial agenda'.[9] In other words, the editorial line taken by Murdoch's newspapers supports his larger business interests.

So, although the general consensus is that we have a free press and broadcasting in the West, it is conceded even by mainstream journalists that the nature of media ownership may compromise editorial freedom. But could there be more to it than that?

The propaganda model: an overview

In their 1988 book *Manufacturing Consent – The Political Economy of the Mass Media*, Edward Herman and Noam Chomsky introduced their 'propaganda model' of the media. The propaganda model argues that there are five classes of 'filters' in society that determine what is 'news'; in other words, what gets printed in newspapers or broadcast by radio and television. Herman and Chomsky's model also explains how dissent from the mainstream is given little, or zero, coverage, while governments and big business gain easy access to the public in order to convey their state-corporate messages – for example, 'free trade is beneficial', 'globalisation is unstoppable' and 'our policies are tackling poverty'.

Ownership

We have already touched upon the fact that corporate ownership of the media can – and does – shape editorial content. The sheer size, concentrated ownership, immense owner wealth, and profit-seeking imperative of the dominant media corporations could hardly yield any other result. It was not always thus. In the early nineteenth century, a radical British press had emerged which addressed the concerns of workers. But excessive stamp duties, designed to restrict newspaper ownership to the 'respectable' wealthy, began to change the face of the press. Nevertheless there remained a degree of diversity. In postwar Britain, radical or worker-friendly newspapers such as the *Daily Herald, News Chronicle, Sunday Citizen* (all since failed or absorbed into other publications) and the *Daily Mirror* (at least until the late 1970s) regularly published articles questioning the capitalist system.[10]

The well-known Australian journalist John Pilger joined the *Mirror* in 1963 and worked there for over 20 years. Pilger later claimed that 'The *Mirror* was the first popular paper to encourage working-class people to express themselves, for whatever reason, to *their* newspaper'. Luckily for him, 'Irreverence and a certain anarchy were encouraged'. Later, when Robert Maxwell took over ownership of the newspaper, Pilger was personally assured that his job was secure: 'Eighteen months later, after relentless interference from Maxwell, I was sacked.'[11]

The media typically comprise large conglomerates – News International, CBS (now owned by Westinghouse), Turner Broadcasting (now merged with Time-Warner) – which may belong to even larger parent corporations such as General Electric (owners of NBC). All are tied into the stock market. Wealthy people sit on the boards of these major corporations, many with extensive personal and business contacts in other corporations. Herman and Chomsky point out, for instance, that: 'GE [General Electric] and Westinghouse are both huge, diversified multinational companies heavily involved in the controversial areas of weapons production and nuclear power.'[12] It is difficult to conceive that press neutrality would not be compromised in these areas. But more widely, press freedom is limited by the simple fact that the owners of the media corporations are driven by free market ideology. How likely is it, then, that such owners would happily allow their own newspaper, radio or TV station to criticise systematically the 'free market' capitalism which is the source of their material wealth?

Advertising

The second filter of the propaganda model is advertising. Newspapers have to attract and maintain a high proportion of advertising in order to cover the costs of production; without it, the price of any newspaper would be many times what it is now, which would soon spell its demise in the marketplace. There is fierce competition throughout the media to attract advertisers; a newspaper which receives less advertising business than its competitors is at a serious disadvantage. Lack of success in raising advertising revenue was another factor in the demise of 'people's newspapers' in the nineteenth and twentieth centuries. It is clear, therefore, that for any publication or commercial radio or TV station to survive, it has to hone itself into an advertiser-friendly medium. In other words, the media has to be sympathetic to business interests, such as the travel, automobile and petrochemical industries. Even the threat of withdrawal of advertising can affect editorial content. A letter sent to the editorial offices of a hundred magazines by a major car producer stated: 'In an effort to avoid potential conflicts, it is required that Chrysler corporation be alerted in advance of any and all editorial content that encompasses sexual, political, social issues or any editorial content that could be construed as provocative or offensive.'[13] In 1999, British Telecom threatened to withdraw advertising from The *Daily Telegraph* following a number of critical articles. The journalist responsible was suspended.

A 1992 US study of 150 news editors found that 90 per cent said that advertisers tried to interfere with newspaper content, and 70 per cent tried to stop news stories altogether. 40 per cent admitted that advertisers had in fact influenced a story.[14] In the UK, £3.2 billion is spent on newspaper ads annually and another £2.6 billion on TV and radio commercials, out of a total advertising budget of £9.2 billion.[15] In the US, the figure is tens of billions of dollars a year on TV advertising alone.[16] An advertising-based system makes survival extremely difficult for radical publications that depend on revenue from sales alone. Even if such publications survive, they are relegated to the margins of society, receiving little notice from the public at large. Advertising, just like media ownership, therefore acts as a news filter.

Sourcing of news

The third of Herman and Chomsky's five filters relates to the sourcing of mass media news: 'The mass media are drawn into a symbiotic relationship with powerful sources of information by economic necessity and reciprocity of interest.'[17] Even large media corporations such as the BBC cannot afford to place reporters everywhere. They therefore concentrate their resources where major news stories are likely to happen: the White House, the Pentagon, No 10 Downing Street, and other centralised news 'terminals'. Although British newspapers may occasionally object to the 'spin-doctoring' of New Labour, for example, they are in fact highly dependent upon the pronouncements of 'the Prime Minister's personal spokesperson' for government-related news. Business corporations and trade organisations are also trusted sources of stories considered newsworthy. Editors and journalists who offend these powerful news sources, perhaps by questioning the veracity or bias of the furnished material, can be threatened with the denial of access to their media life-blood – fresh news.

Robert McChesney, a professor of communications at the University of Illinois at Urbana-Champaign, points out that 'Professional journalism relies heavily on official sources. Reporters have to talk to the PM's official spokesperson, the White House press secretary, the business association, the army general. What those people say is news. Their perspectives are automatically legitimate.' Whereas, according to McChesney, 'if you talk to prisoners, strikers, the homeless, or protesters, you have to paint their perspectives as unreliable, or else you've become an advocate and are no longer a "neutral" professional journalist.' Such reliance on official sources gives the news an inherently conservative cast and gives those in power tremendous influence over defining what is or isn't 'news'. McChesney, author of *Rich Media, Poor Democracy*, warns: 'This is precisely the opposite of what a functioning democracy needs, which is a ruthless accounting of the powers that be.'[18]

Flak

The fourth filter is 'flak', described by Herman and Chomsky as 'negative responses to a media statement or [TV or radio] program. It may take the form of letters, telegrams, phone calls, petitions, law-suits, speeches and Bills before Congress, and other modes of complaint, threat and punitive action'.[19] Business organisations regularly come together to form flak machines. Perhaps one of the most well-known of these is the US-based Global Climate Coalition (GCC) – comprising fossil fuel and automobile companies such as Exxon, Texaco and Ford. The GCC was started up by Burson-Marsteller, one of the world's largest public relations companies, to rubbish the credibility of climate scientists and 'scare stories' about global warming (see Chapter 4).

In her 1997 book *Global Spin,* Sharon Beder documented at great length the operations of corporations and their hired PR firms in establishing grassroots 'front movements' to counter the gains made by environmentalists. One such coalition, the Foundation for Clean Air Progress, is 'in reality a front for transportation, energy, manufacturing and agricultural groups'. The Foundation was established to challenge the US Clean Air Act by 'educating' the public about the progress made in air quality over the previous twenty-five years. As Beder notes, the Foundation's 'focus is on individual responsibility for pollution, as opposed to the regulation of industry to achieve further improvements.'[20] The threat – real or imagined – of law-suits can be a powerful deterrent to media investigation. In the UK, environmental journalist Andrew Rowell notes that, 'Britain's archaic libel laws prevent much of the real truth about the destructive nature of many of [the] UK's leading companies from ever being published or broadcast. Very few people within the media will take on the likes of Shell, BP or [mining company] RTZ'.[21]

Anti-communism / demonisation

The fifth and final news filter that Herman and Chomsky identified was 'anti-communism'. *Manufacturing Consent* was written during the Cold War. A more apt version of this filter is the customary Western identification of 'the enemy' or an 'evil dictator' – Colonel Gaddafi, Saddam Hussein, or Slobodan Milosevic (recall the British tabloid headlines of 'Smash Saddam!' and 'Clobba Slobba!'). The same extends to mainstream reporting of environmentalists as 'eco-terrorists'. The *Sunday Times* ran a particularly nasty series of articles in 1999 accusing activists from the non-violent direct action group Reclaim The Streets of stocking up on CS gas and stun guns.

The demonisation of enemies is useful, essential even, in justifying strategic geopolitical manoeuvring and the defence of corporate interests around the world, while mollifying home-based critics of such behaviour. The creation of an 'evil empire' of some kind, as in postwar Western scaremongering about the 'Soviet Menace' or earlier talk of the 'Evil Hun', has been a standard device for terrifying the population into supporting arms production and military adventurism abroad – both major sources of profit for big business. Iraq's Saddam Hussein has been a useful bogeyman for US arms manufacturers who have notched up sales of over $100bn to Saddam's neighbours in the Middle East.[22] The fifth filter also applies to media demonisation of anti-globalisation protesters – often described as 'rioters' – and anyone else perceived as a threat to free-market ideology.

This brief description of the propaganda model hardly does justice to the sophisticated and cogent analysis presented by Herman and Chomsky. The interested reader is urged to consult their book directly. Its particular relevance here is that it explains how and why the status quo of corporate power is maintained in modern society, the dominance of the neoliberal agenda of free trade with its automatic rejection of alternatives (Margaret Thatcher's 'There Is No Alternative'), and the emasculation of dissident viewpoints which are variously labelled as 'biased', 'ideological' or 'extreme'. How likely is it that anyone calling for radical change in society – whether environmentalists, human-rights activists or opponents of the arms trade – will be consistently and fairly reported by corporate news organisations? How much more likely is it that their arguments will be vilified, marginalised or simply ignored?

The propaganda model: behind the veil

A standard reaction on meeting the propaganda model for the first time is a mixture of incredulity and scorn, typified by author Tom Wolfe's statement that this is 'the old cabal theory that somewhere there's a room with a baize-covered desk and there are a bunch of capitalists sitting around and they're pulling strings ... I think this is the most absolute rubbish I've ever heard.'[23] Herman and Chomsky anticipated this kind of response, refuting the notion that big business controls news outlets through conspiratorial means:

We do not use any kind of 'conspiracy' hypothesis to explain mass media performance. In fact, our treatment is much closer to a 'free market' analysis, with the results largely an outcome of the workings of market forces.[24]

As we saw above in the discussion of the model's five filters, these market forces operate via the usual capitalist mechanisms such as advertising, the integration of media companies into the stock market, and the overriding imperative to generate profit. The writer David Edwards emphasises that the notion of thought control in a democracy 'not only does not propose a conspiracy but actually requires the *absence* of any such conspiracy'. It would be impossible to achieve, never mind maintain, the required level of advanced thought control through any kind of conspiracy. Such a system would quickly be exposed and so made largely impotent as was the case, for example, in the Soviet Union. Edwards points out that 'thought control of the modern kind is dependent, not on crude conscious planning, but on the human capacity for self-deception.'[25] As George Orwell remarked in his – originally unpublished – preface to *Animal Farm*: 'The sinister fact about literary censorship ... is that it is largely voluntary. Unpopular ideas can be silenced, and inconvenient facts kept dark, without any need for any official ban.'[26]

The ability to think truly independent thoughts is perhaps the highest expression of the human brain. We all have that potential to a greater or lesser extent, and even if we do not exercise it, we certainly like to maintain within ourselves that we can do so at will. However, it is noteworthy that the dominant institutions in society have a remarkable and disturbing propensity for reducing independence of thought. Chomsky gives an example from his own university, the Massachusetts Institute of Technology, where a referendum was held in the 1970s on the proposal to effectively turn a third of the nuclear engineering department over to the government of Iran for the training of a large number of Iranian nuclear engineers. Students voted four to one against such a move, while faculty members were four to one in favour. Only a few years separated the two groups in terms of age. Chomsky concluded on the basis of this case, and others, that somehow 'incorporation into the institution has a tremendous effect on determining attitudes towards such matters'. He continued, 'the natural ... and instinctive commitment to justice and truth and decency that one finds in a mind that hasn't yet been corrupted by its institutional commitments, very rapidly attenuates when those institutional commitments take over'.[27]

The propaganda model has been repeatedly applied in analysis of post-World War Two political developments, particularly in the role of the Western powers around the world. It is worth pursuing this further here for at least two reasons. First, the following examples from the sphere of foreign policy demonstrate the explanatory power of the propaganda model which – as Edwards, Beder and others have argued – applies equally to the reporting of environmental issues. Second, the foreign policies pursued by the Western powers have been undertaken hand in hand with policies of economic globalisation, in order to ensure access to natural resources – such as oil – and markets in the developing world, thus ensuring that our rich lifestyles are maintained. Economic dominance and military dominance are intimately linked. In attempting to elucidate this phenomenon, historian Mark Curtis, author of *The Ambiguities of Power*, suggests that two approaches are possible:

> In the first, one can rely on the mainstream information system, consisting primarily of media and academia, where commentators are presumed to provide analyses of current affairs independent of the reasoning and priorities of the state. This is deemed to be consistent with notions of a 'free press' and 'political science'. In the second approach, by contrast, one can consider the facts of the real world.[28]

Herman and Chomsky considered the facts of the real world in their examination of Guatemala and El Salvador where the US-supported regimes 'could indulge in torture, rape, mutilation, and murder on a daily and massive basis without invoking remotely proportional attention, indignation, or inferences about the quality of these regimes [in the Western press]'.[29] On Vietnam: '... it was standard practice throughout the Indochina war for journalists to report Washington pronouncements as fact'[30] – little has changed there in the intervening years – and '... it was the American invaders who were regarded as the victims of the "aggression" of the Vietnamese, and the war was reported from their [the invaders'] point of view, just as subsequent commentary, including cinema, views the war from this perspective'.[31]

During the Cold War, Western politicians and military planners justified intervention around the globe under the guise of protecting 'the free world' from 'Communist aggression', aided by sympathetic media coverage. As Curtis explains, 'recourse to the "Soviet threat" was useful in providing the ideological background to policy carried out for other purposes', namely ensuring that the economic and political 'development' was pursued which benefited elite interests in the West. Anglo-American objectives were the expropriation of economic resources in the South and the 'consolidation' of the West under US auspices. Control of the global economy was threatened above all by independent, national forces [in other words, *not* Soviet-sponsored Communists as alleged by Western politicians and media] in the Third World, especially in the Middle East where the crucial oil resources lay.[32]

Britain was not afraid to go it alone in flexing her military muscle, 'restoring order' during the 'emergency' or 'counter-insurgency' campaign in Malaya between 1948 and 1960; 'civilising' the natives of Kenya in the destruction of the 'communist' Mau Mau movement in the 1950s; and in 1953 overthrowing the democratically-elected government of British Guyana led by nationalist leader Cheddi Jagan who was declared to be 'an agent of the international communist conspiracy'. In fact, formerly secret government documents reveal that the British Secretary of State for the Colonies noted at the time that Jagan's policies were 'no more extreme' than those of the British Labour Party.[33]

John Pilger provides further examples of British abuses abroad, such as the actions of the Wilson government in the 1960s. Rather than promote human rights around the world, a common refrain heard to this day, the government 'supported the American invasion of Vietnam, sold arms to racist South Africa and armed and conspired with the Nigerian military regime to crush Biafra'.[34] Then there is Indonesia. In 1965, the pro-West General Suharto (who himself was forced out of office in 1998 following massive civil unrest) came to power in a bloody coup, overthrowing the non-aligned, nationalist General Sukarno. Declassified Foreign Office files reveal that Britain aided in the slaughter of more than half a million Indonesians. 'I have never concealed from you my belief', cabled the British ambassador in Jakarta, Sir Andrew Gilchrist, in 1965, 'that a little shooting in Indonesia would be an essential preliminary to effective change'. Covert British operations were directed from Singapore in support of the 'little shooting'. Hundreds of thousands of people were murdered.[35]

Curtis reports that declassified US documents indicate that the US, like Britain, not only looked with favour upon Suharto's coup, but actively supported it. The CIA gave the Indonesian army a hit list of 5,000 PKI [the Indonesian Communist Party] supporters, including party leaders, regional committee members and heads of labour, women's and youth groups, who were sought and then killed. A US embassy official, who spent two years drawing up the hit list, observed afterwards that it was a 'big help to the army'. He added, 'I probably have a lot of blood on my hands, but that's not all bad. There's a time when you have to strike hard at a decisive moment'.[36]

Western support for Indonesia's brutal domestic violence is matched by its condoning – and active backing via arms exports – of Indonesia's illegal annexation of East Timor in December 1975. In subsequent years, over 200,000 East Timorese – around one third of the population – lost their lives as a result of the Indonesian invasion. Official documents reveal that Indonesia's annexation of East Timor was supported by the West. In July 1975, the British ambassador in Jakarta informed the Foreign Office that 'the people of Portuguese Timor are in no condition to exercise the right to self-determination' and 'the arguments in favour of its integration into Indonesia are all the stronger'.[37]

It was not just the US and the UK that were happy to see East Timor being swallowed up by Suharto's Indonesia. The Australian government was also complicit. Richard Woolcott, the Australian Ambassador in Jakarta in 1975, was tipped off by the Indonesians that the invasion was about to take place. Woolcott secretly cabled the Department of Foreign Affairs, proposing that '[we] leave events to take their course ... and act in a way which would be designed to minimise the public impact in Australia and show private understanding to Indonesia of their problems.'[38] This 'private understanding' clearly assisted in the subsequent carving up between Australia and Indonesia of the considerable oil and gas reserves covered by the Timor Gap Treaty, signed in 1989. Indonesia under Suharto was a significant market for Western arms sales. But by providing 'political stability', Suharto also offered Western business interests the opportunity to benefit from the country's extensive mineral resources. A few months before the invasion of East Timor, a Confederation of British Industry report noted that Indonesia presented 'enormous potential for the foreign investor' and that, according to one press report, the country enjoyed a 'favourable political climate' and the 'encouragement of foreign investment by the country's authorities'.[39]

Curtis notes that 'RTZ, BP, British Gas and Britoil are some of the companies that have since taken advantage of Indonesia's "favourable political climate" '.[40] An honest appraisal of the historical record reveals, therefore, that the establishment of political conditions conducive to Western corporate interests – using military power either directly, or indirectly with the aid of proxy forces, as in Suharto's Indonesia – is a necessary condition for economic globalisation. In 1999, when Western governments finally intervened in the East Timor bloodbath, following the Indonesian regime's murderous response to the overwhelming vote for Timorese independence in August, it was only because of the unstoppable momentum of public demand in the West, particularly in Australia, for action.

The issue of the environment

Former British Prime Minister Margaret Thatcher once famously declared that 'we're all green now'. Indeed, opinion polls regularly suggest that the majority of British people regard themselves as 'environmentalists'. Surely this has been a sign of the green movement's success? A qualified 'yes' is in order. Public awareness of environmental problems in the modern era can arguably be traced back to the publication of Rachel Carson's seminal 1962 book, *Silent Spring,* which eloquently and authoritatively warned of the growing dangers of DDT and other chemicals in the environment. Fears regarding exhaustion of the earth's natural resources, pollution of the seas and extinction of species attracted some media attention in subsequent decades. In the 1980s, public concern was heightened by news of the destruction of the ozone layer and the possibility of devastating climate change. Since then, however, there has been a dearth of sustained public debate on environmental topics – except for genetically modified food, which we will consider in a moment.

Business has helped shape the terms of this non-debate. If we examine the corporate sector, as Andrew Rowell did in *Green Backlash* and Sharon Beder in

Global Spin, we see that it has become the norm for business to adopt a green veneer, courtesy of expensive public relations, without actually replacing damaging business practices with ecologically sustainable activities. US business spends an estimated $500 million every year in greenwashing.[41] In 1998 it was reported that Shell and BP 'spend seven times more on advertising their green credentials than they spend on environmental projects'.[42]

As with industry PR, so it is with the media's apparent reflection of public concern about green issues: more gloss than substance. Whenever the mainstream media serve up stories about 'the environment', a curious blinkered view prevails. First, the environment is tidily swept into a corner away from the 'real' bread and butter issues: interest rates, superpower posturing, corporate take-overs and personality politics. Instead, environmental stories are prostituted into bland news-bites or media-friendly picture stories, and often portrayed as the remit of 'single-issue' (media-speak for 'narrow-minded') mainstream environmental pressure groups such as Greenpeace, Friends of the Earth and the World Wide Fund for Nature. Second, the media – and for that matter, the worlds of business and conventional politics – appear incapable of treating the environment as a core political theme. The green view that 'the environment' encapsulates humanity's intimate relationship with the planet is one which the media seem incapable of acknowledging, far less portraying in depth.

Take climate change: the greatest environmental threat facing humanity. The 2,500-member Intergovernmental Panel on Climate Change estimates that stabilising global temperatures requires a 60-80 per cent cut in the emission of greenhouse gases. At Kyoto in 1997 developed countries struggled to agree on a 5.2 per cent cut. And even that puny target has yet to be ratified by the requisite number of governments. Meanwhile, according to climate scientist Mike Hulme of the University of East Anglia, we are already in a new climate regime that has been 'tainted' by industrial society. 'There is no longer such a thing', says Hulme, 'as a purely natural weather event'.[43]

Do broadcasters and newspapers reflect the scale and urgency of this problem? Not at all. The respected London-based Global Commons Institute estimates that there will be more than two million deaths from climate change-related disasters worldwide over the next ten years. Damage to property will amount to hundreds of billions of dollars.[44] How many people know that even though the Kyoto deal is often lauded as a 'vital first step', it falls vastly short of the cuts in fossil-fuel use that have to be made now in order to stabilise global warming? The occasional superficial newspaper report of climate scientists' warnings or dramatic footage of hurricane devastation on TV is a pitiful response.

And yet, the media prides itself on its 'balance'. A revealing view of just where this balance lies was given by David Edwards following the broadcast of the anti-green Channel 4 series *Against Nature* in the UK.[45] Responding to criticism, Michael Jackson, Chief Executive of Channel 4, wrote: 'The small but significant group of people who hold views opposed to the environmental lobby have rarely been seen on British television'. As Edwards adds wryly, 'Can we assume, then, that TV advertisers – say, petrochemical, automobile, atomic energy, fast food and retail corporations – are not expressing views "opposed to the environmental lobby"?'.[46]

For the environmental lobby, making an impression on the mainstream media is a constant battle involving clever campaigning, dramatic photo-opportunities, a never-ending stream of professional press releases, constant badgering of journalists (and supporters for yet more donations) and, often, sophisticated research which is more credible than government or industry pronouncements. It is a competition that pressure groups with scant resources can ill afford to participate in, while the larger groups rarely question the terms of the media game in which they are trapped, usually unwittingly.

Why should this be so? To answer this, we must return to the propaganda model which explains the 'specific inability of the mass media to report the systematic links between the West and human rights abuses in the Third World'.[47] Such abuses aside, what about reporting of industrial pollution, the worldwide loss of biodiversity and global warming? Edwards' answer is disturbing: 'The same is true for business-unfriendly environmental issues. Environmentalists – no matter how accurate or brilliant their facts and ideas – will always encounter obstacles to the communication of messages which threaten state and business interests'.[48] Investigative journalism into corporate greed for profit at the expense of people and the planet is therefore largely missing from our news reports.

Is it not significant that even the largest non-governmental organisations with relatively secure funding – Oxfam, Friends of the Earth, Greenpeace, WWF – constantly struggle to attract media coverage in the belief that we have a free press? As Peter Melchett, then executive director of Greenpeace UK, wrote in 1998, 'it's been a good year, but what's been frustrating is that we're not doing enough to get the message of our successes over in the media, or to people more generally'.[49] It's a perfect example of activists not recognising the structural constraints of the media, and heaping blame upon themselves for 'not doing enough'. One wonders whether Greenpeace, Friends of the Earth and other NGOs shouldn't devote at least some of their campaigning skills to lifting the lid on the 'free' press. The propaganda model reveals that constraints in the mass media necessarily limit the impact of environmental activism. Surely this is of crucial importance to environmentalists? A twin-pronged approach is advisable whereby pressure groups campaign on environmental issues using the mass media where possible – there *are* sympathetic journalists and editors – but also highlight mass media biases, omissions and deceptions. Most NGOs ignore or neglect the latter. When I asked Friends of the Earth's press officer why this was so, I was told that the pressure group would 'have to divert scarce campaigning resources' and that, in any case, FoE's current media strategy enables them 'to punch above their weight'.[50] To accept the argument that the mass media is an integral component of mass human and environmental rights abuses, and yet refrain from bringing it to the public's attention, is surely an odd position. Would it really involve so many precious resources to raise the topic amongst NGO supporters, publish the occasional article in their own newsletters or magazines, mention it in context when being interviewed, and so on? One wonders whether there has ever been any major debate in any of the NGOs about the propaganda model.

Greens, anti-globalisation activists and corporate critics are used to minimal or zero coverage. So any media coverage tends to be received gratefully, even if it is inadequate given the appalling seriousness of the human-rights abuses and environmental threats facing us. Nonetheless, a basic understanding of the propaganda model should be in the tool kit of every socially-engaged citizen. Campaign issues such as pollution, global warming, ozone depletion or species loss are important. But also important is the structure of the corporate media which processes, filters and distorts these issues. This structure is a crucial cog in the profit-driven system that created the need for such campaigns in the first place. Only by understanding this can we hope to overcome the systemic bias of the corporate media which continues to block public understanding of the plunder of the planet and ways to combat it.

However, it is extremely difficult to break through the prevalent belief that the mass media represent a reasonably level playing field of news, opinions and ideas. Confronting one's own deeply-held assumptions about the world around us can be disconcerting, even traumatic. It is therefore not surprising that campaigners are often unwilling to contemplate the notion that there is an inherent media resistance to their message. It is also not surprising that activists who may be aware of the propaganda model, have often not grasped it. They have gleaned from the mass media the damning but false impression that 'big companies try to control the news in their favour'.[51] This is the 'conspiracy' charge that Herman and Chomsky cogently refuted from day one. The view of Andy Neather, then editor of *Earth Matters*, Friends of the Earth's magazine, is illustrative:

> All national papers and most regional dailies, as well as all serious national broadcast news media, have environmental correspondents; a sheaf of cuttings on environmentally-related stories, many of them generated by environmental pressure groups, lands on my desk every morning.[52]

The proliferation of environmental correspondents and 'environmentally-related stories' is tendered as proof positive that all is basically well in the media world; but the content, context and depth of the reporting – or lack thereof – is apparently not of primary concern. Moreover, the number of environment correspondents is far outweighed by the number of news, business and financial correspondents promoting business as usual. In any case, as Beder points out: 'Environmental reporting emphasizes individual action rather than underlying social forces and issues'. She provides an example: 'A current-affairs TV show may expose corporation X for spewing toxic waste into the local waterway, but it will seldom look at the way corporations have lobbied to weaken the legislation preventing such dumping'.[53]

GM? More grist to the mill

Have I exaggerated the media problem? Is it really that awful? Some will counter that the issue of genetically modified food – an environmental *cause célèbre*, if ever there was one – has been one of the biggest media stories of recent years. Well, there is no denying the explosion of newsprint and airtime devoted to GM issues, at least in Europe, beginning in 1998. Many sections of the mainstream media quickly picked up on the public's unease about genetic engineering and ran with it. It was significant that in the UK even the right-wing *Daily Mail* and the *Daily Express*, not normally noted for their environmental stances, took up a very clear anti-GM position. Biotech corporations – Monsanto, in particular – were hammered. New Labour – and Prime Minister Tony Blair himself – had the biggest PR disaster to date. Surely the media handling of the GM story blows the propaganda model out of the water? Not at all. Recall that we are not talking here about blatant, crude suppression of radical and green views. Nor is the press uniformly submissive to business interests, especially when confronted by massive public concern on an issue.

But is it not significant that even major pressure groups had to campaign solidly against genetic engineering for anything up to 10 years before much media interest was generated? Sue Mayer worked on GM issues with Greenpeace in the early nineties when they were struggling to attract any media attention at all. Mayer says that 'They [the press] had to reflect the interest and information from public interest groups forcing it onto the agenda'. Previously the media 'were extremely unwilling to look behind the hype of the companies and the hype of the scientists until they were forced to'.[54]

Moreover, much of the mainstream reporting on GM – again there are exceptions – treated it as a consumer story. Issues relating to the undermining of Third World agriculture and corporate dominance of the food chain were underreported – in particular, moves by Western corporations to control the supply of seed to peasant farmers. Significantly, negative reporting of activists who destroyed GM crops at test sites was common in the press, with much bandying around of pejorative terms such as 'vandals' and 'terrorists'. Looking more broadly, Andrew Rowell notes that: 'It is becoming increasingly difficult to get hard-hitting current affairs stories that have an in-depth understanding of environmental, development or human rights issues into the media, especially broadcast media.' Rowell, who has worked for *The Guardian* newspaper in Britain, added, 'All too often environmental issues are still ignored as editors fight for a quick popular headline'.[55]

The dismissive response of many activists, such as FoE's Andy Neather, to the propaganda model is telling. It is consistent with the notion that to those inside the media system – whether journalists, PR executives or even well-intentioned professional environmentalists – not only is the freedom of the press taken more or less for granted, but that the very concept of a propaganda model can be rejected without thought. In an interview, Chomsky commented as follows on the reaction of 'liberals' and others who fail to engage with the argument that there are structural constraints in the media which limit the impact of dissident thinking and activism:

> Somehow they have to get rid of the stuff [dissident arguments]. [They] can't deal with the arguments, that's plain, for one thing you have to know something, and most of these people don't know anything. Secondly, you wouldn't be able to answer the arguments because they're correct. Therefore what you have to do is somehow dismiss it. So that's one technique, 'It's just emotional, it's irresponsible, it's angry'.[56]

Throughout this book, I frequently cite mainstream news sources: the BBC, *The Independent* and *The Guardian*, for example. Other media critics, such as Chomsky, also reference mainstream press and broadcasting for at least some of their facts. This encourages dismissive critics of the propaganda model to conclude triumphantly that the model is false, and that media coverage of crucial issues is indeed reasonably fair and accurate. But as Herman and Chomsky point out, this is a 'classic *non sequitur*'. The important point here is: what context and attention are provided by the mass media for any given fact? What is the framework within which it is presented? Are related facts, which might elucidate or contradict the meaning, presented also? An honest appraisal would conclude that 'there is no merit to the pretense that because certain facts may be found in the media by a diligent and skeptical researcher, the absence of radical bias and de facto suppression is thereby demonstrated'.[57]

In *The Compassionate Revolution,* David Edwards draws parallels with the lack of mainstream scrutiny of corporate abuse of people, and corporate abuse of the environment, while emphasising that the mass media are not 'monolithic'. Occasionally, the truth does shine through, but with one important proviso:

'Reporting will ... always be sporadic and lacking the sort of historical background and rational framework that might allow us to understand the systemic and institutionalized links between the West and Third World human rights abuses'[58] or, for that matter, between the West and global environmental degradation.

Killing the children of Iraq

The malaise of self-deception afflicts even such celebrated journalists as the BBC's Fergal Keane. Mainstream journalists tend to rise through the ranks, or receive accolades from their peers, by conforming to the narrow statutes of the mass media. And so, when Keane wrote that 'the first casualty of television's ratings war is too often the truth'[59] it was hardly news. In fact, it is far more insidious than he allows. As we have seen above, the 'news' which the public receives has been filtered by economic and political forces operating in a profit-maximising society. Real politics, news and analysis are anathema to the mainstream news corporations which are vulnerable to any radical shifts in society. Instead, truly critical news analysis is marginalised while mainstream news sources act as PR machines for Western governments, military adventurism and corporate interests.

John Pilger devotes a full chapter in *Hidden Agendas* to numerous cases where the mainstream portrayal of major news stories was heavily biased. The BBC, because of the widespread misconception that it represents the very pinnacle of impartiality, comes in for particularly heavy criticism. As Pilger noted, its reporting on Vietnam, the Falklands War, the Gulf War and subsequent US attacks on Iraq, including devastating economic sanctions, have all provided tacit approval of British and American government policy while relegating opposition viewpoints to the sidelines or, worse, a news blackout.

Pilger pointed out that during the Gulf War – which was about access to oil and maintaining 'stability' favourable to Western interests, rather than the spin of 'defending human rights' – the mainstream media propagated the myth that by virtue of 'surgical' application of new 'smart' bombs there would be a 'miraculously small number of casualties'. Even today, how many people in Britain or the United States or elsewhere in the West are aware that more than 100,000 Iraqi soldiers were slaughtered and twice that number of civilians? These figures do not even include the half a million Iraqi children under the age of 5 – probably more than a million Iraqis in all – who have died as a direct result of economic sanctions imposed by the UN Sanctions Committee (with the US and UK governments its most influential and unyielding members).[60] In January 1999, Noam Chomsky, Edward Herman, Edward Said and Howard Zinn drew attention to the harsh reality of sanctions which were continuing to kill 4,500 Iraqi children under the age of 5 every month.[61] In March 2000, with the sanctions still in place, John Pilger's documentary, *Paying the Price: Killing the Children of Iraq*, was broadcast on ITV. He interviewed Scott Ritter, a former UN weapons inspector, who stated that after years of sanctions and weapons inspections there is now 'zero threat' from Saddam, undermining the alleged motivation for the economic embargo. Pilger also revealed the barely reported war being waged by the West's air forces against the innocent people of Iraq, with around 24,000 combat missions flown between May 1998 and January 2000.

In 1998, Denis Halliday, assistant Secretary-General of the UN, who had been based in Baghdad to administer the humanitarian 'oil for food' programme, resigned in protest at the West's 'genocide' of the Iraqi people. In February 2000, Hans von Sponeck, Halliday's successor as humanitarian coordinator in Iraq, also resigned in protest. Halliday told David Edwards in an interview the following month:

> Washington, and to a lesser extent London, have deliberately played games through the Sanctions Committee with this ['oil for food'] programme for years – it's a deliberate ploy. That's why I've been using the word 'genocide', because this is a deliberate policy to destroy the people of Iraq.[62]

Halliday refuted the claim made by the British and US governments that Saddam had deliberately blocked or diverted food and medicine: 'There's no basis for that assertion at all. The [United Nations] Secretary-General [Kofi Annan] has reported repeatedly that there is no evidence that food is being diverted by the government in Baghdad.'[63]

Demonising Saddam, but ensuring that he remains in place, provides marketing opportunities in the Middle East for Western weapons manufacturers. Over $100 billion of US military hardware has been sold to Iraq's 'threatened' neighbours: Saudi Arabia, Kuwait, the Gulf States, Turkey and Israel. Halliday said, 'It's thanks to Saddam ... [he] is the best salesman in town'. As for media coverage of the whole affair, Halliday singled out the BBC for criticism: 'I'm very disappointed with the BBC. The BBC has been very aggressively in favour of sanctions.'[64]

The BBC presents itself to this day as the upholder of Lord Reith's 'three truths' of 'impartiality', 'objectivity' and 'balance'. Former BBC political editor John Cole wrote approvingly in *The Guardian* that the BBC is 'obsessed about its reputation for impartiality'.[65] The corporation's political news editor Ric Bailey continued the propaganda campaign in *The Independent* a few days later, saying that impartiality is 'obsessively important'.[66] BBC trailers continually exhorted viewers to trust the organisation for its 'honesty' and 'integrity'. At sensitive times, however, the Reithian ideals are quietly dropped. As Pilger notes, during the Falklands War in 1982:

Leaked minutes of one of the BBC's Weekly Review Board meetings showed BBC executives directing that the reporting of the war should be concerned 'primarily with government statements of policy' while impartiality was felt to be 'an unnecessary irritation'.[67]

Smoothing public opinion in Nato's favour

The BBC's reporting of the 1999 Nato bombing campaign in the Balkans was another example of this august institution's abdication of its public responsibilities; in particular, the station's reluctance to bring home to the viewer the inconsistencies and deceit implicit in Nato's pronouncements, as well as Nato's terrorist actions in bombing civilian targets. Although BBC reporter John Simpson upset government spin doctors with his frank reports from Belgrade, the BBC did not inform its viewers and listeners of the ridiculous terms of the Rambouillet peace treaty (see below); nor did it query Nato's claims about the Serbian 'war machine' being 'degraded'; nor, worst of all, did it systematically question the politicians and military planners about the many non-military targets being hit – atrocities routinely presented by Nato and the BBC (and the media as a whole) as 'blunders'.

The BBC was not alone in acting as mouthpieces for Nato. Indeed, when the bombing was over, several journalists praised themselves for smoothing public opinion in Nato's favour. Channel 4 correspondent Alex Thomson wrote, 'So, if you want to know why the public supported the war, thank a journalist, not the present government's propagandist-in-chief [Alastair Campbell, the Prime Minister's press secretary]'.[68] The *Guardian*'s Maggie O'Kane made the same point: '… Campbell should acknowledge that it was the press reporting of the Bosnian war and the Kosovar refugee crisis that gave his boss the public support and sympathy he needed to fight the good fight against Milosevic.'[69] Even the BBC's John Simpson spoke up for the media's support of Nato: 'Why did British, American, German, and French public opinion stay rock-solid for the bombing, in spite of Nato's mistakes? Because they knew the war was right. Who gave them the information? The media.'[70]

Most commentators in the British media accepted the Foreign Office line that Nato attacks had been justified because of the Serb refusal to sign the peace treaty drafted in February 1999 at Rambouillet, just outside Paris. They also accepted the spin that the West's aim was to bring peace and autonomy to Kosovo. In fact, as Pilger wrote:

Anyone scrutinising the Rambouillet document is left in no doubt that the excuses given for the subsequent bombing were fabricated. The peace negotiations were stage-managed and the Serbs were told: Surrender and be occupied, or don't surrender and be destroyed. The impossible terms, recently published in full in *Le Monde Diplomatique*, but not in Britain, show that Nato's aim was the occupation not only of Kosovo, but effectively all of Yugoslavia.[71]

The Rambouillet Agreement called for the complete military occupation of, as well as considerable political control over, Kosovo by Nato and, in effect, military control over the rest of the Federal Republic of Yugoslavia (FRY). In Appendix B, headed 'Status of Multi-National Military Implementation Force', a crucial paragraph read:

> NATO personnel shall enjoy, together with their vehicles, vessels, aircraft, and equipment, free and unrestricted passage and unimpeded access throughout FRY including associated airspace and territorial waters. This shall include, but not be limited to, the right of bivouac, manoeuvre, billet, and utilisation of any areas or facilities as required for support, training, and operations.[72]

In Pilger's words, 'No government anywhere could accept this. It was an outrageous provocation'.[73] Chomsky observed that: 'In the massive US coverage of the war, I found no report of [Nato's] terms that was near accurate, notably the crucial article of Appendix B'; and so 'it was impossible for the public to have any serious understanding of what was taking place'.[74] The public also had no inkling of a serious alternative to Nato's accept-or-be-bombed proposal. The Serbian National Assembly responded to Nato's ultimatum by issuing a resolution on March 23. It rejected the demand for Nato military occupation, and called on the Organisation for Security and Cooperation in Europe and the UN to facilitate a peaceful settlement. The National Assembly resolution called for negotiations leading 'toward the reaching of a political agreement on a wide-ranging autonomy for Kosovo and Metohija [the official FRY name for the province], with the securing of a full equality of all citizens and ethnic communities and with respect for the sovereignty and territorial integrity of the Republic of Serbia and the Federal Republic of Yugoslavia'.[75]

Of the Serbian National Assembly resolution, Chomsky noted, 'Several database searches have found scarce mention, none in the national press and major journals'.[76]

> The two peace plans of March 23 thus remain unknown to the general public, even the fact that there were two, not one. The standard line is that 'Milosevic's refusal to accept ... or even discuss an international peace-keeping plan [namely, the Rambouillet Agreement] was what started NATO bombing on March 24'.[77]

If we turn to the Kosovo Accord of 3 June, following the defeat of Milosevic, it is actually a compromise between the two peace plans of March 23. Chomsky explained that, at least on paper, the US/Nato abandoned their major demands [cited above from Appendix B] which had led to Serbia's rejection of the ultimatum. Serbia in turn agreed to an 'international security presence with substantial Nato participation [which] must be deployed under unified command and control ... under UN auspices'.[78]

An addendum to the Accord made clear that Russian troops would not be under Nato command, nor were there terms permitting access to the rest of Yugoslavia for Nato or the 'international security presence'. The Accord declared that political control of Kosovo would *not* be under the auspices of Nato, but of the UN Security Council, just as the Serbian resolution of March 23 requested. The withdrawal of Yugoslav forces was not specified in as much detail as in the Rambouillet Agreement, but is similar, if 'accelerated'. The rest of the terms 'is within the range of agreement of the two plans of March 23'. Chomsky concluded: 'The outcome suggests that diplomatic initiatives could have been pursued on March 23, averting a terrible human tragedy with consequences that will reverberate in Yugoslavia and elsewhere, and are in many respects quite ominous.'[79]

'Humanitarian intervention' and the politics of deception

It is instructive to consider the roles of Nato and the Western media during the bombing campaign. On 25 March, the day after the bombing began, UK Defence Secretary George Robertson described Nato's aim as 'clear cut'. It was, he said, 'to avert an impending humanitarian catastrophe by disrupting the violent attacks currently being carried out by the Yugoslav security forces against the Kosovan Albanians'.[80] A CIA warning to President Clinton, leaked to the American press, made clear that the bombing was likely to spark mass ethnic cleansing. And indeed this is what happened. On 27 March, US-Nato Commanding General Wesley Clark claimed that it was 'entirely predictable' that Serb terror and violence would intensify after the Nato bombing. He emphasised the point shortly after when he announced that he was not surprised by the sharp escalation of Serb terror after the bombing began: 'The military authorities fully anticipated the vicious approach that Milosevic would adopt, as well as the terrible efficiency with which he would carry it out.'[81] The timing of the bombing and the flood of refugees is of particular interest. Prior to the bombing, and for two days following its onset, the United Nations High Commissioner for Refugees (UNHCR) reported no data on refugees. On March 27, three days into the bombing, UNHCR reported that 4,000 had fled Kosovo to Albania and Macedonia. By April 5, the *New York Times* reported 'more than 350,000 have left

Kosovo since March 24'. When 78 days of bombing ended, the UNHCR reported that 671,500 refugees had fled FRY. According to the Yugoslav Red Cross, over a million people were displaced within Serbia, along with many who had left Serbia.[82] The West's leaders told us that the bombing was taken in 'response' to expulsions of Kosovar Albanians and to 'reverse' the flow. But there was scant mention anywhere in the mainstream media that the Nato bombing actually precipitated a huge flood of refugees.

Instead, the line dutifully reported by the media was that the Serb violence would have been 'even worse' if the bombing had not gone ahead. Despite a general acquiescence amongst the press and broadcasters, or even active support for Nato's line (as we saw above), there was considerable disquiet amongst the British public with little-reported anti-war demonstrations taking place throughout the bombing campaign. A group of Labour MPs even voted against the government, earning the wrath of Clare Short, Secretary of State for International Development, who compared them to appeasers of Hitler and Nazi Germany.[83] As the bombing raids went on, and the targets were broadened from military to 'economic' and 'propaganda machine' targets, the offices of Serbian state TV were deliberately targeted, killing technicians and a make-up lady. Short declared the building a 'legitimate target'.[84]

The media expressed horror at a whole series of apparent Nato 'blunders'. These included 18 hospitals and clinics and at least 200 nurseries, schools, colleges and students' dormitories, as well as housing estates, hotels, libraries, youth centres, theatres, museums, churches and fourteenth-century monasteries on the World Heritage list.[85] Behind the scenes at Nato, there may well have been consternation that a few days of bombing was insufficient to make President Slobodan Milosevic give in. Nato's spokesman Jamie Shea claimed, 'This was never an operation that was planned for only two or three days'[86] – not something that was stated before Nato went to war. Throughout the campaign, Nato told the public that the Milosevic 'war machine' was being 'severely degraded'. Nato Air Commodore David Wilby said: 'We continue to systematically degrade and to diminish the military, paramilitary and special forces of the former Republic of Yugoslavia.'[87] The truth was rather different. When, after 78 days of intense Nato bombing, the Serbs capitulated and their army withdrew from Kosovo, there was little evidence that the Milosevic 'war machine' had been 'degraded' at all. There were reports that, in fact, Nato had been duped by decoy tanks and installations. According to Robert Fisk of *The Independent*: 'The Serbs, interestingly enough, say they lost 19 tanks – but Nato officials now privately think they only destroyed 13!'[88]

Fisk, who had been critical of Nato throughout the Kosovo crisis, later analysed the media handling of the bombing campaign. He was scornful of the almost universal acceptance by his fellow reporters of the Nato line spun to them:

'...most of the journalists at Nato headquarters were so supine, so utterly taken in by Nato's generals and air commodores that their questions might have been printed out for them by Nato in advance.'[89]

Fisk summed up what had happened in the Balkans campaign:

> Nato's bombing brought a kind of peace to Kosovo – but only after it had given the Serbs the opportunity to massacre or dispossess half the Albanian population of the province, caused billions of dollars in damage to Yugoslavia's infrastructure, killed hundreds of Yugoslav civilians, destabilised Macedonia and gravely damaged relations with China. And the media called this a successful war.[90]

Those are hardly the words you would have heard in BBC news reports. Nor was there much attention given to a scathing report issued by Médecins sans Frontières on the failure of Nato and UN to protect Kosovo minorities more than a year after the 'peace accord' of June 3, 1999. 'The action of the international community in Kosovo is ineffective', said Dr James Orbinski of MSF. 'There is no true environment of security, there exists a climate of impunity. There has been no systematic and effective response to violence'.[91]

In the UK, the all-party Commons select committee on defence produced a damning report in October 2000 attacking the British government's handling of the war. 'It was unwise for politicians within [Nato]', concluded the committee, 'to either have thought or ever suggested that a humanitarian disaster on the ground could be averted from the air. On the contrary, all evidence suggests that plans to initiate the air campaign hastened the onset of the disaster'. The report also noted the 'distressingly low' success rate of 1,000lb unguided bombs confirmed as hitting their targets: 2 per cent. However, the committee did not condemn the use of cluster bombs, beyond saying that they were of 'questionable legitimacy'. Nor did it castigate the use of depleted uranium which has been linked to increased cancer rates amongst Gulf War veterans, Iraqi civilians and, recently, military personnel who served in the Balkans, not to mention local inhabitants. As a British Harrier pilot observed, 'after a while you've got to ignore the collateral damage and start smashing those targets'.[92]

Ever since the end of the Kosovo bombing, Western journalists have been flailing around doing their utmost to help the US and Britain justify Nato's action which, according to Amnesty International, led to 'serious violations of the laws of war leading in a number of cases to the unlawful killings of civilians'. Thus, the principle of retrospective justification has been deployed. When, in September 2000, Slobodan Milosevic was toppled and replaced by Vojislav Kostunica, this provided for some the long-awaited glorious outcome of Nato's action. No matter that, according to news analyst Martin Sieff, Kostunica 'regularly denounces the

NATO bombing of Yugoslavia last year as "criminal",' 'implacably opposes having Milosevic or any other prominent Serb tried as a war criminal,' and worse still from the Clinton-Blair point of view, 'does appear to accurately express the democratic aspirations of the Serbian people'. As for the help granted by Nato's illegal bombing, as a Belgrade university student told the BBC: 'We did it on our own. Please do not help us again with your bombs'. Reaffirming this conclusion, a correspondent for the opposition daily newspaper *Blic* wrote that, 'Serbs felt oppressed by their regime from the inside and by the West from the outside'. She also condemned the US for having 'ignored the democratic movement in Yugoslavia and failing to aid numerous Serbian refugees' – by far the largest refugee population in the region, as Chomsky notes.[93]

As David Edwards concluded of the whole affair, 'The real question not just for future historians, but for all thinking people, is how so many respected journalists, could yet again be so readily taken in by the deceptions of Western power?'[94]

No news can mean bad news

In the summer of 1999, the British press was awash with glowing tributes to George Robertson, the UK Minister of Defence with 'the granite accent', on his unanimous approval as the new Nato Secretary-General. 'Rock-steady', 'tough-talking', 'trusted' – and British to boot. This was the same George Robertson who had stated in March 1999 that Nato bombing raids against Serbia 'will hit heavily at Milosevic's ability to pursue his murderous campaign in Kosovo' and that 'these air strikes have one purpose only: to stop the genocidal violence'.[95] It turned out that he was wrong on both counts. But that was quickly forgotten by the media in their praise of one of the chief architects of Nato's 'victory against Milosevic'.

Robertson had been so impressive as a propaganda merchant for Western powers during the post-Gulf War bombing of Iraq, which had resumed in December 1998 and continues to this day, that comedian and former *Guardian* columnist Mark Steel declared him 'stupid enough to believe his own bullshit'.[96] Steel's sharp political pieces in *The Guardian* were liberally sprinkled with such remarks, which seemed breathtaking to the reader simply because hard-hitting, truthful observations about our political leaders occur so rarely in the press. Steel wrote about workers who faced up to globalisation; in particular, the Liverpool dockers and the strikers on London Underground's Jubilee Line. But in the end it was all deemed too 'Old Labour' for *The Guardian* which 'was preparing to realign itself politically'[97] and Steel was told that his services were no longer needed. He currently writes a column in *The Independent*.

As for Robertson, he is a master of Orwellian doublespeak, as befits a man in his position. In a newspaper article while still UK Defence Secretary, he provided a classic, if disturbing, example of how powerful politicians sweep aside truth and compassion in the interests of propaganda. He made the grandiose claim that British foreign policy protects 'a secure and prosperous Britain in a world where democracy and liberal economics continue to spread'.[98] But Mark Curtis has shown in *The Ambiguities of Power,* based on a careful examination of the historical record, that the primary aim of UK government foreign policy has been – and remains – to secure British profits and economic interests abroad, at the expense of human rights, social justice and environmental sustainability. Britain's postwar role in the Middle East, southeast Asia and elsewhere – often as the adjutant to the United States – is shameful.[99]

One has only to look at Britain's aiding of Indonesia's brutal suppression of East Timor, or human rights abuses perpetrated by our arms customers in Saudi Arabia, Turkey and Malaysia, to see that the 'defence' policy of Robertson and his predecessors is a smokescreen for sales of British weapons and torture equipment.[100] The security of the British people is subordinate to the expansion of British corporate activities, all with the creation of profit as their prime motive. As activist Angie Zelter wrote in *The Guardian*, 'If our democratic and legal institutions worked properly, the British government would be prosecuted for supplying weapons to [former Indonesian President] Suharto'.[101] Sadly, a change of government from Tory to Labour in 1997 did nothing to promote ethical concerns above business priorities.

Robertson maintained that Britain is 'willing and able to play a leading role' in a 'strong world community'.[102] But there is one particular step in the direction of genuine security that he never took as Defence Secretary. On 8 July, 1996, the International Court of Justice in The Hague published an Advisory Opinion in which it found no lawful circumstance for any threat, let alone use, of nuclear weapons. Moreover, in the Court's judgement 'there exists an obligation to pursue in good faith and bring to a conclusion negotiations leading to nuclear disarmament'.[103] Given such a momentous ruling, one might have expected the media to give considerable coverage to the story. Instead, a few paragraphs in the broadsheets summed up the court's judgement and the generally dismissive response from governments, and there has been little – if any – media follow-up. As a result, pressure on world powers to disarm has dropped off. And now that he is comfortably ensconced as Nato's top official, George Robertson, who is presumably aware of the Court's ruling, is even less likely to respond positively, or even refer to it at all.

Since the mainstream media are reluctant to highlight the UK's illegal nuclear 'deterrent', or are at least oblivious to its illegality, it is hardly surprising that there should be a virtual news blackout of direct campaigning against the Trident nuclear weapons system. One story that largely escaped the media's attention in August 1998 concerned five women peace activists from the direct action group

Trident Ploughshares 2000, who were detained following an anti-nuclear action and subsequently strip-searched and held naked in solitary confinement in a British prison. Their 'crime' was to attempt to disarm the illegal Trident system at Coulport, a nuclear submarine base on the west coast of Scotland.

In a separate incident a month later, another woman peace activist was dragged from her car in the early hours of the morning, handcuffed and charged with vagrancy. She had been waiting to join the CND 'Citizens Inspection Team' which planned to inspect Barrow nuclear submarine dockyard for weapons of mass destruction later that morning. A fellow CND activist later said, 'This was an act of intimidation against a single woman who offered no threat or argument and it demonstrates how desperate the authorities have become since the launch of Trident Ploughshares 2000'.[104]

It is often the important stories that go unreported in the mass media. No news, unfortunately, often means bad news.

A world of dissent

Media conglomerates, formed through mergers or the absorption of smaller companies, are leading the charge to introduce new technology in an attempt to maintain and boost audiences. Domination of the press and terrestrial television is now expanding into cable and satellite television, with a digital gateway provided by 'black box' technology – controlled by media tycoons such as Rupert Murdoch – sitting atop your television. Giant corporations are taking over the information channels which broadcast to the majority of the population. As channels multiply and audiences fragment, ownership is becoming more concentrated in the hands of a wealthy few. Media analyst Colin Leys notes that 'the differences between the media are getting smaller ... text, sound and images are all increasingly produced and accessed through the same digital technology'.[105]

The current plethora of docusoaps, pet, household, cookery and gardening programmes on television decries the mantra that competition improves product quality. Substantive news reporting and analysis has lost out to cosy, comfortable and cut-price entertainment. As writer and activist Katharine Ainger says, 'In this virtual fantasy world, the environment features only as a series of cow-lifting tornadoes and exploding volcanoes in cheap "Real Life Disaster" shows'.[106] Ainger points to the decline of in-depth media coverage of international issues – around 80 per cent of TV programmes on developing countries consists of glossy wildlife shows – thereby diminishing any coherent frame of reference for a sensible analysis of economic globalisation. It has simply fallen outside the media's narrow field of vision.

Granville Williams, of the London-based Campaign for Press and Broadcasting Freedom, not only points out the urgent need for a broad coalition in campaigning for media reform, but identifies four main policy issues on which to base such a campaign. First, defence of public service broadcasting. Second, challenging media concentration by breaking up powerful media conglomerates and limiting cross-media ownership. For example, the public interest would be better served by splitting up the small number of burgeoning media empires, thus allowing a greater diversity of views to proliferate. Third, new forms of regulation to ensure that digital technology serves people not business. And fourth, media law reform to ensure that journalists are protected from proprietorial and editorial pressures.[107] If such a campaign fails, it opens the door for continued planet-consuming globalisation promoted by a powerful media network which is owned by, or allied with, identical corporate interests.

Is the situation hopeless? Not if more people recognise that the media is an integral part of the institutionalised system of greed and violence that is destroying cultures and ecosystems around the planet. And not if public pressure encourages the media industry to report more of what the US comedian and broadcaster Michael Moore ironically calls 'the awful truth'. What does this mean in practical terms? Recall that the mainstream media are not uniformly servile to business interests. There *are* outspoken editors and journalists, many of whom are aware of the nature of the system in which they are working and who try consciously to overcome the obstacles preventing full and truthful reporting. (Noam Chomsky has said on several occasions that many of the best journalists, with whom he is personally acquainted, have a far more cynical attitude to the media than he does). Activists ought to establish and maintain good links with sympathetic journalists, feeding them reliable information and supporting them in a hostile media environment. As far as other journalists are concerned, the public should regularly highlight their omissions and biases, gently but relentlessly chivvying them along in the direction of unbiased reporting.

The US-based media watchdog, Fairness and Accuracy In Reporting (FAIR), has been offering well-documented criticism of media bias and censorship since 1986. FAIR campaigns 'for greater diversity in the press' and is constantly 'scrutinizing media practices that marginalize public interest, minority and dissenting viewpoints'. The group exposes 'important news stories that are neglected and defends working journalists when they are muzzled'.[108] A central feature of FAIR's work is the dissemination of e-mail addresses and phone numbers of publishers, editors and journalists, thereby encouraging members of the public to highlight distortions and omissions, ask difficult questions and generally cajole the mainstream to toe a less business-friendly line. Because a central feature of corporate propaganda is flak – bombarding the media with protests – activists need to respond in kind. It's also worth keeping in mind that journalists and editors often have limited access to dissident ideas; exposure to such ideas can have a highly beneficial effect.

As well as maintaining pressure on the mainstream media, we should be developing alternative frameworks to raise and maintain awareness of the truth that so often goes unreported. Alternative media sources may be tiny, but do play an important role. One avenue is the internet which, like most technology, is a double-edged sword. When Chomsky was interviewed in 1996 for BBC2's *The Big Idea* by *Independent* journalist Andrew Marr, now the BBC's political editor, he warned that the internet, like any new technology 'has a liberatory potential, but it also has a repressive potential, and there's a battle going on about which way it's going to go, as there was for radio, and television, and so on'.[109] As Chomsky pointed out in the interview, the internet remains an elite operation: most of the world's population has never picked up a telephone, never mind surfed the web. But for the moment it remains effectively free from censorship and campaigning groups have found it to be the most effective means of quickly disseminating information to a wide audience. Its speed and power were dramatically highlighted by the grassroots spread of worldwide opposition to the notorious Multilateral Agreement on Investment (see Chapter 1). Drafts of the secretive treaty circulated in cyberspace. Groups such as the Washington-based Public Citizen, the International Forum on Globalisation, the World Development Movement in London and Third World Network in Malaysia informed their own supporters and other campaigners around the globe via e-mail and website updates, forming a loose but effective coalition which took politicians and corporations by surprise.

Also making good use of the internet is the *Justice?* collective based in Brighton, which produces a sharp, entertaining and irreverent weekly look at the world in SchNEWS, which is obtainable in print, on their website[110] or via email. The wording of their 'disclaimer' – published at the end of each issue – varies but is usually a pithy epigram of the form: 'The SchNEWS warns all readers not to attend any illegal gatherings or take part in any criminal activities. Always stay within the law. In fact please just sit in, watch TV and go on endless shopping sprees, filling your house and lives with endless consumer crap. Then you will feel content. Honest.'

SchNEWS regularly covers an impressive range of topics: the harmful effects of economic globalisation on people's rights and the environment; the dangers represented by the nuclear industry; other forms of industrial pollution; accounts of non-violent direct action; big business and government promotion of genetically modified foods; injustice in the court systems; police brutality and harassment (including a 'Crap Arrest of the Week feature'); and oil company duplicity in human right abuses and environmental degradation. In short, the kind of news which is lacking on the BBC and CNN, in *The Times* and *The Washington Post* and in all the other conventional news sources which we are encouraged to consider as objective and authoritative.

The internet is playing an increasingly important role in facilitating global resistance to the damaging impacts of transnational corporations, as well as in promoting eco-friendly alternatives to consumer capitalism. The McSpotlight site on McDonald's has chalked up millions of hits; the OneWorld 'supersite' (www.oneworld.org) hosts an array of pressure groups and alternative media outlets; GreenNet (www.gn.apc.org) is an umbrella site for yet more campaigning groups; ZNet (www.zmag.org) in the United States has a remarkable collection of resources, including regular contributions from a formidable stable of writers such as Noam Chomsky, Edward Herman, Howard Zinn, Robin Hahnel, David Edwards and John Pilger.

But more traditional methods of distributing progressive thinking are still invaluable: magazines, leaflets, newsletters. *The Big Issue*, a street magazine sold by homeless and 'vulnerably housed' people in the UK (with spin-offs elsewhere, such as the United States and the Netherlands), has become very popular – almost mainstream – while still carrying challenging and thoughtful articles. There is a plethora of penetrating periodicals: *Red Action, Socialism Today, Living Marxism, Green Line, Car Busters, Living Earth, Poverty, Red Pepper, Green World, New Internationalist, Le Monde Diplomatique, Adbusters, The Ecologist, Z Magazine.* Earth First's annual publication *Do or Die* regularly features incisive critiques of economic globalisation. The impressive range of such material on offer reflects a modicum of good health in the state of dissent today.

Sometimes the alternative press feels big business breathing down its neck. In 1998, a special issue of *The Ecologist* focused on the US biotech corporation Monsanto which had just launched a £1 million advertising campaign in the UK to promote genetically modified food.[111] As the magazine reminded us, this is the same company responsible for such environmental nightmares as recombinant Bovine Growth Hormone, Agent Orange (used to poison Vietnam), and the worldwide release of 1.2 million tonnes of toxic polychlorinated biphenyls. Oddly, the first print run of 20,000 copies of the issue ended up as pulp, after the printing company took fright at the possibility of legal moves against them by Monsanto. According to the magazine's co-editor (now editor), Zac Goldsmith, 'We have a long history of being forthright about issues and attacking powerful firms, yet not once in 29 years has this printer expressed the slightest qualms about what we were doing'.[112] The printer's fear of a potential libel action was indeed curious. The UK Defamation Act 1996 introduced an 'innocent dissemination' defence for printers who have taken 'reasonable care' and 'were not aware of' the libellous nature of the matter they may have printed. Monsanto's UK spokesman Daniel Verakis claimed to be mystified by the printer's action. 'The fact that the edition has been pulped is news to me. We had nothing to do with it'.[113] True or not, as Chapter 7 shows, it appears that Monsanto and others of their ilk are losing the battle to palm off GM food in Europe. That is testimony to the power of public resistance.

The media jungle is anything but green

If you still harbour doubts that the mass media, through structural constraints but certainly not by conspiratorial means, limit the impact of any citizen activism that seriously challenges the status quo, consider the following question. What constitutes adequate coverage of environmental issues? If we once again turn our attention to climate change, it is noteworthy that broadcasters and newspapers may report the dry facts, then return to business as usual. It is truly surreal. Even when the message gets through, it is heavily weighted towards the need to adapt to human-induced climate change, rather than the pressing need to make the necessary cuts that scientists have estimated are necessary to stabilise rising concentrations of greenhouse gases. By comparison, consider the outpourings we used to endure in the West about the 'Communist menace'. The media brought the 'red scare' to a remarkable pitch, promoting the notion of a Soviet conspiracy working ceaselessly to weaken our defences in order that a surprise attack could be launched at any moment.

As work by historians such as Mark Curtis has shown, state documents released since the end of the Cold War have confirmed that Western governments had little or no fear of Soviet invasion. The 'threat' was fraudulent – for public consumption only. But the promotion of terror boosted the huge arms industries and strategic interests of Western nations. Today, whose interests would be served by a similar treatment of the 'climate menace'? Certainly not those of the business corporations and their political allies, all of them happy to promote a life-threatening addiction to our fossil fuel-based economy. It is not just the infamous 'carbon club' of the Global Climate Coalition that opposes ratification of the Kyoto Protocol by the United States (see following chapter), but mainstream business itself, in the form of the US Chamber of Commerce and National Association of Manufacturers, representing virtually every major US company. How many of us know the huge efforts made by such corporations to stop any action being taken to mitigate climate change? Where have the cynical activities of industry lobbyists been exposed? Where are the massive media campaigns to highlight these issues?

Unless we have fallen prey to the propaganda system, there is no doubt that dissent from the mantra that 'globalisation is good' is grossly under- and misrepresented in the mainstream media. But while dissent is necessary, so is the development of solutions. As this book aims to show, there are practical and sustainable alternatives to the policies driving today's runaway global economy. But to whom should one be addressing one's message? Should it be to the holders of political office and the heads of powerful corporations, as suggested by the Quaker slogan: 'Speak truth to power'? Probably not. As Chomsky said: 'The audience is entirely wrong, and the effort hardly more than a form of self-indulgence.' It is a waste of valuable resources to 'speak truth' to Tony Blair, the managing directors of arms companies 'or others who exercise power in coercive institutions – truth that they already know well enough, for the most part'. Instead, suggests Chomsky, we should try to engage with 'an audience that matters – and furthermore, it should not be seen as an audience, but as a community of common concern in which one hopes to participate constructively. We should not be speaking *to* but *with*'.[114] Throughout this book are examples of how this process of constructive participation is taking place around the world – in a benign form of globalisation.

Notes

1 Chomsky, *Powers and Prospects,* p. 91.
2 ZNet daily commentary (www.zmag.org), 17 March, 2000.
3 Quoted in Norman Solomon, ZNet daily commentary (www.zmag.org), April 4, 2000,
4 Quoted in Edwards, *The Compassionate Revolution,* p. 60.
5 *Ibid.,* p. 60.
6 Quotes from journalist Andrew Marr in his interview with Noam Chomsky, *The Big Idea,* BBC2, 14 February, 1996.
7 *Independent on Sunday,* 13 December, 1998.
8 Curran and Seaton, *Power without Responsibility,* p. 82.
9 Personal communication, 5 August, 1999.
10 Curran and Seaton, *Power without Responsibility,* chapters 1-7.
11 Pilger, *Hidden Agendas,* pp. 374, 375, 424.
12 Herman and Chomsky, *Manufacturing Consent,* p. 12.
13 Edwards, *The Compassionate Revolution,* p. 59.
14 Beder, *Global Spin,* pp. 180-181.
15 Colin Leys, *Red Pepper,* April 1998, p. 14.
16 Beder, *Global Spin,* p. 180.
17 Herman and Chomsky, *Manufacturing Consent,* p. 18.
18 Interview by Robert Jensen, *The Sun* magazine (Baltimore), September, 2000.
19 *Ibid.*
20 Beder, *Global Spin,* p. 35.
21 Andrew Rowell, interviewed by David Edwards on 8 May, 2000.
22 Denis Halliday, former UN Assistant Secretary-General, interviewed by David Edwards, 17 March 2000, for *The Big Issue.*
23 Quoted in Achbar, *Manufacturing Consent – Noam Chomsky and The Media,* p.61.
24 Herman and Chomsky, *Manufacturing Consent,* p. xii.
25 Edwards, *The Compassionate Revolution,* pp. 78-79.
26 Quoted in Chomsky, *Rogue States,* p. 125.
27 Milan Rai, *Chomsky's Politics,* Verso, 1995, p.199, notes.
28 Curtis, *The Ambiguities of Power,* p. 1.
29 Herman and Chomsky, *Manufacturing Consent,* p. 93.
30 *Ibid.,* pp. 176-177.

31   *Ibid.*, p. 177.
32   Curtis, *The Ambiguities of Power,* p. 49.
33   *Ibid.*, pp. 56-86.
34   Pilger, *Hidden Agendas*, p. 139.
35   *Ibid.*, p. 139.
36   Curtis, *The Ambiguities of Power,* p. 218.
37   *Ibid.*, p. 219.
38   Pilger, *Hidden Agendas,* p. 256.
39   Curtis, *The Ambiguities of Power,* p. 225.
40   *Ibid.*, p. 225.
41   Gelbspan, *The Heat Is On*, p. 56.
42   Alasdair Clayre of the Oxford-based lobby group Millennium Energy Debate, quoted in *The Guardian,* 12 November, 1998.
43   *The Guardian*, 15 March, 2000.
44   Global Commons Institute, letter to *The Guardian*, 14 March, 2000. Full text of letter at www.gci.org.uk/guardlet.html
45   The three-part *Against Nature* series, produced by Martin Durkin and RDF Television, was broadcast in the UK in December 1997. Its crude anti-green stance, scientifically weak material, and manipulation of interviewed environmentalists was described as 'an appalling stitch-up' by David Aaronovitch, former TV critic of the *Independent on Sunday* (21 December, 1997). The programme makers were also required by broadcasting regulators to issue an apology for its treatment of interviewees.
46   *The Ecologist*, Vol 28 No 4, pp. 201-203.
47   Edwards, *The Compassionate Revolution,* p. 72.
48   *Ibid.*, p. 73.
49   Greenpeace UK Annual Review 1998.
50   Ian Willmore, Friends of the Earth press officer, email, 4 August, 2000.
51   Personal communication from Andy Neather, Friends of the Earth, 31 August, 1999.
52   *Ibid.*
53   *New Internationalist*, July 1999, p. 30.
54   Interview with David Edwards, 8 May 2000.
55   Interview with David Edwards, 8 May 2000.
56   Chomsky, *Deterring Democracy*, p.79.
57   Herman and Chomsky, *Manufacturing Consent*, p. xv.
58   Edwards, *The Compassionate Revolution,* p. 73.
59   *The Independent,* 25 July, 1998.
60   Arnove, *Iraq Under Siege, passim.*
61   *The Independent*, 21 January, 1999.
62   Interview with David Edwards, 17 March 2000 for *The Big Issue.*
63   *Ibid.*
64   *Ibid.*
65   *The Guardian*, 19 May, 2000.
66   *The Independent*, 23 May, 2000.
67   Pilger, *Hidden Agendas,* p. 492.
68   Quoted by Charles Glass, ZNet daily commentary (www.zmag.org), 1 August, 1999.
69   *Ibid.*
70   *Ibid.*
71   *Sydney Morning Herald*, 14 May, 1999.
72   Chomsky, *The New Military Humanism*, p.107.
73   *Sydney Morning Herald*, 14 May, 1999.

74   Chomsky, *The New Military Humanism*, pp.107-108.

75   *Ibid.,* p. 109.

76   *Ibid.*, p. 109.

77   Chomsky, *Z Magazine*, July/August 1999, p. 41.

78   *Ibid.*

79   *Ibid.*

80   Quoted in. *Sydney Morning Herald*, 14 May, 1999.

81   Chomsky, *The New Military Humanism*, p.21.

82   Figures cited in Chomsky, *The New Military Humanism,* pp. 16-17.

83   *The Independent*, 21 April, 1999.

84   *The Independent*, 24 April, 1999.

85   *Sydney Morning Herald*, 14 May, 1999.

86   *The Independent,* 5 April, 1999.

87   *The Independent,* 9 April, 1999.

88   *The Independent,* 29 June, 1999.

89   *Ibid.*

90   *Ibid.*

91   *The Independent*, 17 August, 2000.

92   *The Independent,* 25 October, 2000.

93   Noam Chomsky, ZNet daily commentary (www.zmag.org), 12 October, 2000.

94   David Cromwell and David Edwards, ZNet daily commentary (www.zmag.org), 24 October, 2000.

95   *The Independent,* 29 March, 1999.

96   Quoted in *The Independent*, 13 April, 1999.

97   *Ibid.*

98   *The Independent,* 14 July, 1998.

99   Curtis, *The Ambiguities of Power,* and Pilger, *Hidden Agendas.*

100 *The Independent*, 23 May, 1997.

101 Quoted in Edwards, *The Compassionate Revolution,* p. 126.

102 *The Independent,* 21 April, 1999.

103 *Financial Times,* 9 July, 1996; Briefing from the International Peace Bureau, The Hague/Oslo, 29 July, 1996.

104 *Conscience* – Newsletter of the Peace Tax Campaign, Autumn 1998, No. 102.

105 *Red Pepper,* April 1998, p. 14.

106 Katharine Ainger, personal communication, 31 October, 1999.

107 *Red Pepper,* April 1998, pp. 17-18.

108 www.fair.org

109 Noam Chomsky interviewed by Andrew Marr, *The Big Idea*, BBC2, 14 February, 1996.

110 www.schnews.org.uk

111 *The Ecologist,* Vol 28, No 5.

112 *SchNEWS,* Issue 184, 25 September, 1998.

113 *Ibid.*

114 Chomsky, *Powers and Prospects,* pp.60-61.

4

FOSSIL FUEL DINOSAURS

Slow to respond to climate change

The issue of global economic inequity is as critical as the carbon balance to the stability of the planet's atmosphere.

Ross Gelbspan, US journalist[1]

The alliance between oil and auto companies is one of the most powerful alliances in the world. It can paralyse governments.

Mustafa Tolba, head of the United Nations Environment Programme[2]

Global warming hits home

Ever since the West's industrial revolution in the nineteenth century, mankind has been sending heat-trapping gases – carbon dioxide (CO_2), methane, nitrous oxide and others – into the atmosphere by destroying forests and burning fossil fuel. A few facts and figures are in order at this point. Each year, approximately 6 billion tonnes of carbon in the form of CO_2 is released into the earth's atmosphere from the combustion of coal, oil and gas. Over the last few decades, these emissions have increased by around 2 per cent per year.[3] Pre-industrial levels of CO_2 stood at around 280 parts per million by volume (ppmv). It now stands at 367 ppmv – the highest for 20 million years.[4] Even if emissions were stabilised at present rates, atmospheric CO_2 concentration would continue to increase for several centuries, breaking the 500 ppmv level around 2100. At the same time, global warming has proceeded apace. According to the World Meteorological Organisation, the Earth's global surface temperature in 1998 was the highest since reliable records began in 1860: 0.57°C above the recent long-term average based on the period 1961 to 1990. The global temperature is almost 0.7°C warmer than at the end of the nineteenth century.[5]

The warmest years of the twentieth century all occurred in the 1990s. 1999 was the twenty-first consecutive year with an above-average global surface temperature. For the United States, it was the second warmest year on record since 1880, while in central England it was the warmest year since records began in 1659. Peter Ewins, head of the UK Meteorological Office and James Baker, his US counterpart, wrote in an open letter to the press that 'new data and understanding now point to the critical situation we face: to slow future change, we must start taking action soon'. Ominously, they added, 'Ignoring climate change will surely be the most costly of all possible choices for us and our children'.[6]

In the Pacific Ocean, the strongest *El Niño* of the century had a dramatic impact on the lives of hundreds of millions of people. It led to extremely dry conditions and fires in Indonesia, drought in Papua New Guinea, and large-scale flooding in Ecuador, Peru and Kenya. In Central America, Hurricane Mitch caused the deaths of more than 11,000 people. Following the hurricane there were outbreaks of cholera, dengue fever and malaria. In eastern Africa, extreme weather events exacerbated the incidence of cholera, Rift Valley fever and malaria. In China, 25 million hectares were flooded and the death toll exceeded 3,000. Floods in India and Bangladesh killed 2,800 people.[7]

By mid-1998, the central equatorial Pacific had switched from *El Niño* conditions to *La Niña*, when colder-than-normal sea surface temperatures occur. Around the same time, extremely heavy rainfall hit the western Pacific, triggering landslides and floods in Indonesia. Impoverished people continued to be the most vulnerable to severe weather events. In October 1999, the heaviest rains in 30 years caused severe flooding in northern Ghana, killing at least 70 people and displacing more than 280,000 persons.[8] In the same month a devastating cyclone hit Orissa, India – the worst in 30 years – leaving around 10,000 people dead. In December 1999, 20,000 people were killed in floods in Venezuela. Two months later, severe flooding and a wave of tropical cyclones left Mozambique and Madagascar struggling to cope, with hundreds of thousands made homeless.

In addition to considerable loss of life, extreme weather events cause devastating destruction of infrastructure and property which, especially in poor regions, are often under- or uninsured. In insured regions, insurers are now worried about 'billion dollar cats'. Early examples of these include the October 1987 storm in northwest Europe ($2.5 billion), Hurricane Hugo in September 1989 ($5.8 billion), and European storms early in 1990 with total losses of over $10 billion. In September 1991, the strongest typhoon to hit Japan in 30 years cost almost $5 billion.

In August 1992 came the costliest storm event yet. Hurricane Andrew blasted into Florida, leaving behind a $16.5 billion insurance bill. The total cost, including uninsured losses, was around $30 billion. As former Greenpeace climate campaigner Jeremy Leggett said, 'Had the storm hit downtown Miami, just 30 kilometres further north, the bill would have been well over $50 billion'.[9] The following year, at the US National Hurricane Conference, the general manager of one of the Caribbean's biggest insurance brokers told delegates: 'If anyone had told the reinsurers ten years ago that they could face $20 billion in insured catastrophic losses in one year, they would have been laughed at.'[10]

The losses continued to mount. Between 1980 and 1989, the insurance industry paid out less than $2 billion a year, on average, for non-earthquake, weather-related property damage. But in the seven years between 1990 and 1997, the hurricanes, cyclones, and floods in Europe, Asia, and North America cost the industry an average of more than $12 billion a year, according to the large German-based reinsurance firm Munich Re.[11] It was not for nothing that Franklin Nutter, the president of the Reinsurance Association of America, warned that climate change 'could bankrupt the industry'.[12] Unsurprisingly, therefore, the insurance sector joined forces in the 1990s with a growing broad-based constituency demanding tough action from governments to agree binding cuts in greenhouse gas emissions.

New science, new responsibilities

In 1988, in response to mounting concern about global warming, the United Nations established the Intergovernmental Panel on Climate Change (IPCC). The IPCC comprises three working groups investigating, respectively, climate science; impacts, adaptations and mitigations related to climate change; and social and economic dimensions of climate change. The IPCC works to the highest levels of rigour and probity, but it has been subject to immense pressure from an unholy alliance of oil-rich nations, corporate representatives from the coal, oil, electricity, chemical and automobile industries, and fossil fuel-funded sceptic scientists. How and why this has happened is worth considering in a little detail.

In 1990, the IPCC issued its first Scientific Assessment Report which was warmly described by the then UK Prime Minister Margaret Thatcher as 'an authoritative early-warning system: an agreed assessment from some three hundred of the world's leading scientists of what is happening to the world's climate. They confirm that greenhouse gases are increasing substantially as a result of man's activities, that this will warm the Earth's surface with serious consequences for us all.'[13] The IPCC stated that an immediate minimum cut of 60 per cent in greenhouse gas emissions would be required to stabilise atmospheric concentrations at then-current levels.[14]

Over the next few years, IPCC scientists continued to investigate global warming and, in particular, the evidence for an anthropogenic fingerprint on climate change. By 1995, there was a remarkable convergence of the relevant science. Researchers at American Telephone and Telegraph Company's Bell Laboratories reported a strong correlation between global warming and a decrease in the temperature difference between winter and summer. This disproved the claims of sceptics that changes in solar output, and not rising industrial activity, was to blame for observed warming. Meanwhile, the US National Climatic Data Center revealed that the US climate was moving towards 'greenhouse' conditions. In Germany, scientists at the Max Planck Institute for Meteorology published an analysis showing that there was only one chance in 40 that natural climate variability could explain the warming over the previous 30 years.

Moreover, research led by the Lawrence Livermore Laboratory in California demonstrated that climate modelling which took into account the short-term cooling effect of sulphate aerosols (which are mainly produced by burning coal, but also by volcanic eruptions such as Mount Pinatubo in 1991) revealed a clear greenhouse signal since about 1950. As Dr Michael McCarthy, chair of one of the IPCC's working groups put it: 'If everyone in the world could magically [remove the sulphates from coal and oil], you would see the fingerprints of warming in a very short time.'[15] In the UK, scientists at the Meteorological Office included the effect of sulphates in a sophisticated coupled model (in which the atmosphere and the ocean are dynamically linked) and managed to simulate past climates, thus boosting confidence in the predictive power of such models in looking at future climate change.

An unprecedented consensus on climate science had thus emerged, enabling the IPCC's Working Group I on science to conclude famously in its 1996 Second Assessment Report that 'the balance of evidence suggests a discernible human influence on global climate'.[16] The scientists confirmed their earlier mid-range estimate of an average global temperature increase of 2°C by 2100, with a low-to-high estimate range of 1-3.5°C (as we will see below, the IPCC now predicts even higher temperature rises). The sea-level rise mid-estimate was 50 cm by 2100, with a range of 15–95 cm.

The report also warned: 'Future unexpected, large and rapid climate system changes (as have occurred in the past) are by their nature difficult to predict. This implies that future climate changes may also involve "surprises". ' Such surprises may occur as a result of so-called 'positive feedbacks': effects which mutually reinforce each other, leading to a runaway climate change ('negative' feedbacks would tend to dampen, rather than amplify, changes). One example is that of cloud feedbacks, currently a source of uncertainty in climate models. Thin high-altitude clouds in a warming world may trap more heat than the lower-altitude clouds which reflect heat back into space. Another possible positive feedback mechanism is the melting of the Arctic ice cap. Were this to happen, a smaller Arctic ice cap would result in a lower Earth albedo (reflectivity), meaning that more heat would be absorbed by the planet.

Yet another possibility, emphasised amongst others by Jeremy Leggett, is that of the release of immense volumes of methane, a more potent greenhouse gas – molecule for molecule – than CO_2, from the melting of methane hydrates in reservoirs under the Arctic tundra and shallow Arctic seas. Although nobody knows exactly how much hydrate there is around the Arctic, it probably amounts to tens if not hundreds of billions of tonnes. Atmospheric methane currently holds only 5 billion tonnes of carbon. Not much methane hydrate would need to be melted, therefore, to make global warming more severe.[17]

A paradoxical consequence of global warming, by now rather well-known to the general public, is that temperatures in northwest Europe may plunge by 5°C or more as a result of the possible weakening, or even shutdown, of the thermohaline (i.e. driven by differences in heat and salt content) ocean circulation in the North Atlantic.[18] While the IPCC cautiously spoke of the 'scope for surprises' in the climate system, it did not actually spell out any worst-case scenarios in which positive feedbacks could accumulate and lead to runaway global warming. A truly precautionary approach by politicians would certainly have to address the need to insure against the risk of such a catastrophic possibility. The IPCC has warned that future climate change 'is likely to cause widespread economic, social and environmental dislocation' and that '… potentially serious changes have been identified, including an increase in some regions of the incidence of extreme high temperature events, floods, and droughts, with resultant consequences for fires, pest outbreaks and ecosystem[s]'.[19]

Vulnerability to climate change will hit hardest in those regions where food and water shortages are already major threats, principally in the developing world. Crop production may be acutely sensitive to changes in temperature. According to US-based researchers Cynthia Rosenzweig and Daniel Hillel, cereal grain yields are projected to decline in the vulnerable countries of the South. Meanwhile, agricultural exporters in the middle and high latitudes, such as the United States, Canada, and Australia, will profit from the higher prices they will be able to command. Countries with the lowest incomes are therefore likely to be the hardest hit as climate change continues.[20] US journalist Ross Gelbspan referred to an 'extraordinarily well-ignored report' by Oxford researchers Norman Myers and Jennifer Kent which showed that changes in the monsoons that bring India 70 per cent of its rainfall will cause severe food shortages: 'Even a half-degree Celsius increase will reduce the wheat crop at least 25 per cent'.[21]

The IPCC has also warned that 'climate change is likely to have wide ranging and mostly adverse impacts on human health with significant loss of life'.[22] As Gelbspan points out, citing the hundreds of heat-related deaths in the United

States and India in the summer of 1995, there have already been such impacts. But an even greater threat is the spread of infectious diseases including malaria, dengue, yellow fever, cholera, hantavirus and encephalitis. If the IPCC's projected level of warming holds, the 'epidemic potential of the mosquito population' in tropical regions would double, while in the temperate regions – including the United States and most of Europe – it would rise a hundred times. Researchers warn that an increase of 3°C, inside the range projected by the IPCC, could cause up to 80 million extra cases of malaria annually around the world.[23]

IPCC scientists have just completed the Third Assessment Report on climate change. In advance of the completed report, BBC environment correspondent Alex Kirby noted that, compared to 1996's report, there was more emphasis on the potential for nasty shocks in the climate system. Scientists spoke of climate 'thresholds' – the levels of environmental disruption or pollution below which no observable effect occurs. But exceeding the threshold could trigger major climatic changes in short periods of time. Examples include the collapse of the west Antarctic ice sheet and, as we saw above, the breakdown of the thermohaline ocean circulation which warms western Europe.[24] In January 2001, the contribution of Working Group I to the Third Assessment Report was published. The main new finding was deeply disturbing: that the atmosphere could warm at twice the rate anticipated in 1996, leading to global temperature rises by 2100 – in the worst-case scenario – of almost 6°C. The predicted range of temperature rise of 1.4° to 5.8 °C was described by the IPCC as 'potentially devastating'.[25] Sea levels are projected to rise by between 9 and 88 cm from 1990 to 2100. Although temperature projections were higher than in 1996, sea level projections were slightly lower than the range projected earlier, largely due to the use of improved models, which give a smaller contribution from glaciers and ice sheets.[26] Michael McCarthy, *The Independent's* environment correspondent, remarked of the upwardly revised warming rate: 'This implies absolute disaster for billions of people'.[27]

It is worth pointing out that global human population has now exceeded the 6 billion mark and, according to UN figures, is scheduled to reach somewhere between 7.2 and 8.5 billion in 2020.[28] In such a world, where there is already incredible pressure on natural resources, the additional threats represented by the spectre of climate change could create unprecedented political and social upheaval. Will national governments adopt new authoritarian measures to limit personal consumption, mobility and privileges? Or, as Susan George conjectures in her disturbing book, *The Lugano Report,* will the corporate forces behind economic globalisation adopt uncompromising and awful measures to preserve global capitalism in the twenty-first century, keeping the gains to themselves and locking out the rest of us – 'the victims'? Whatever happens, 'The stress caused by climate change', warns Gelbspan, 'is lethal to democratic political processes and individual freedoms'.[29]

Killing Kyoto

Progress towards making any significant emission cuts has been painfully slow. The Third Conference of the Parties (COP-3) to the UN Framework Convention on Climate Change, held in Kyoto in December 1997, represented a nominal step forward. The overall agreement at Kyoto was a 5.2 per cent cut in annual emissions of greenhouse gases by the developed world by 2012, compared with a 1990 baseline. The European Union agreed to an 8 per cent cut, the United States to 7 per cent and Japan to 6 per cent. Australia was allowed to increase its emissions by 8 per cent. Green lobbyists were disappointed by the deal at Kyoto, but not surprised. In the months leading up to COP-3, environmentalists had been trying, more or less unsuccessfully, to raise the profile of the climate threat and highlight the duplicity of the fossil fuel lobby in blocking moves to combat it.

In the summer of 1997, Greenpeace activists occupied an oil platform bound for BP's Foinaven field in the 'Atlantic Frontier', the potentially fossil fuel-rich region west of the British Isles. The action achieved precious little media coverage until BP took the decision to sue Greenpeace for disrupting the oil company's operations, a move which could have bankrupted the campaigning group. It was a godsend to Greenpeace. The threat yielded a media-friendly David and Goliath story that finally generated the publicity the pressure group had been ardently seeking. BP promptly backed off. Geoffrey Lean, environment editor of the *Independent on Sunday,* later reported that relations between John Browne and Peter Melchett – heads of BP and Greenpeace UK respectively – had remained genial throughout and that they were even due to dine *à deux* shortly after the stand-off.[30] Greenpeace claimed that their dramatic action was necessary to focus attention on the increased risk of destructive climate change as a direct result of extracting and burning yet more fossil fuels. They had some hard scientific evidence too, as we shall see.

IPCC emissions scenarios are projections of future greenhouse gas and sulphate emissions based on various assumptions, including industrial and agricultural development. Using these emissions scenarios, Greenpeace had worked out a 'carbon budget'. They estimated that no more than 225 billion tonnes of carbon can be safely burned if global warming is to be limited to an increase of 1°C above pre-industrial levels. This carbon budget figure assumes, however, that major international action is taken to halt deforestation (forests release carbon into the atmosphere when destroyed by burning). If current trends of deforestation continue, the carbon budget drops to 145 billion tonnes.

The proposed ceiling on a global temperature increase of 1°C is far from arbitrary. In 1990, the UN Advisory Group on Greenhouse Gases had concluded that temperature increases beyond this limit could lead to rapid and unpredictable changes to ecosystems, resulting in extensive damage. Another important factor is the rate of increase of global mean temperature: above 0.1°C per decade could result in major ecosystem damage, as well as increasing the likelihood of climate 'surprises'. The total mass of fossil fuels currently due to be extracted is in the order of 1,000 billion tonnes, which if consumed would therefore result in a dangerous temperature rise. Coal, which is rich in carbon, predominates in this total of fossil fuel reserves, comprising more than half. But even economically recoverable reserves of oil alone are perilously close to the carbon budget limit, with gas reserves not far behind. Nature's arithmetic appears compelling: we can afford to burn no more than a quarter of existing total fossil fuel reserves if we are to avoid dangerous climate change.[31] Even if society switched instantly from coal to either oil or gas, the associated carbon budget would still be unacceptably risky. The conclusion is clear. There has to be a major shift to renewables in the short term, not just over the next 50 years, which is the extent of the ambition of even the greenest oil companies, such as BP and Shell.

Regardless of whether the Atlantic Frontier will, if exploited, play a 'marginal role' in the world supply of oil (as oil companies have tried to claim), eco-campaigners argued that a line must be drawn somewhere and that that line would be here. They have had some success. In November 1999, Greenpeace won a High Court case against the UK government for putting coral reefs, dolphins and whales at risk. The government had not upheld the EU Habitats Directive in awarding offshore licenses to oil companies prospecting in the region. There was no govern-ment appeal against the judgement; perhaps ministers feared a public trial of national energy policy. The government had to extend the domain in which it applied the Habitats Directive from 12 nautical miles offshore to 200 miles.

Having lost the case, the Department of Trade and Industry moved quickly to downplay the consequences of defeat. Government spin doctors claimed that the ruling would not have a significant impact on the oil and gas industry. In court, civil servants had said the reverse. Applying the Habitats Directive offshore, they had claimed, 'would cause massive disruption to the British economy'. The truth probably lies somewhere between the two. While the corporate push 'to indus-trialise the Atlantic Frontier' will undoubtedly continue, the court decision gives hope to green campaigners.[32]

Aside from dramatic stories of environmental protesters facing up to giant oil companies, it has proved immensely difficult to get the media to cover climate change and, more importantly, what should be done about it. As we saw in the previous chapter on the role played by the mass media in promoting economic globalisation, Herman and Chomsky's propaganda model explains why this should be so. In essence, the corporate-owned media are extremely unlikely to present a sustained and accurate analysis of the climate problem and its root causes. If there is no international climate summit round the corner, human calamity as a result of extreme weather events, or a dramatic report from a pressure group relating global warming to species loss, the short attention span of editors and journalists darts around elsewhere. Any coherent, consistent and maintained media inquiry into the economic and political system that has put the climate system at risk is structurally impossible and essentially taboo.

Jeremy Leggett's book *The Carbon War*, which details the background to the UN climate negotiations over almost 10 years, is full of examples of the media's reluctance or incapacity to address seriously the prospects of devastating climate change and what should be done to minimise the risks. In 1993, for example, Leggett tried to interest the press in the global warming implications of a free-trade deal agreed by the G7 as aid for Russia:

> An agency journalist from UPI, who was one of the few who phoned me and with whom I did a 30-minute interview, told me that his editor had gutted his story. 'They took out all the references to global warming,' he told me. 'The editor told me it is too controversial.' He shook his head. 'You are fighting an uphill battle, you know.'[33]

Leggett was also unable to sway a *Financial Times* journalist who 'couldn't add [Greenpeace's] perspective to his report'.[34] Another noteworthy case was when Leggett travelled to Siberia to take part in an episode of the 8-part Hollywood-financed PBS/BBC serialisation of Daniel Yergin's Pulitzer Prize-winning history of the oil industry, *The Prize*. Leggett was filmed talking to a representative of a local Siberian tribe about the impact of oil companies operating there, and warning of the 'dangerous game of roulette' humanity would be playing 'if we burnt even a fraction of the world's oil reserves'. Gregory Hood, the producer of the Siberian episode, telephoned Leggett around a year later to relate how the film had been coming along. Apparently, the series producers disliked the first cut of Hood's episode, saying that it had 'a heavily environmental slant'. Hood was sent back to the cutting room to produce a revised film. The series producers did not like that either. Finally, the film was taken out of Hood's hands.[35]

In the United States, journalist Ross Gelbspan observed that the major environmental groups concerned about climate change – the Environmental Defense Fund, Greenpeace, the Natural Resources Defense Council, the Sierra Club and the Union of Concerned Scientists – 'have been repeatedly frustrated in their efforts to get their message across to the American public'.[36] Such groups rarely, if ever, appear to contemplate the possibility that there may be deep-seated reasons for media indifference or antipathy. Even when climate change hits the front pages, there is a dearth of journalistic scratching beneath the surface of likely future global warming scenarios or extreme weather events to the meaty questions of what is to be done, and who is blocking action. Gelbspan notes that news stories about climate change 'generally evoke an eerie silence'.[37] He makes an impassioned plea for more substantive debate:

> Let the media cover the scientific evidence of climate change the way they now cover political campaigns. As scientists gain new understandings of the rates and specific impacts of climate change, they should be featured prominently in the news media. So should new signals of stress from the forests and the oceans and the plains. Let academic consortia and business round-tables and congressional committees and television talk shows put the precarious condition of our beleaguered planet in the spotlight of public attention.[38]

This is, in all probability, a forlorn hope in view of the structural constraints on the mass media. An 'eerie silence' on any issue requiring radical action, whether it be climate change, poverty reduction, or the West's role in arming dictators around the world, is the norm – the status quo – enjoyed by the corporate forces, including the media industry, now permeating modern society. On climate change, the flagbearers of corporate industry, such as *The Economist*, are keen to exaggerate scientific uncertainty and to promote business-as-usual: 'Most actions would pose a bigger threat to human well-being than does global warming. Consider first, the uncertainty of scientists about the extent of global warming. Despite recent advances, science still understands little about the world's climate.'[39] Such an attitude, in denial of both overwhelming scientific evidence and the common sense of a precautionary approach, is a corporate diversionary tactic in the face of risky climate change. It is this business obstructionism to which we now turn our attention.

Profit before humanity

From the very first days of the climate talks, a curious coalition of oil-rich nations and private corporations from the coal, oil, gas, electricity and automobile industries have waged a war to prevent, or at least stall, international agreements to make significant binding cuts in greenhouse gas emissions. Because of this, and more importantly because of what is at stake – the future habitability of the planet – the climate system is where economic globalisation is impacting in the most damaging ways. Robin Hahnel, professor of economics at American University in Washington DC, correctly sees this phenomenon as a natural extension of the way capitalism has traditionally abused the environment: 'As long as globalization brings more decisions into the market nexus and increases pressures on countries to reduce environmental regulations to the lowest common denominator, globalization will aggravate global warming, just as it aggravates other forms of environmental degradation.'[40]

Matthew Spencer, senior climate campaigner at Greenpeace UK, succinctly expresses the specific link between the fossil fuel industry, and the risk of climate catastrophe:

> Globalised competition fuels a carbon arms race against the atmosphere because it creates the incentive for companies to increase production from existing reserves and to discover and open up new ones. Competition, and the technology-push it generates, has every company frantically trying to keep up with competitors on new reserve additions and guaranteeing massive atmospheric overload of carbon in the future.[41]

Free trade and the threat to the stability of the climate system are coupled. Leggett described a G7 summit at which $610 million of an aid package to Russia had been disbursed, via the World Bank, to that country's oil-producing sector. 'That was what it came down to: a direct link between economic well-being and oil production'.[42]

Just as it is clear what has to be done to minimise the risk of potentially cata-strophic climate change – dramatically reducing fossil fuel combustion and deforestation, combined with a major shift to renewables and energy conserva-tion – so is it clear that powerful companies are opposing such moves. In essence, they are holding humanity to ransom for the sake of their own short-term private gains.

The Carbon Club

Such influence is pervasive. Leggett revealed how, under pressure from the 'carbon club', the conclusions of the authoritative IPCC Second Assessment Report were watered down. The original draft had a section titled, 'The changes point towards a human influence on climate'. The next day it read more cautiously: 'The balance of evidence points towards a human influence on climate.' Bob Watson, head of the US negotiating team, proposed: 'The balance of evidence suggests an appreciable human influence on global climate.' When the meeting was over, the weakened title read: 'The balance of evidence suggests a discernible human influence on global climate.' The header at the top of the executive summary – 'Significant new findings since IPCC 1990' – had disap-peared completely. Leggett stated, 'This watering-down was achieved entirely by the carbon club, the Saudis and the Kuwaitis, who knew the scientists would have to exercise compromise while at the same time racing against the clock'.[43] Mohamed Al-Saban, leader of the Saudi Arabian delegation, later told the journal *Nature* that the IPCC report was 'now balanced and cautious enough not to mislead policymakers'. When asked to explain his tireless obstructive tactics, Al-Saban responded, 'Saudi Arabia's oil income amounts to 96 per cent of our total exports. Until there is clearer evidence of human involvement in climate change, we will not agree to what amounts to a tax on oil.'[44]

Leggett reserved particular ire for Don Pearlman, a corporate lawyer heading the Climate Council, a carbon-fuel front group. Pearlman's talents had been honed at the Washington law firm Patton, Boggs & Blow whose major clients included Sony, American Express, the Haitian dictator Duvalier, and the Guatemalan military. According to observers at the climate negotiations, Pearlman shamelessly used the oil-rich Saudi and Kuwaiti delegations as proxies for the fossil fuel industry. At a Swedish climate summit in 1990, Leggett clearly overheard the lawyer talking with five Arab diplomats as they pored over the draft negotiating text for an IPCC report, saying 'if we can cut a deal here ...'. During negotiations for the Berlin Mandate in 1995, the Kuwaiti delegation actually submitted amendments in Pearlman's handwriting. Perhaps the most troubling revelation is the hold which Pearlman had over US negotiators. When the final set of talks in the approach to the Rio Earth Summit in 1992 went badly for the fossil fuel industry, Leggett observed Pearlman publicly accosting Dan Reifsnyder, then head of the US team, and likened the lawyer's behaviour to an 'incandescent headmaster [giving] a severe finger-lashing' to a 'recalcitrant schoolboy'.[45]

Arguably, the most notorious and powerful member of the carbon club is the Global Climate Coalition which was set up in 1989 by the PR company Burson-Marsteller to discredit climate scientists' warnings of the need to combat global warming. The GCC includes representatives from the American Petroleum Institute, Arco, Dow Hydrocarbons, DuPont, Exxon, Phillips and Texaco. The US subsidiaries of BP and Shell were members until October 1996 and April 1998 respectively, withdrawing from the GCC following public pressure on them to do so. The GCC also represents various companies from the coal, chemical and automobile industries, including General Motors. Under continuing public pressure, the Ford company announced its withdrawal in December 1999, as did Chrysler Daimler in February 2000. Both BP and Shell, however, remain members of the American Petroleum Institute which has lobbied the US government not to ratify the Kyoto deal. Indeed, the National Association of Manufacturers, comprising much of mainstream US industry, is forthright in its opposition: 'We oppose the Kyoto Protocol and urge the President and Congress to reject it'.[46] George W. Bush marked his early presidency by doing just that, while proclaiming his 'concern' for climate change.

Dirty tactics

Immediately following the publication in June 1996 of the IPCC's authoritative Second Assessment Report which pointed to the 'discernible human influence on global climate', the GCC, wielding its considerable media influence, mounted a desperate and astonishing series of attacks on the scientists themselves. Industry lobbyists singled out Ben Santer of the Lawrence Livermore Laboratory for particularly heavy criticism. Santer, the lead author of the chapter on climate detection, was attacked in a 9-page analysis by the GCC of changes made by him to that chapter. John Schlaes, GCC executive director, tried to convince the press that Santer's revisions 'raise very serious questions about whether the IPCC has compromised, or even lost, its scientific credibility'.[47]

At a public symposium in which Santer and fellow IPCC scientist Tom Wigley explained the findings of the IPCC report, they were visibly shaken by verbal attacks from Pearlman and William O'Keefe, chairman of the GCC and an official of the American Petroleum Institute. Santer was charged with 'single-handedly suppressing expressions of dissent from other IPCC scientists [and] for eliminating references to scientific uncertainties'.[48] Meanwhile, coal and oil lobbyists placed damaging stories in the *Washington Times* and the trade paper *Energy Daily* accusing Santer of making 'unauthorized' and 'politically motivated' changes to the IPCC report. In an editorial in the *Wall Street Journal,* Frederick Seitz, chairman of the George C. Marshall Institute, a corporate-sponsored think-tank, wrote of '...[a] disturbing corruption of the peer-review process'.[49] The unsubstantiated accusations were then picked up by the *New York Times.* Right-wing US politicians entered the fray, with one of them – Dana Rohrabacher, a Californian Republican congressman – even urging the US Energy Department to withdraw funding from the Lawrence Livermore Laboratory where Santer was based. The IPCC strongly refuted all the charges. In a letter to the *Wall Street Journal,* IPCC chairman Bert Bolin, and Sir John Houghton and Luiz Gylvan Meira Filho, co-chairs of the working group on science, praised Santer's meticulous work on the climate detection chapter: 'No one could have been more thorough and honest.'[50] Santer himself said, 'I am really troubled by what is going on. This appears to be a skilful campaign to discredit the IPCC, me, and my reputation as a scientist'.[51]

The GCC then mounted a major assault on the public consciousness and US politicians in the months preceding the Kyoto summit. $13 million was spent on a massive advertising campaign in an attempt to convince Americans that their jobs and economic welfare would be lost if economic growth was sacrificed for CO_2-cutting measures. Faced with the real prospect of international agreement on binding emission cuts at Kyoto, the GCC circulated scaremongering claims that the following two decades would see as many as 600,000 American jobs being lost each year. O'Keefe opined that, 'global warming remains a possibility, not an established fact; realistically, global warming remains a hypothesis.'[52] Exxon's chairman Lee R. Raymond, a significant figure in the GCC, was adamant: 'United we stand, divided we fall. We simply cannot afford to "fall" on the critical long-term issues facing our industry, such as global climate change.'[53] After progress was made at the 1995 climate negotiations in Berlin, Pearlman claimed: 'It's clear the agreement gives the developing countries like China, India and Mexico a free ride [and] puts US jobs, economic activity and international competitiveness at risk.'[54] In 1997, in a breathtaking Machiavellian move, Raymond exhorted Asian industry at the fifteenth World Petroleum Congress in Beijing to exploit new reserves of hydrocarbon and fight emission regulations, while back home in the United States he denounced proposed cuts in American emissions if there were to be no emission controls in the developing world.

Corporate greenwashing

As Kyoto approached, I was curious to find out the attitude of Shell, my former employers,[55] on climate change. I sent a fax to Shell UK's 'Issues Manager' reiterating Greenpeace's concerns regarding the carbon budget – that humanity can afford to burn no more than a quarter of known carbon fuel reserves (see above). Perhaps Shell did not even dispute the Greenpeace analysis? Moreover, the continuing stockpiling of reserves would cumulatively have more than a 'marginal impact' on atmospheric greenhouse gas concentrations. Shell did not answer my points directly. Instead, they sent me a copy of a speech given by Heinz Rothermund, managing director of Shell UK Exploration and Production, at an oil and gas conference in London on 23 September 1997. The crux of Rothermund's argument for continuing to exploit more reserves was: 'don't forget that the contribution which secure oil and gas supplies make to the GDP will increase the country's ability to invest in progress towards sustainable development and in addressing the challenge of global climate change.' In other words, Rothermund's strategy for averting dangerous climate change was to call for more investment in the fossil fuel industry – a major contributor to the problem! Yet in the same speech, Rothermund made this green-sounding statement: 'Extravagant or wasteful energy consumption, whether by burning oil, coal, gas or even the use of renewable sources, is symptomatic of a non-sustainable society.'[56] This phrase sounded curiously familiar to me. After a bit of scratching around in my files, I realised it was – virtually word for word – the closing sentence of a letter of mine that *The Times* had published a month earlier. It would appear that Shell management is not averse to turning green statements to their own advantage, without actually undertaking any shift in their core business. It was a wonderful example of what writers such as Andrew Rowell and Sharon Beder refer to as 'corporate greenwash'.[57]

At first sight, though, oil companies in Europe appear to have been engaged in a competition to out-green each other. BP's chief executive John Browne said in a major industry speech at Stanford University in 1997:

There is now an effective consensus among the world's leading scientists and serious and well-informed people outside the scientific community that there is a discernible human influence on the climate, and a link between the concentration of carbon dioxide and the increase in temperature ... It would be unwise and potentially dangerous to ignore the mounting concern.[58]

Not to be outdone, Cor Herkströter, chair of the Committee of Managing Directors of Shell, described climate change as 'the most intractable challenge to sustainability.'[59] But according to Herkströter – and Browne – it is obviously not so serious a problem as to warrant interfering with conventional economic growth.

Of course, oil companies deny that their green rhetoric is unmatched by green actions. BP – which has since merged with Amoco – aims to increase the sales of its solar energy technology to $1 billion a year by 2010.[60] Meanwhile, Shell International – in an attempt to catch up with BP's solar power initiatives – finally made a significant move into the market for renewable energy sources in October 1997. The Anglo-Dutch group announced that it would be investing $500 million over the following five years with the aim of capturing at least 10 per cent of the world market for solar and photovoltaic cells by 2005.[61] However, these initiatives from corporate giants wishing to capitalise on potential future market winners barely dent the 'business as usual' motorcade. Shell's investment in renewables is only 10 per cent of the oil giant's spending on hydrocarbon exploration ($1 billion annually), 0.8 per cent of its global investment ($12 billion) and only 0.06 per cent of its global sales ($171 billion): a drop in the barrel, in other words.[62] Other companies such as the combined Exxon-Mobil, the world's largest oil corporation, are doing even less.

Unsurprisingly, company mergers have become a notable feature of the oil industry, with the pressures of economic globalisation increasing the incentive to become 'competitive' and 'reduce inefficiency'. Job losses in the industry have been severe, even in traditionally paternalistic companies such as Shell, which has so far resisted any merger deal. In July 1999, TotalFina – itself an amalgamated company – was reported to have made a hostile £27.5 billion bid for fellow French oil company Elf.[63] BP Amoco financial experts claimed that their own merger would generate savings of $2 billion by 2000. It was coolly reported that 'the existing cost reduction plan involves 10,000 redundancies, of which 6,000 have already been achieved'.[64]

BP Amoco is now in the process of acquiring the US company Atlantic Richfield (Arco), which is a significant gas enterprise itself. Indeed, a shift in emphasis from oil to less carbon-intensive gas is being exploited by oil company PR departments to portray themselves as 'green', even though they remain in the hydrocarbon business. In September 2000 it was reported that BP Amoco were rebranding themselves as a 'green company', complete with the Helios mark – a 'vibrant sunburst of green, white and yellow' named after the sun god of ancient Greece. Environmentalists retorted that BP now stood for 'Burning the Planet'.[65]

Shell's 1998 annual report *Profits and Principles – does there have to be a choice?* argued that the company was responding to worries over global warming by 'concentrating on low-carbon materials such as gas and renewables'.[66] Andrew Rowell, author of *Green Backlash* and an experienced observer of the oil business, is justifiably scathing:

> The idea that gas exploration is eco-friendly is ludicrous. The only moral and rational reaction to global warming is disinvestment in the processing of all fossil fuels.[67]

A BP Amoco Arco conglomerate could end up having a near-monopoly in some areas of hydrocarbon exploration around the world, such as the North Slope reserves of the Alaskan Arctic. In June 1999, the European Commission, voicing concerns of reduced competition, launched an in-depth investigation into the takeover of Arco by BP.[68] If a sustainable future is to be based on decentralised renewable energy (see next chapter), then we are moving in the wrong direction.

Subsidising climate disaster

Few people are aware that taxpayers are still funding fossil fuel expansion through government rewards for companies actively exploring and developing oil and gas reserves, in the form of favourable tax treatment or low royalties. According to Gelbspan, in the United States, 'The federal government spends more than $20 billion a year to subsidize the development of oil, coal and natural gas. It spends more than $10 billion to subsidize nuclear energy'.[69] The IPCC estimates that the effect of removing such energy subsidies worldwide would be a cut in CO_2 emissions of up to 18 per cent. Greenpeace reports that more than 90 per cent of direct subsidies from European governments to the energy industry goes to fossil fuels (63 per cent) and nuclear power (28 per cent).[70] The equivalent of more than $15 billion of European taxpayers' money is being spent every year to subsidise energy systems which accelerate climate change and increase the risk from nuclear power. In stark contrast, only 9 per cent – around $1.5 billion a year – is provided for clean renewable energy sources, such as solar electricity and wind power.

Unsurprisingly, the oil industry is reluctant to admit that the economics of the energy markets are heavily loaded in their favour. At an industry conference in 1997, Shell's Heinz Rothermund stated categorically, 'It is a hard fact of life that renewable energy sources are not economically viable'.[71] Oil executives are always reluctant to acknowledge the huge public subsidies made to their industry when they trumpet the free market; instead they ruefully shake their heads at the 'unfavourable economics' of renewable energy.

At the Kyoto Climate Summit in 1997 some fossil fuel lobbyists were at least open about their tactics. John Grasser of the US National Mining Association and Global Climate Coalition asserted:

> We think we have raised enough questions among the American public to prevent any numbers, targets or timetables to achieve reductions in gas emissions being achieved here. What we are doing, and we think successfully, is buying time for our industries by holding up these talks.[72]

In the approach to Kyoto, some American trade union leaders stood alongside corporate chiefs in calling for stringent carbon limits to be set on developing, as well as developed, nations. According to the American Federation of Labor, '[carbon dioxide] emission limits are harsh, arbitrary, and show no regard for industrial workers'. Otherwise, claims the AFL, 'regressive energy taxes [will encourage] corporations ... to locate new capacity offshore, in countries with no carbon reduction commitments'.[73]

In the UK there is perhaps a greater willingness on the part of the trade union movement to accept the need to phase out fossil fuel use. According to Dick Barrey, policy and research officer of UNISON: 'We actively support energy efficiency, conservation and renewables as an alternative to fossil fuel electricity generation, as long as employment effects are benign.'[74] The UK has had some success in reducing carbon dioxide emissions in the 'dash for gas', but this has been at the expense of large chunks of the coal industry with the loss of hundreds of thousands of jobs. Dave Feickert, TUC's European Officer in Brussels, argues, 'the industrial sector in the UK has borne the brunt of carbon dioxide cuts until now. The next phase – to achieve the UK's target of a 20 per cent reduction on 1990 levels by 2010 – ought to come primarily from the transport and domestic sectors'. Feickert accepts, however, that there is much scope for 'clean electricity generation' and highlights the likely increased role of combined heat and power stations.[75] Unfortunately, although a boon to energy efficiency, most CHP stations still consume fossil fuels.

In some quarters of British industry there was a backlash against government plans to introduce a 'climate change levy' when it was announced by Gordon Brown, the Chancellor of the Exchequer, in his budget of March 1999, with it coming into effect in April 2001. Representatives of steel, chemicals, paper, glass, food manufacturing and other energy-intensive industries all complained that the new carbon business tax was not 'fiscally neutral' and would render them 'uncompetitive'.[76] Over the summer of 1999, the government appeared to be holding firm on the tax, with Deputy Prime Minister John Prescott retorting that the industries had already benefited from substantial reductions in energy prices. At the same time, Brown was backing away from the 'petrol escalator tax' – the commitment to raise petrol duty by 6 per cent each year on top of inflation in order to cut pollution and greenhouse gas emissions. There was even a brief media-reported spat between Prescott and Prime Minister Tony Blair that was at least partly fuelled by Prescott's failure to get the Treasury backing and the parliamentary time he needed to push through legislation, effective or otherwise, on integrated public transport. In the autumn 1999 budget Brown did indeed drop the petrol escalator tax and – following intense corporate lobbying, particularly from the Confederation of British Industry – scaled down the climate change levy from £1.7 billion to £1 billion. This was despite a report by the World Wide Fund for Nature estimating that businesses employing 93 per cent of the UK workforce would either be unaffected or would gain from the levy.

In March 2000, John Prescott unveiled a 'blueprint' for cutting UK greenhouse gas emissions by 21.5 per cent by 2012, exceeding its Kyoto commitment of 12.5 per cent. Prescott announced that the target would be achieved by imposing the climate change levy; negotiated agreements with the energy intensive sectors; voluntary agreements with car manufacturers to cut engine emissions; the integrated transport white paper; an obligation on suppliers to deliver 10 per cent of the UK's electricity from renewable sources by 2010; new funding for energy efficiency programmes; and a new target to double the capacity of combined heat and power by 2010.[77]

As we will see in the following chapter, a target of 10 per cent of electricity from renewables by 2010 is actually rather a modest one. Prescott's strategy gave little hope to the beleaguered British wind, wave and solar industries, while leaving the country's fossil fuel dependence firmly in place. The captains of the oil industry could breathe a sigh of relief. However, the Royal Commission on Environmental Pollution (RCEP) told the British government in June 2000 that carbon dioxide emissions must fall by at least 60 per cent. Presently, the government's pledge is to reduce such emissions by only 20 per cent by 2012. Sir Tom Blundell, chair of the RCEP, emphasised the need for 'huge cuts' if there was to be any realistic possibility of 'a tolerable effect on the climate'.[78]

Climate change is a grave threat to which the current political and economic system is structurally incapable of responding adequately. The fact that cuts were agreed by the developed countries at Kyoto was testament to the immense public pressure on politicians to make any progress at all. However, the figures were exceedingly modest, with questions of implementation remaining unanswered, and with ratification by the US now rejected by President Bush. Professor Martin Parry, of the University of East Anglia, told the BBC just how ineffectual the proposed cuts are: 'If the provisions of the Kyoto Protocol on climate change were implemented they would reduce the expected rise in temperature by 2050 of one to two deg C by only about 0.06 deg C.'[79] The fact that 'progress' in the international climate arena has been nowhere near enough to significantly reduce the risk of climate catastrophe highlights how far government policy and business obstructionism diverge from public aspirations and from a genuine path of sustainable development.

The failure of government policy

A major reason why energy consumption is wasteful in today's industrialised countries is our dependence on fossil-fuel-driven transport networks serving centralised centres of population. Economic globalisation has led to an enormous increase in the volume of raw and processed goods being carried between far-flung corners of the globe, requiring huge numbers of ships, aircraft, trains and lorries. Indeed, transport is the most energy-intensive sector of an industrialised economy. Trade transport uses one eighth of the world's oil production and although 90 per cent of goods are carried by ships, air transport is taking an increasing proportion and uses 47 times as much energy.[80] According to a 1999 report from the IPCC, air travel is an important and growing cause of global warming. Greenhouse gases from airliners are responsible for 3.5 per cent of global emissions, but this could rise to 15 per cent by 2050.[81] More efficient engines, better air traffic control and other operational improvements will not stop emissions rising, simply because the number of people flying is growing so rapidly: by nearly 9 per cent a year since 1960, according to the report. The IPCC report called for subsidies to be withdrawn from the aviation industry, for new taxes on flying and for rail journeys to be encouraged as an alternative to short flights. For several years, environmentalists such as Friends of the Earth have highlighted the bizarre anomaly that airlines pay no duty on aviation fuel and have called for an internationally agreed aviation tax. Clearly, government action is required to tackle the problem.

But biting the climate bullet means intervention in the global marketplace, transforming the powerful vested interests that are leading us to disaster. In Britain, sadly, the Labour government's corporate instincts easily override any feeble green leanings it may possess. The signs so far – including a weak white paper on transport in the summer of 1998 and a lack of any real commitment on ecotax reform – are that it is incapable of meeting the climate challenge. The following episode illustrates the point.

Early in 1999, Robin Cook unveiled a new environmental initiative in front of a mixed audience of business, non-governmental organisations, civil servants and journalists.[82] It was Cook's first major speech on the international environment since becoming Foreign Secretary 18 months previously. Under the prosaic title of 'Energy Challenge for Business', the government announced a green fund worth £500,000 to spend on climate-saving projects in various developing countries. Each energy project, claimed Cook, would encourage that particular country to move away from polluting industries that pump out global warming gases to less carbon-intensive economic growth. China, for example, had already indicated that it would welcome British assistance in making the shift from carbon-intensive coal to gas for heating and cooking. Other countries lining up to take advantage of the scheme were India, South Africa, Brazil and Indonesia. Cook brimmed with enthusiasm: 'By working with business, the environment movement and developing countries, we can break the myth of conflict between the green agenda and the growth agenda'.[83]

British businesses were encouraged to contribute matching funds. Indeed, the government was keen to emphasise the growth opportunities for companies exporting clean energy technology as part of the Kyoto Protocol's clean development mechanism. According to a Foreign Office spokesman, Cook's 'Energy Challenge' will 'help us raise the UK profile and hopefully increase our influence among those concerned with climate change or related areas in the target country'.[84] In fact, the 'Energy Challenge' is a minuscule drop in the ocean when set against the massive subsidies received each year by the fossil fuel industry, as we saw above. Not only that, but the net effect will be to export jobs to locations with cheap labour, a defining characteristic of today's global economy. The main benefits will accrue to transnational corporations which will extend their domains of influence in the vulnerable South. For this reason alone, one can only be sceptical of Cook's claim that developing countries will receive a boost for genuine sustainable development. Some environmentalists may have seen the scheme charitably as a small step towards joined-up, green-tinged government taken by a Labour administration which had once boasted unconvincingly that it would form the 'first truly green government in this country'.[85] In reality, initiatives such as Cook's 'Energy Challenge' leave the cancerous capitalist market intact, preserving the inequities between the rich North and the poor South.

However, Cook was to some extent well-intentioned. Together with Prescott and Environment Minister Michael Meacher, Cook recognises that a central factor in tackling climate change is to get the Americans on board (something which singularly failed to happen at the climate talks in The Hague at the end of 2000). By seeking a solution within the framework of economic globalisation – exporting clean technology to developing nations – the Foreign Secretary was arguably trying to generate inspiring leadership for the UK in showing the US and the rest of the world the positive benefits of cutting greenhouse gas emissions. The stumbling block at present is that, before committing themselves to any cuts in emissions, the US is demanding the 'meaningful participation' of 'key' developing countries – for which read China and India. On the other hand, developing countries have retorted that the US – which is responsible for around 25 per cent of greenhouse gas emissions – and the other rich nations of the West caused the problem of climate change in the first place. *They* – in particular, the US – should act first. Stalemate.

Contraction and convergence

Behind the scenes, British climate negotiators were already exasperated at American stonewalling,[86] even before President Bush ditched the Kyoto agreement. Cook's initiative, which was jointly agreed with John Prescott's Department of the Environment, represented one possible way to get the developing world and, by implication, the US, on board the climate train. However, it is not the only way or, for that matter, the sustainable way. Environmentalist Aubrey Meyer believes that he has a more comprehensive 'world-saving idea' that could really cut the Gordian knot of international climate negotiations. Under the auspices of the Global Commons Institute,[87] the London-based lobbying group he helped to set up with friends from the Green Party in 1990, Meyer has been promoting a simple and powerful concept which has already had a major impact on senior politicians and negotiators.

What it boils down to is that everyone in the world, according to the GCI, has an equal right to a share of greenhouse gas emissions. Taking as their starting point the IPCC figure of 60 per cent cuts to stabilise atmospheric carbon dioxide levels, Meyer and mathematician friend Tony Cooper calculated what level of greenhouse gas pollution each nation would be allowed. Their eye-catching computer graphics illustrate past emissions and future allocation of emissions by country, achieving per capita equality by 2030, for example. After this date, emissions drop off to reach safe levels by 2100. This so-called 'contraction and convergence' in emissions has gathered the support of a majority of the world's countries, including China and India. It may be the only approach that developing countries are willing to accept.

But will the Americans, who would have to make real cuts, buy it? Not so far. At climate talks in November 1999 in Bonn, they said that they would not match moves by Europe and Japan to ratify the Kyoto Protocol by 2002;[88] the US Congress first 'wants more action from developing countries'.[89] The previous year, this was set down by the Byrd-Hagel resolution – which states that the United States should not be signatory to any protocol which excludes legally binding commitments from developing countries, or which would seriously harm the US economy. The resolution was passed by a vote of 95-0 in the Senate. So much for President Clinton's warning on Earth Day (April 22), 1992, that 'our addiction to fossil fuels is wrapping the earth in a deadly shroud of greenhouse gases'. As David Edwards has pointed out, the Global Climate Coalition is not the only US business group that opposes the Kyoto protocol. The United States Chamber of Commerce and the National Association of Manufacturers, representing 'the interests of just about every large corporation you've ever heard of', have both urged Congress to reject the agreement reached at Kyoto. In other words, the mainstream US business community *en masse* is implacably opposed to even modest measures to combat climate change.[90] In this context it is hardly surprising that Bush took the stance he did. It remains to be seen whether other countries will press on without the US.

Climate threat: just another business opportunity?

The buzz phrase of the Kyoto Protocol, with its hundred-odd unsettled decisions, is 'flexible marketing mechanisms'. These 'market-based solutions' are the trading of emission credits, by which rich countries can buy 'licenses to pollute' from industry-deficient countries, and joint implementation (JI) measures. JI would allow industrialised countries to obtain credit for investing in reductions overseas; for example, by means of the 'clean development mechanism' involving energy efficiency or renewables projects in developing countries. However, JI need not involve green energy. It includes energy conservation and efficiency technologies, as well as tree planting and forest conservation, as ways of limiting atmospheric levels of carbon dioxide. Such 'solutions' would enable polluting countries to desist from cutting emissions at home. However, as Ross Gelbspan warns:

> Ultimately, any emissions-trading-rights plan is unmonitorable and unenforceable. And it in no way addresses the conundrum at the center of the climate change issue: the massive economic inequality between the world's minority of wealthy nations and its majority of poor ones.[91]

JI is the 'market-based plan of choice of the oil and coal industries',[92] allowing polluting industries to continue to profit from their activities at the expense of people and the environment. Before the Climate Summit in Buenos Aires in 1998, the US Business Roundtable (BRT), comprising chief executives of more than 200 large corporations (many of them also members of the Global Climate Coalition), sent a letter to the US climate negotiating team, spelling out its demands. These included the instruction not to accept limits on the use of market solutions. In particular, the BRT suggested that emissions trading could meet 80 per cent or more of the country's commitments. Developing countries should be fully involved, they said, even though – and this is welcome honesty from the corporate sector – 'participation in full global trading actually puts southern countries at a competitive disadvantage'.[93]

In November 2000, the climate talks at COP-6 collapsed in The Hague, without agreement on the details of implementing the Kyoto Protocol agreement, paltry as it is. The British media delighted in the bitter recriminations that were exchanged between John Prescott, Britain's 'macho' environment minister, and Dominique Voynet, his 'tired' French counterpart. Meanwhile, the US delegation managed to slouch off back home, feeling self-righteous after supposedly making 'enormous concessions'. Efforts to get the negotiations back on track before Bill Clinton made way for George W. Bush came to nothing.

Beyond such bare facts there was precious little substance to most media coverage of the talks. Tony Blair's statement following meltdown in The Hague that Mr Prescott did an 'extraordinary job getting so close to an agreement' was dutifully reported and amplified approvingly in mainstream comment pieces. The Prime Minister's statement was clearly part of a damage-limitation exercise. There were reports about a deal having been struck three years earlier in Kyoto between the Americans and the Europeans.[94] This was allegedly to allow the US to make generous use of 'loopholes' in meeting their emissions targets. Was this the hidden agenda in The Hague?

The media-friendly stories were the 'battle' between the US and the EU, and the 'spat' between Prescott and Voynet. But a multitude of questions remained. Why grant a huge free gift to the US for using its existing forests and farmlands as carbon 'sinks'? Why allow forest projects under the clean development mechanism when its original purpose was to promote renewables and energy efficiency? FoE warned that this giant treaty loophole would encourage 'the destruction of old growth forests and their replacement by monoculture planta-tions'.[95] How reliable is the science of carbon sinks? What happens if forests later release their stock of carbon, if and when they burn, as they are more likely to do in a warming world?

There remains the possibility that nuclear power could make a comeback through the backdoor, courtesy of the joint implementation mechanism. This would allow developed countries to offset obligatory cuts in emissions by promoting the use of nuclear power in former Soviet and Eastern European coun-tries, for example. However, one positive outcome of climate talks in The Hague was 'that nuclear power was dealt a firm (if not decisive) "no" and is now unlikely to qualify' as an emissions reduction policy under the Kyoto Protocol.[96] That remains to be seen, given that the nuclear industry has considerable lobbying resources. Then there is the putative global market in hot air trading which will be exploited for profit by multinational companies such as DuPont and Texaco: 'the very companies', pointed out FoE, ' that did so much to create pollution from fossil fuels in the first place'.[97]

At root, nothing has changed: power still lies in the hands of unaccountable transnational corporations – and the politicians unwilling to confront them. These are the forces which are dictating the world's inadequate response to the threat of cataclysmic climate change.

Buddhist economics – have Shell's eyes been opened?

I was intrigued to learn in September 1998 that Shell had hired a Buddhist monk to lead 550 senior managers in meditation.[98] Several years previously, as an employee of Shell International, I had suggested in a memo that senior managers could benefit from attending courses such as 'Buddhist Economics' at Schumacher College in Dartington, Devon. No doubt this latest development was pure coincidence: I had only ever received a polite, non-committal response from the company.

It was the late E. F. Schumacher, author of the seminal 1973 book, *Small is Beautiful – A Study of Economics as if People Mattered*, who coined the term Buddhist Economics to describe a worldview which, by emphasising Right Livelihood, would promote human fulfilment and a sustainable environment, in contrast to the global economic apartheid and environmental destruction of today's growth-obsessed consumerist society. Today, Schumacher's views are even more compelling than ever. But how many corporate managers are aware of such views, far less try to translate them into action in their work? The sad truth is that business decisions are mostly taken subject to the unquestioned expediency of profit, and often short-term profit at that. Shell have tried to claim that there is no need to choose between profits and principle, but their record reveals otherwise.[99] So how do transnational corporations such as Shell initiate new recruits into their corporate culture? The following tale may shed some light on the matter...

It was the end of another week of intensive assimilation of Earth sciences. Not the science of Gaia[100] – the interconnectedness of Earth processes as though the planet were a single organism – but the science of oil and gas extraction. A detective story spanning hundreds of millions of years with clues revealed in the shape of the land and the texture of the rock; as much art and intuition as science and technology. But now it was time for a shift of perspective.

This Friday evening's briefing session at the training centre meant that the weekend would not be spent idling in and out of cafés, museums and each other's well-appointed apartments in The Hague. Instead, our assignment was spelt out by the training centre's geologist and geophysicist: to travel overnight to a remote location in the Belgian Ardennes, under strict instructions to arrive by 10 o'clock the next morning. We were split into four teams – each with an identical financial budget – travelling independently but in competition, amassing points by performing as many set tasks as possible along the way: taking a stranger out for a meal, collecting a bottle of sea water, using as many different modes of transport as possible, and so on. But no private transport was allowed – in other words, we couldn't simply drive down in our cars, which would have been far too easy! Around 15 hours later, my team glimpsed the remote adventure centre for the first time. There were also the smiling faces of two new instructors. After breakfast came the first of many review sessions: how well had we performed, and how could we improve in the future? Plan. Action. Review.

In the midst of the beautiful Ardennes we undertook a planning exercise for an imaginary exploration drilling location: geological setting, soil types, vegetation and surface waters. Bird and wildlife sanctuaries; breeding seasons. Site layout, camp and rig sites. Blowouts, pollution and contingency procedures in an emergency. Access roads and impact on the local communities and the environment. Landowner permission. Reinstatement of the site on completion of drilling. Total budget required. And then a final presentation was made to the 'exploration manager' for quality control of both the site report and the well proposal. A practice run for real-life cases in the Netherlands, Britain, Thailand, Oman, Venezuela, Nigeria...

The weekend was a blur of early rises, teamwork exercises, long review sessions, brief unsatisfying meals and late nights. 'They're trying to brainwash us!' laughed one of my colleagues, only half-joking. The smiley-faced new instructors dominated the review sessions. What would you do differently in future exercises? Which decisions must you stick by? What's important to you and to the team? Which criteria are essential and which merely desirable? Examine options and test the risks!

Towards the end of the weekend everyone had had enough. Under the restricted terms of the training course the sessions had been a success. Despite a more than healthy dose of scepticism, the new recruits had actually attempted to apply in the teamwork exercises those management tools – the 'hamburger model', the 'U-model' and other quaintly-named concepts – which had been discussed in the review sessions. The soft social science of the instructors had made some inroads into the rock-hard mentality of the trainees.

If one single word encapsulated all the qualities looked for in budding top Shell managers it was, and perhaps still is, 'heli-view': the ability to zoom in quickly to examine the details of a problem and zoom out again to grasp the whole picture. This is the quality prized above all others and occupying pride of place on Shell staff evaluation forms as we all later discovered on being assigned to our first postings. Heli-view: a poor cousin of holistic thinking to the ecologically-minded.

But ironically and significantly, the better ideas thrown up during the course had not been used to question the very basis of why such a hydrocarbon enterprise exists. Hardly surprising, really. Business objectives would quickly distil down to profit, profit and more profit. Endless business growth to ensure investor confidence. There is no perceived need, nor methodology, for recognising the desirability of a healthy diverse ecology or the soaring spirit in that calculation. And by not explicitly acknowledging the natural cycles of birth, growth and decay upon which the whole enterprise is ultimately based – how else did the fossil fuels get there? – the business activities are locked into a dead-end route. Dead-end? Yes, because the drive towards ever-increasing consumption contains within it the seeds of its own destruction. In a world of finite resources and gross inequalities, we are already becoming trapped and suffocated by unaccountable authority and by our own greed, ignorance and delusions. Given that David Korten and others warn of the 'cancer of capitalism', shouldn't we be rethinking how we train our future managers? Indeed, shouldn't we be rethinking the whole educational process, from early schooldays onwards?

Although Mark Moody-Stuart, the outgoing Shell chairman, took a few small steps in the right direction, such as instigating annual audits of the group's economic, environmental and social performance, it was not nearly enough. For one thing, such audits must be stringently and independently verified. But more than that, it is the very nature of Shell's business – and the whole undemocratic fossil fuel economy – that is in question. The Earth's rapidly changing climate is poised to make life very difficult indeed for many species, our own included.

As we saw earlier, Greenpeace have shown that we can afford to burn no more than a quarter of the known reserves of fossil fuels without risking dangerous climate change. As we will see in the following chapter, countries such as Denmark have demonstrated that there is economic benefit in taking action to slow global warming by boosting renewable energy. And yet senior Shell executives continue to maintain that the importance of oil and gas is likely to increase rather than diminish in the twenty-first century. Shell's flirtation with Buddhism may lead to a softer company image. However, what we need from this oil giant is a fundamental transformation to an ecological outlook and practice. Arguably such large corporate structures are beyond reform and should be split into smaller publicly-accountable units working on renewables and energy conservation. The example of anti-trust legislation invoked in the United State in 1911, which led to the complete divestiture of John D. Rockefeller's Standard Oil, the forerunner of today's Exxon, is an inspirational precedent.

If we are true to ourselves and our planet, we will recognise that there can be no long-term future for commerce, never mind ourselves, while there is this endless business-promoted depletion of natural resources with its associated social, economic and environmental damage. We are consuming the capital of the world's embarrassment of riches at a phenomenal, ever-increasing rate. The dragon is eating its own tail. How much time do we have left?

Notes

1   Gelbspan, *The Heat Is On,* p. 112.
2   Quoted in Leggett, *The Carbon War,* p. 16.
3   Hare, *Fossil Fuels and Climate Protection.*
4   *The Independent,* 17 August, 2000.
5   World Meteorological Organisation statement on the status of the global climate in 1998, WMO-No. 896, 1999.
6   *The Independent,* 23 December, 1999.
7   *Ibid.*
8   Environmental News Service at http://ens.lycos.com/ens/oct99/1999L-10-27-05.html
9   Leggett, *The Carbon War,* p. 103.
10   *Ibid.,* p. 121.
11   Gelbspan, *The Heat Is On,* p. 10.
12   *Ibid.,* p. 87.
13   Quoted in Leggett, *The Carbon War,* p. 4.
14   Because emissions have continued to rise in the intervening years, it now appears that 60 per cuts would only be enough to ensure that concentrations levelled off at around twice pre-industrial levels. Cuts of 80-90 per cent are probably required to stabilise concentrations at 1990 levels.
15   Quoted in Gelbspan, *The Heat Is On,* p. 20.
16   IPCC, *Climate Change 1995.*
17   Leggett, *The Carbon War,* p. 46.
18   T. H. Guymer, A. L. New and H. Cattle, 'A statement on the UK contributions to CLIVAR (Climate Variability programme) with particular focus on Atlantic climate variability and change and its effect on Europe', prepared on behalf of the Royal Society Global Environmental Research Committee for the International CLIVAR conference, Paris, 2-4 December 1998.
19   IPCC Working Group II, *Summary for Policymakers: Scientific-Technical Analysis of Impacts, Adaptations and Mitigation of Climate Change,* November 1995.
20   Quoted in Gelbspan, *The Heat Is On,* p. 160.
21   *Ibid.,* pp. 160-161.
22   *Ibid.,* p. 147.
23   *Ibid.,* p. 148.
24   http://news.bbc.co.uk/hi/english/sci/tech/newsid_526000/526690.stm
25   Environment news service: http://ens.lycos.com/ens/jan2001/2001L-01-22-02.html
26   *Ibid*
27   *The Independent,* 14 November, 2000.
28   Cited in George, *The Lugano Report,* p. 68.
29   Gelbspan, *The Heat Is On,* p. 154.
30   Geoffrey Lean, *Independent on Sunday,* 24 August, 1997.

31   Hare, *Fossil Fuels and Climate Protection.*
32   Greenpeace UK, *Frontier News – The Farewell Issue,* 12 November, 1999.
33   Leggett, *The Carbon War,* p. 140.
34   *Ibid.,* p. 140.
35   *Ibid.,* pp. 70-71.
36   Gelbspan, *The Heat Is On,* p. 91.
37   *Ibid.,* p. 172.
38   *Ibid.,* p. 194.
39   Quoted in Leggett, *The Carbon War,* pp. 198-199.
40   Hahnel, *Panic Rules!,* p. 23.
41   Matthew Spencer, *The Ecologist,* Vol. 29, No 2, pp. 127-128.
42   Leggett, *The Carbon War,* p. 138.
43   *Ibid.,* p. 229.
44   *Ibid.,* p. 230.
45   *Ibid.,* p. 90.
46   National Association of Manufacturers website: www.nam.org
47   *Ibid.,* p. 242.
48   Gelbspan, *The Heat Is On,* p. 79.
49   *Ibid.,* p. 80.
50   *Ibid.,* p. 81.
51   Leggett, *The Carbon War,* p. 243.
52   Quote from the October 1997 Global Climate Coalition website, www.globalwarming.org
53   Lee Raymond, speech in Beijing, 13 October, 1997.
54   Quoted in Leggett, *The Carbon War,* p. 203.
55   I was employed as a geophysicist by Shell International between January, 1989 – August, 1993, and was based in The Netherlands.
56   Heinz Rothermund, 'Challenges for the UK Oil and Gas industry: a partner for tomorrow's children', speech to the UK Oil and Gas Industry Conference, London, 23 September, 1997.
57   Rowell, *Green Backlash*; Beder, *Global Spin.*
58   John Browne, climate change speech at Stanford University, 19 May, 1997.
59   Cor Herkströter, 'Contributing to a sustainable future – the Royal Dutch/Shell Group in the global economy', Erasmus University, Rotterdam, 17 March, 1997.
60   Letter to author from Andrew Harper, BP Communications Manager, 15 October 1997.
61   In 1999, Shell's renewable division and BP Solar closed down headquarter operations in the UK and moved abroad, highlighting their lack of commitment to job creation in the renewable energy sector in Britain.
62   Shell International, *Profits and Principles,* pp. 9, 37, 47.
63   *The Independent,* 6 July, 1999.
64   *The Independent,* 13 July, 1999.
65   *Independent on Sunday,* 3 September, 1999.
66   Shell International, *Profits and Principles,* p. 35.
67   Quoted in *The Big Issue,* 15-21 February, 1999.
68   *The Independent,* 9 July, 1999.
69   Gelbspan, *The Heat Is On,* p. 180.
70   Greenpeace International, *Energy Subsidies in Europe.* Report prepared by the Institute for Environmental Studies of the Vrije Universiteit, Amsterdam on behalf of Greenpeace International, 1997.
71   Rothermund, 'Challenges for the UK Oil and Gas Industry'.
72   Quoted in Leggett, *The Carbon War,* p. 301.

73   Quote from the American Federation of Labor website, www.aflcio.org, in October 1997.

74   Telephone interview, 28 October, 1997.

75   Telephone interview, 28 October, 1997.

76   Revenues from the carbon tax are to be returned to industry through a reduction in employers' national insurance contributions. However, British Steel claimed that 'in the worst case', the new tax would cost them up to £300 million, with only a £5 million saving on its national insurance bill, *The Independent*, 30 March, 1999.

77   DETR press release, 9 March, 2000.

78   BBC news online, www.bbc.co.uk/news, 10 May, 2000.

79   http://news.bbc.co.uk/hi/english/sci/tech/newsid_505000/505115.stm#top

80   *Globalisation and Climate Change*, Chris Keene, anti-globalisation campaigner, report prepared for the Green Party of England and Wales, May 1999.

81   IPCC press release on 4 June, 1999, www.unep.ch/ipcc/press/pr6-99.html

82   'Britain and the global environment', speech by Robin Cook to the Green Alliance, London, 15 February, 1999.

83   *Ibid.*

84   *Ibid.*

85   Michael Meacher and Robin Cook, speeches given at 'A Green Labour Government?', conference organised by the Socialist Environment and Resources Association, London, 25 January, 1997.

86   Personal communication, London, February, 1999.

87   Global Commons Institute website: www.gci.org.uk

88   In order for the Kyoto Protocol to come into effect, 55 countries representing at least 55 per cent of carbon dioxide emissions must ratify it. No developed county has yet done so.

89   http://news.bbc.co.uk/hi/english/sci/tech/newsid_505000/505017.stm

90   David Edwards, *The Ecologist,* Vol. 30, No. 3, p. 52.

91   Gelbspan, *The Heat Is On,* p. 128.

92   *Ibid.,* p. 128.

93   Letter from Robert N. Burt, BRT Chairman of the Environmental Task Force, addressed to US climate negotiator Stuart Eizenstat, 10 November 1998, leaked to Friends of the Earth, and quoted in Balanyá *et. al.*, *Europe, Inc.,* ch. 17.

94   Geoffrey Lean wrote in the *Independent on Sunday* (26 November, 2000) that the US 'wanted to be able [to] count both the financing and planting of forests in developing countries and part of the carbon dioxide absorbed by managing its own existing forests against its target of reducing its CO2 emissions by 7 per cent below their 1990 levels. It said, and Mr Prescott confirmed, that it had *only agreed the Kyoto target on the understanding that it could do something like that'* [my italics].

95   Friends of the Earth press release, 24 November, 2000.

96   Oliver Tickell, *The Independent*, 15 December, 2001, global warming supplement, p. 2.

97   *Ibid.*

98   *The Independent*, 29 August, 1998.

99   Shell Nigeria's alleged role in the 'judicial murder' of Ken Saro-Wiwa and eight other Ogoni activists in November 1995 is perhaps the most well-known example. See, for example, Rowell, *Green Backlash.*

100   Lovelock, *Gaia.*

5

THE CONTROL OF ENERGY GENERATION

Can alternative energy sources ever break through?

Our aim must be to greatly reduce our use of fossil fuels, indeed eventually to phase them out.

John Battle MP, Energy Minister[1]

Democracy is a false promise if it does not include the power to steer the energy economy.

Daniel Berman and John O'Connor[2]

Local energy, local democracy

As we saw in the previous chapter, climate change is the greatest environmental problem facing humanity. Society's addiction to fossil fuels is driving us relentlessly down a highway of self-destruction, thanks to corporate greed and political short-sightedness, not to mention government handouts to the fossil fuel industry in the form of generous tax benefits and subsidies. The thesis of this chapter is that diverting from such a suicidal course requires a twin revolution: switching to renewable energy generation and, at the same time, boosting the power of local democracy. This may seem an odd combination at first sight, but the reasoning behind it encapsulates precisely why opposing economic globalisation and replacing it with an ecological and socially-just alternative is so important for the well-being of people and the planet. This chapter also examines the evolving electricity market in the UK, which has potentially seismic implications for renewable energy generation. There is no space here to give an exhaustive review of renewables. We will touch, however, on both solar and wave power, while focusing on offshore wind as an example of a potentially important renewables business, particularly for Britain.

As noted already, the unsustainable expansion of corporate activities into ever-larger markets means that there is an almost irresistible force driving the formation of mega-companies. Growth demands further growth; if companies do not expand in today's 'internationally competitive' markets they tend to stagnate and die.[3] Smaller enterprises are swallowed up whole or trampled underfoot in the stampede to maintain or increase returns on short-term investment, or even simply to repay loan capital. The business of generating electricity is no different in such matters from other industrial operations; there is an inherent trend away from small-scale, localised enterprises towards large-scale, centralised operations. It should therefore come as no surprise that power companies are engaged in a frenzy of mergers, in a similar manner to oil companies, news corporations and biotech enterprises. By 1998, more than half the UK's electricity industry had been swallowed up by American utility companies. But the US invasion, even on its own terms of empire-building, was a mixed success. Two of the eight British regional electricity companies were actually later sold back, another was split in half, and a further three were on the verge of collapse.

Meanwhile, a British electricity company was moving into the power market in the US. In December 1998, ScottishPower announced a £4.4 billion takeover bid for the Oregon-based electricity company PacifiCorp. As one analyst said, 'ScottishPower would have had to do a deal soon or it would have run out of steam'.[4] The deal, approved by the American regulatory authorities a year later, will deliver 1.4 million customers in 6 US states, and includes interests in 10,000 megawatts of coal-fired generation – enough to power over 5 million households – and a number of coal mines. But the expanded empire is not limited to US soil. Thanks to PacifiCorp's earlier empire-building, ScottishPower also inherited Powercor in Australia. Back home in the UK, ScottishPower's acquisitions already included Southern Water, Scottish Telecom, the regional electricity company Manweb, plus interests in gas supply businesses. Then, in May 2000, ScottishPower announced that it would axe 1,600 jobs at PacifiCorp – one-fifth of the workforce. At the same time, it was requesting regulatory approval to increase its prices by 10 per cent in four of the six states it 'serves' – Utah, Wyoming, Oregon and Washington. According to Sir Ian Robinson, chief executive of ScottishPower, such moves would make PacifiCorp 'one of the 10 most efficient US utilities'.[5]

Another UK regional electricity supplier, the Eastern group, moved into the Spanish power market, forming an alliance with Cantabrico, Spain's fourth-largest utility company.[6] The three largest utility companies in Spain had already allied themselves with foreign companies, a trend the Spanish government encouraged by opening 40 per cent of the domestic market to foreign competition. A Madrid-based analyst proclaimed that Cantabrico represented an excellent 'port of entry' into the Spanish market for the Eastern group.[7] Eastern, in turn, is a wholly-owned subsidiary of Texas Utilities.

These examples are typical of the complex web of acquisitions, mergers and alliances which plague the electricity market and, indeed, the global economy. Decisions affecting how electricity is delivered to local communities – such as whether it is generated by nuclear energy, fossil fuels or renewable sources – are taken, or at least strongly influenced, by executives sitting in corporate head-quarters thousands of miles away. Such a global arrangement may benefit company managers and shareholders, but it is rarely conducive either to job security for lowly employees (mergers typically lead to considerable job losses) or to the self-reliance and stability of the communities to which electricity is being supplied. As the economist Richard Douthwaite explained in *Short Circuit*, sustainable communities cannot be based on imported energy for three reasons. The first is that substantial use of fossil fuel – and most energy imports are of the fossil variety – is not itself sustainable, as we saw in the previous chapter. The second reason for aiming for community energy self-reliance is that imported fuel supplies are unreliable. The third reason is that energy prices are very erratic.[8]

Douthwaite argues that for much of the rich North, imported power is vulnerable to military conflicts and political instability in those regions which have traditionally supplied it with fuel, primarily the Middle East. We saw in Chapter 3 how this relates to US and British interventionist foreign policy, with the mass media faithfully playing a supporting role. For example, the Gulf War of 1990-91 was fought to ensure a reliable source of oil for the First World (as well as to maintain its traditional requirements for dominance and 'political stability' in the Middle East). However, the rich North's struggle to ensure a relatively stable source of fossil fuels – while riding roughshod over human rights and the global environment – is constantly undermined by erratic changes in energy prices. Fluctuations in oil prices, especially evident since the early 1970s, not only affect energy markets but disturb the entire economy. In other words, the whole structure of price relationships in the economy is affected by changing energy prices. This occurs because different products require different amounts of energy to be created, and so need to be raised or lowered in price by different amounts. Some goods and services become relatively cheaper, so that people begin to use more of them instead of the more expensive ones. This changes the entire make-up of an economy's output, encouraging expansion in some areas and contraction in others. The wasteful end result is that machinery is scrapped and factories are demolished before the end of their useful lives, resulting in job losses.[9]

It is almost a quarter of a century since the energy analyst Amory Lovins argued that the only viable long-term energy policy is a 'soft energy path' based on decentralised, renewable energy from the sun. 'An affluent industrial economy', wrote Lovins, 'could advantageously operate with no central power stations at all!'[10] Lovins emphasised that there is no obligatory link between increases in energy consumption and higher living standards or GNP. In fact, the opposite effect is more likely: to maintain the 6 per cent annual increase in energy production in the United States since 1945 through almost universal nuclear- and coal-fired electrification would suck up three quarters of the country's investment capital and impoverish the rest of the world.[11]

Rather than pursuing such a damaging energy policy, society ought to be using local renewable energy sources. These come in many forms: wind, wave, solar, geothermal, small-scale hydro, biomass fuels. Some of these are available at every location around the globe. Consequently, small-scale decentralised economies would be able to make use of a range of local energy sources. On the other hand, large industrialised economies with urbanised centres are locked into centralised power sources that convert fossil fuel or nuclear power into electricity, which is then transmitted over hundreds or even thousands of miles. This is extremely wasteful: two-thirds of the energy in fossil fuels is lost in the production and transmission process. Moreover, as Lovins explains, electricity is an indefensible luxury for 90 per cent of energy uses. Lighting and heating homes, for example, can be made much more energy-efficient by adopting 'passive' solar building designs, low-energy lights and tight insulation.

Energy efficiency is vastly underexploited at present. The economics panel of the Intergovermental Panel on Climate Change has identified a number of steps, called 'no regrets' policies, that at virtually no cost at all could reduce greenhouse gas emissions by around 20 per cent. Journalist Ross Gelbspan refers to such measures as 'a bridge to a new energy era'. They include such simple steps as implementing known efficiency and conservation techniques, planting more trees (to absorb carbon dioxide), and instituting international standards for energy-efficient appliances. Such measures should go hand in hand with a switch to green energy. Diverting the fossil fuel and nuclear tax credits and subsidies that currently promote – as Friends of the Earth (FoE) put it, 'the destruction of the global environment' – to windmill farms, home-based fuel cells, photovoltaic panels and hydrogen fuel plants 'would provide the liftoff boost to propel renewable energy into the big league of global industry'.[12]

FoE has performed research which shows that by improving energy efficiency and shifting to renewables such as solar, wind and wave power, the British government's modest target of a 20 per cent reduction in CO_2 emissions by 2010 could be easily achieved and would, at the same time, create an additional 226,000 jobs.[13] According to Matthew Spencer of Greenpeace, a higher target for CO_2 emission reductions is feasible: 'The UK could reduce its dependence on fossil fuels by up to a third [by 2010] without pain and with much economic gain.' He called for the British government to 'start the switch from fossil fuels to solar, wind and wave energy'.[14] But the government's long-awaited climate change programme, which was published in November 2000, was criticised by Greenpeace 'for doing little to break our economy's dependence on fossil fuels or to build a strong UK renewable energy industry'. Spencer rightly pointed out that: 'The Labour government is still dining out on the accidental carbon dioxide reductions that came from Thatcher's battle with the miners.'[15] 'There are not enough climate pollution penalties nor incentives to help industry and house-holders go green', warned FoE's director Charles Secrett. 'This leaves a gaping hole in the strategy. It looks like the Environment Department's plans have been scuppered by other Government departments.'[16]

Just days before the government's climate change programme was published, Gordon Brown, the Chancellor, had buckled under pressure from the 'people's fuel lobby' – largely a front for the road haulage industry – and announced a cut in fuel duty in a pre-budget statement. FoE warned that the cut would lead to more traffic and increased emissions of carbon dioxides. It was noteworthy that the government had failed on a number of critical policy measures: no carbon-based taxes for industry, vehicle and household energy use; no immediate obligation for strict energy conservation ratings for offices and homes; and insufficient funding to boost renewable energy such as offshore wind, and solar homes. Secrett warned that 'much more is needed to combat the awesome threat posed by climate change'.[17] The government appears unwilling, or unable, to accept the argument that moving to a clean and efficient energy strategy will boost jobs and the economy. In the United States, renewable energy analyst Scott Sklar has estimated that for every million dollars spent on oil and gas exploration, only 1.5 jobs are created; for every million on coal mining, 4.4 jobs. But for every million spent on making solar water heaters, 14 jobs are created. For manufacturing solar electricity panels, 17 jobs. For electricity from biomass and waste, 23 jobs.[18]

'A passionate public fight'

In today's capitalist society, the population tends to cluster in large cities in which a high-consumption lifestyle is encouraged. Profligate energy use, international trade and the concentration of millions of people in urban centres are intimately linked. This is why a decentralised, solar-based economy must go hand in hand with a revitalised locally-based democracy; one cannot succeed without the other. What would such a society look like? Based on detailed proposals made by Berman and O'Connor in *Who Owns the Sun?* and others, such as the former

German energy minister Hermann Scheer,[19] a blueprint for a solar society would incorporate:

- Public 'ownership' of energy – just as is the case with water or schools in some countries and US states.
- Massive investment in renewable energy technologies and building design, by diverting tax breaks and subsidies from fossil fuel and nuclear energy.
- Access to loans, tax credits and rebates for photovoltaics, solar water heating, wind and small-scale hydro generators, and other forms of renewable energy-generating and energy-saving technologies.
- Net metering (i.e. monitoring electricity flows) and rate-based incentives, so that independent home- and business-based electricity producers are paid the same price for electricity they supply to the grid as they would be required to pay for the grid power if they used it.
- Partnerships between industry, government and local communities to oversee the new 'green' industries, in order to ensure that the public knows what is being produced in a factory, by what means, and how any wastes and by-products will be managed.
- New government legislation to ensure that all this is carried out.

None of the above will happen if we simply leave it to the giant oil corporations to tinker with solar renewables – as we saw Shell and BP Amoco doing in the previous chapter – while they bulldoze ahead with exploration and production of new oil and gas reservoirs. Citizen control over a decentralised solar economy is in direct competition with the profit imperative of large companies. As Berman and O'Connor put it:

> To turn the tools of a solar transition over to utilities and fossil-fuel corporations, which is the present policy of the [US] government and mainstream environmental organisations, is to guarantee that the coming Solar Age will arrive a century behind its time, and that it will be every bit as autocratic as today's fossil-fuel economy. We believe that a solar revolution will necessarily occur at the expense of the private energy monopolies, and that such a revolution will not take place without a passionate public fight for more democracy and participation.[20]

Not many commentators have picked up on it yet, but this 'passionate public fight' is a necessary step to combat human-induced climate change. Even relatively progressive business forces could scupper such moves. In the United States, a coalition of large industry players called the International Climate Change Partnership (ICCP) has been attempting to take a lead corporate role in the climate change debate. The ICCP, which includes such companies as AT&T, Dow Chemicals, Electrolux, Enron and General Electric, accepts the reality of climate change and even the need for binding cuts in greenhouse gas emissions. However, the coalition aims to make sure that its members are poised to achieve dominance in the energy sector should the market for alternative sources take off. According to Ross Gelbspan, 'make no mistake – the business opposition to the fossil fuel industries is driven first and foremost by considerations of the bottom line ... the ICCP sees the coming energy transition as a way to reinforce the dominance of transnational corporations over governments'.[21]

Energy deregulation – a foot in the door?

Despite its urgent nature, the climate crisis has yet to impact in a commensurate way on governmental energy policy. Let us first consider the energy market in the UK, where a small step has been taken to provide green power to people – at a price. Until recently, British homes had to take whatever electricity was supplied to them by local electricity companies. But with the opening up of domestic gas and electricity markets to full competition in May 1999, 25 million customers were, in principle, able to buy electricity from any company they wished. Friends of the Earth had already compiled league tables ranking the environmental and ethical performances of the various electricity suppliers with a view to persuading their supporters to switch to green energy. The only catch is that most consumers of renewably-generated power are subject to a 'green tariff', typically a premium of around 10 per cent. The justification given by the utility companies for this extra cost is that they 'need to invest' in renewable energy generating capacity. Few of them felt that their existing large profits had been sufficient to provide such investment. On the other hand, the Renewable Energy Company based in Gloucestershire offered customers 'green electricity for the price of brown', meeting at least half the demand from renewable sources. Also in the green corner was the oddly-named Unit[e] (pronounced 'unity'), which offered 100 per cent green electricity.

Matching green demand and capacity has been hindered by the hugely complex trading system of the electricity pool – the wholesale power market. In October 1998, John Battle, then UK energy minister, announced a review of the workings of the pool. This led to new legislation on utilities in 2000. The motivation, however, was not to ensure a ready supply of green electricity, but rather to honour a Labour election manifesto commitment to provide cheaper electricity to customers. Indeed, there had been persistent criticism from consumer groups about the rigging of high energy prices by electricity companies.[22] Under the pool system, the National Grid determined a single wholesale price based on offers placed each day by electricity generating companies. Under the new electricity trading arrangements (NETA), the pool is to be replaced by a market-based trading system similar to those used in commodity markets; electricity will be traded using forward and future markets. A central feature of NETA is a 'balancing mechanism' to ensure a consistent supply of electricity. Contracts between companies buying and selling electricity will involve fines to penalise those who fail to provide the secure generation promised. However, the government's energy regulator, Callum McCarthy, was prevented by the Competition Commission from imposing 'good behaviour' clauses in the licences of the major electricity generators. Such clauses were planned in order to give the energy regulator powers to clamp down on companies engaged in price-rigging (setting prices artifically high). McCallum was reportedly 'furious' at being rebuffed saying that, 'This is not a good day for consumers. This decision has removed a very powerful weapon from our armoury.'[23]

NETA will have serious consequences for renewable energy generation. Renewable energy schemes in the UK started up in 1990 following privatisation of the electricity industry. Such schemes were supported by a small levy of less than 1 per cent on electricity bills. The levy, known as the Non Fossil Fuel Obligation, was also used to prop up the expensive nuclear industry. At the same time, the number of wind turbine farms and other green energy sources grew to around 150,000 households' worth of renewable energy capacity, though still falling far short of the UK's immense potential, as we will see below. Without substantial expansion of the NFFO subsidy, the onus of supporting, and improving upon, 150,000 households' worth of renewable energy capacity falls upon the green tariff. Suppliers will be obliged to deliver 10 per cent of the UK's electricity from renewable sources by 2010, thus satisfying Labour's previously announced target. But Greenpeace warned: 'This means suppliers will go for the cheapest technologies like landfill gas, waste incineration and onshore wind, and expensive technologies will be left out in the cold.'[24] In other words, renewables such as wave, solar and offshore wind would not get the kickstart that would allow their enormous potential to be realised. According to Greenpeace, 'The DTI's favourite, a renewables percentage obligation on electricity suppliers, would leave wave, solar and offshore wind completely out in the cold.'[25]

As far as the green tariff was concerned, the World Wide Fund for Nature (WWF) warned, 'any scheme would need rigorous auditing to ensure customer demand to buy only green power had been fully matched with renewable energy generation'.[26] South Western Electricity was the first UK company to offer a green tariff to customers through its Green Electron scheme, which provides power from small hydro-electric projects and landfill gas generators. According to a company spokesman, the project needs 10,000 customers paying a 10 to 15 per cent premium to break even. Although the scheme was theoretically available to all its 1.3 million customers, the company could give no guarantee of sufficient green generation projects in the event of high demand, as warned by WWF and other environmental groups.[27]

Indeed, because NETA places considerable emphasis on electricity 'supply security', there were serious concerns that renewable energy may actually suffer a devastating setback. The British Wind Energy Association warned that NETA 'could have profound implications for small, intermittent generators such as wind.' Moreover, the wind industry 'is concerned that the new proposals will discriminate in favour of flexible fossil-fuel generators because of their ability to predict and match demand'.[28]

Centrica, the gas trading and supply arm of the former British Gas, adopted a sluggish approach to providing green electricity to their customers. Meanwhile, the company was busily acquiring £250 million worth of PowerGen's upstream gas business. The deal included half a dozen gas fields in the southern North Sea, an area in which Centrica previously had no assets. The company continued its expansion in fossil fuel-fired electricity generation by preparing bids for coal-fired power stations that PowerGen and its rival, National Power, were obliged to sell off to meet the demands of the industry regulator on the opening up of competition in the electricity market.[29] In June 1999, the Centrica empire expanded further when it acquired the Automobile Association in a £1.1 billion deal, triggering 'windfall' payments of around £250 for the motoring organisation's 4.4 million full members. The acquisition is yet another example of the overwhelming pressure on competitive companies to maintain growth.

The liberalisation of the gas and electricity markets in the UK was an expensive exercise for consumers: the energy regulator, Callum McCarthy, allowed the industry to pass on £726 million of the costs of the process to the consumer. Even as consumer groups decried this as excessive, companies were pressing the government to be allowed to pass on their full costs – an additional £270 million – to customers. Most of the costs arose, the public was told, because companies did not have their new computer systems ready in time for market liberalisation. Industry and government ducked the question of the 'fuel poor' customers – those finding it too costly to properly heat or insulate their homes – who had benefited least from the whole exercise. Energy minister John Battle cheerfully likened the transition to 'open' markets to 'sending a rocket to the moon'. Meanwhile, concern was expressed that the exercise would lead to the emergence of just a small handful of powerful electricity suppliers. At least four suppliers – owned by Swalec, Norweb, Seeboard and SWEB – were put up for sale not long after National Power bought up Midland Electricity's supply arm. Battle said merely that he had 'an open mind' about mergers.[30] There was hardly any press coverage of the potential, or risks, for new renewable energy schemes, mainly because the whole exercise – from the point of view of both industry and government – was not about expanding opportunities for green energy at all.

The large corporations that dominate the energy market may feel peer pressure to introduce green pricing,[31] but will do so only if it does not threaten their position of control. However, the introduction of a green tariff, even on an international basis, will be insufficient to kick-start a real societal shift from fossil fuels to renewables – a shift that would be significant enough to reduce greenhouse gas emissions to levels that stabilise global climate before it is too late. Unless there is government intervention to truly 'green' the energy market – perhaps first at supranational bloc level (e.g. the EU) with the clout to challenge big business – coupled with the dismantling of transnational energy companies and the devolution of genuine democratic power to local communities, there will be no citizen control of decentralised power, and the dream of a new solar age will remain just that – a dream.

Groundswell of support

The experience of living in a 12- by 6-foot solar-powered survival pod perched on a small, steep-sided rocky island somewhere in the northeast Atlantic is an adventure most of us would happily eschew. But Pete Morris and two other Greenpeace activists did exactly that for 48 days in 1997 on the tiny island of Rockall, west of Scotland, as part of a dramatic protest against opening up the Atlantic Frontier to new oil and gas exploration. Morris later described the experience of being brought to Rockall by ship and left there for a long occupation:

> The three of us were alone and committed on Rockall in the wilderness of the North Atlantic, somewhere between Scotland, Iceland and the Faroes, watching the ship disappear over the horizon and realising that our lives now depended on the pod. When the weather was kind we'd sit outside and be humbled by the size of the sea, becoming blasé about the number of minke whales travelling past and fascinated by the whirling clouds of seabirds constantly circling our little micro-continent, cruising the updraughts just feet away … It was an honour to be the liberators of Rockall, the last and silliest of Britain's imperial conquests.[32]

The name Rockall comes from the Gaelic word for 'roaring' and it was known to Hebridean seafarers as the 'sea rock of Roaring'. In the Second World War it was almost rammed by a British warship that mistook it for a German submarine; at other times, it has been misidentified as an iceberg. In the 1970s, a Rockall Bill was passed by parliament incorporating the island into Scotland. The motivation for the Bill was oil.

The Greenpeace Atlantic Frontier campaign has been a successful and popular one, particularly among the crucial target population of internet-savvy youngsters. Pop stars Kylie Minogue, Blur's Damon Albarn and Pulp's Jarvis Cocker were among 60 artists who backed the environmental group's call for real action on climate change. During the occupation of Rockall, a Greenpeace website allowed armchair activists to monitor the progress of the three pod occupants and even offered passports and citizenship of 'Waveland'. Over 200,000 people signed a petition backing Greenpeace's call for a planned phaseout of fossil fuels and greater government and industry investment in renewable energy.

In 1997, the International Institute for Energy Conservation published a report, commissioned by Greenpeace UK, on the potential for sustainable energy in the UK.[33] One of the principal conclusions was that 'approximately 30 per cent of UK electricity could practicably be supplied from renewables by 2010, given a determined environmentally-driven energy policy'. As we saw earlier, the current Labour government's target for 2010 is a modest 10 per cent. Beyond this date the government has set no targets for renewables, even though a government study in 1998 concluded that half of Britain's electricity could come from renewable energy by 2025.[34] In what follows, we concentrate on just two types of renewable energy which have an enormous potential in Britain: solar and wind energy.

Solar: shining a light on a sustainable future

It may be surprising in a land not known for a sunny climate, but solar power could be of immense benefit in Britain. According to a government-sponsored solar taskforce, solar power is 'the single most important long-term means of reducing [greenhouse] gas emissions.'[35] In actual fact, solar power could become competitive with conventional electricity, even in the short term, if governments and industry exerted the will to make it so. Over the past twenty years, the price of solar electricity has reduced by 500 per cent, and the efficiency of solar panels has improved by 60 per cent.[36] In a report commissioned by Greenpeace, the international business consultant and accountancy firm KPMG stated that one large-scale solar photovoltaic factory manufacturing five million solar panels a year (sufficient to equip 250,000 homes, each with a two kilowatt system) could reduce the cost of solar power by a factor of four. Compared to electricity produced from conventional sources, this would make solar power price-competitive for domestic consumers.[37]

Photovoltaic (PV) cells, like those on cameras and pocket calculators, convert sunlight directly into electricity. There are no major technological or financial barriers to creating a large solar PV factory, costing around £320 million – easily within reach of government support or private investment. As Greenpeace observed: 'For BP, which spent double that amount on its new Foinaven oil development in the Atlantic Frontier, that level of investment would be radical and visionary – but not impossible.'[38]

Even in Britain, sufficient energy could be generated from a solar-tiled roof to provide for a family's needs and still leave enough electricity that could be sold to the local electricity company. A typical roof installation is a two kilowatt system – equivalent to 20 powerful light bulbs, or a 2-bar electric fire. Jeremy Leggett, a former Greenpeace climate campaigner and now director of the green energy company Solar Century, says that on a typical day his roof can create enough power for '350 cups of tea, 70 *Coronation Street* episodes and 800 slices of toast'.[39] The scope for solar energy in the UK is enormous. The Energy Technology Support Unit, the government's own energy advisor, has estimated that the potential of this resource is equivalent to 63 per cent of the country's domestic electricity consumption in 1997.[40]

In the United States, President Clinton launched an initiative in June 1997 to create a million solar-tiled homes by 2010. Germany plans 100,000 such homes by 2005 and Japan planned to have 70,000 by the end of 2000. In the UK, the Department of Trade and Industry plans a mere 100, with no fixed timescale. Leggett blames a reluctant electricity industry:

> No gas, no coal and no nuclear power would be required if every roof was covered with solar tiles. But the power companies have a policy of obstruction. The utilities are lobbying the Government and regulators hard, to stop the authorities allowing customers to get their due.[41]

The introduction of the green electricity tariff in the UK followed a similar initiative in the US where, 'for solar advocates left penniless by the vagaries of energy policy, "green pricing" became the new holy grail'. But this holy grail is illusory. Berman and O'Connor cite one case where public enthusiasm for solar energy was subverted by the utility company Detroit Edison. The company signed up 280 customers at a premium of $6.59 a month for its SolarCurrents programme, which claimed to supply solar electricity from a centralised plant. But no guarantees were given as to whether the participants would actually be using solar electricity in their homes or just 'the ordinary Detroit Edison mix of fossil- and nuclear-generated electricity.' Perhaps those 280 participating households could have made a greater impact on the energy politics of the Detroit area by pooling their $1,845 per month of solar surcharges, and instead founding a 'solar activists club' to monitor the environmental performance of Detroit Edison. SolarCurrents participants could demand that the Department of Energy create a fund for low-interest loans to encourage PV installations, 'rather than channeling its subsidies through Detroit Edison'. This could begin to have a real impact on democratising solar electricity.[42]

The Detroit case study is important because it typifies how, while electricity companies strive to develop a green veneer ('keen to be seen to be green', in the parlance of Friends of the Earth), they are suppressing the rise of a true solar age. The same arguments apply to the large oil corporations. BP Solarex – formed when BP Solar took over the company Solarex – already controls as much as 20 per cent of the world market in solar cells. The goal of energy corporations is the expansion of profit opportunities by replicating profligate northern lifestyles around the world, but still based largely on fossil fuels, putting the climate system at risk. The Devon-based International Society for Ecology and Culture (ISEC) warns that current global energy consumption 'places an unsustainable burden on the biosphere'. ISEC adds: 'Even if the North's energy efficiency were to increase substantially, it is likely that any gains made will be negated by simultaneous efforts to industrialise the more populous South, where the per capita emissions of CO_2 are still only one-tenth what they are in the most industrialised countries.'[43]

Wind power: more than enough

As well as providing direct energy in the form of light, the sun also powers atmospheric circulation which is generated by the temperature difference between the equator and the poles. The wind systems around the globe can be tapped for power. Indeed, wind power was the fastest growing energy source in the world in 1998. Over the previous four years, it had an average growth rate of 40 per cent worldwide with 10,000 megawatts (MW) of installed capacity – enough to power more than six million homes – in over 50 countries, led by Denmark, Germany and Spain. Although supplying nearly 10 per cent of Denmark's electricity needs, wind power's contribution to worldwide energy remains small – a mere 0.15 per cent. However, the European Wind Energy Association (EWEA) and the Forum for Energy and Development have argued that by 2020 wind energy could provide 10 per cent of the world's electricity requirements. By that date a total of 1.2 million MW of wind power could be installed, more than the total electricity consumption in Europe today. If just one-fifth of this total capacity were to be installed in Europe it would create a quarter of a million jobs there.[44] Klaus Rave, president of the EWEA, stated: 'With the political will to create the right regulatory framework the wind industry can become a mainstream power source creating investment, jobs and providing a cost effective solution to the climate change problem.'[45]

Renewable energy specialists Border Wind concluded that in the UK, offshore wind energy alone could easily meet the government's target of 10 per cent of electricity being supplied from renewable sources by 2010 and at the same time create 36,000 new jobs and an annual market worth £2.5 billion.[46] The UK's total wind resource is three times the country's current electricity usage. Despite the fact that the UK has the best offshore resource in Europe, with one-third of the total European potential, the government has no specific plans to capitalise on this potential. Border Wind recommended that the Non Fossil Fuel Obligation (NFFO), which was supposed to encourage renewable energy, be expanded to include offshore wind and other offshore renewables. Britain's first offshore wind farm, capable of supplying electricity to 6000 households, came into operation off the coast of Blyth, Northumberland in December 2000. The £4m scheme was developed by a consortium made up of Border Wind, PowerGen Renewables, Nuon UK and Shell Renewables. Greenpeace said that, 'Blyth is a good start but we need to do much, much more to harness the enormous potential of wind energy in Britain'.[47]

The example of Denmark

There is no reason why the UK cannot duplicate the success of wind power in Denmark. By 2030, wind power is expected to be supplying half of Denmark's electricity and a quarter of its total energy. This is the most ambitious wind target in the world and is part of the Danish government's commitment to a major reduction in carbon dioxide emissions: a 20 per cent cut in the 1988 level of emissions by 2005, and the promise to adopt an action plan by 2030 to cut emissions by half. Over 70 per cent of the country's wind energy in 2030 will come from offshore wind farms.[48] As Svend Auken, Danish Minister for Environment and Energy said: 'Offshore wind energy is a little more expensive than conventional power in Denmark. But if you take the environmental costs of fossil fuels and internalise them, it's very competitive indeed.'[49]

Denmark's success story goes back to 1891, when teacher Poul la Cour realised that the traditional windmill could be adapted from grinding corn to producing electricity. Wind turbines based on his design were used to keep power flowing to rural areas hit hard by fuel blockages during both World Wars. But when supplies of oil and coal were plentiful once again, interest in wind power flagged. That all changed with the Middle East oil crises of the early 1970s, when wind power reappeared on the energy agenda. It offered an alternative to the volatile prices and vulnerable supplies of fossil fuels, was available locally, and did not produce acid rain-poisoned forests, oil-polluted coastlines, or hazardous radioactive waste.

Two very different approaches to wind power emerged: 'bottom-down' and 'bottom-up'. The former was based on the experience of large aerospace companies in the US and Europe, such as Boeing and General Electric, which attempted to tailor the wind turbine to their aerodynamic expertise. Often funded by major government programmes, the corporate philosophy was 'biggest is best'. Conversely, the 'bottom-up' approach, pioneered in Denmark, was rooted in the initiatives of environmental activists and small entrepreneurs. Indeed, the wind turbine industry derived from farm equipment manufacturing, where the emphasis was on low cost, simplicity, reliability and the use of readily available materials. This approach paid off while the aerospace programmes foundered: none of their giant turbines got off the drawing board.

By the 1980s, a healthy home market in wind turbines had been established in Denmark. This was boosted by the California 'wind rush' which, fuelled by tax credits to encourage alternative energy, saw over 7,000 Danish wind turbines going up around the windswept valleys above Los Angeles. Although the Danish turbines were not ideally suited to the local conditions, the technology was essentially vindicated. However, a sudden end to US government support left dozens of failed projects on barren, rocky California hillsides. Nevertheless, valuable lessons had been learned and Danish engineers returned to Europe to further refine the basic wind turbine design into a sleek, aerodynamic structure, its tall tower topped by large fibreglass blades whose regular rotation is converted into kilowatt hours of power.

The statistics make impressive reading. Denmark has around 5,000 wind turbines generating 8 per cent of the country's electricity, a higher percentage than any other nation. In 1998, the Danish wind industry employed 15,000 people in Denmark and almost as many overseas. More than 60 per cent of all wind turbines installed around the world have been built by Danish manufacturers. Their machines have been exported to around 20 countries, including Ireland, Canada, Finland, Japan, Poland, Argentina and the United States.

The goal of the current Danish national action plan on energy is the offcoast installation of the equivalent of more than 2 million households' worth of electricity by 2030. The main advantage of going offshore is the enormous wind resource available. Average wind speeds can be 20 per cent higher, and the resulting energy yield up to 70 per cent greater, than on land. The lack of obstacles such as hills, and the generally smooth surface of the sea, also makes the wind more reliable. In a densely populated country like Denmark, where land is at a premium, going offshore makes sense. Moreover, improved technology is bringing down the cost of offshore schemes, so that soon they can be built just as cheaply as on land.

The Danish action plan calls for a small number of large wind parks at a typical distance of between 7 and 10 kilometres from the coastline. This avoids having a scattering of small-scale developments close to the coast, which would be visually and physically obtrusive. Environmental impact assessments indicate that sea birds, such as diving ducks which use coastal waters to find food in winter when other water is frozen, are unaffected by the presence of turbines. In some locations, turbine foundations have even encouraged fresh colonies of marine animals for birds to feed on.

Other European countries have not been slow to push ahead with offshore wind. In the Netherlands, two wind farms have been built in the shallow waters of the IJsselmeer. A 100-turbine wind park has just been approved off the Dutch North Sea coast. This will generate enough electricity for up to 100,000 households. Meanwhile, Sweden's first offshore wind park, with Danish turbines, was built near the island of Gotland in 1997. An industrial consortium now has plans to construct a wind farm in the sea near the port of Malmö, while another company is aiming for major offshore development.

UK government stalling on renewables

In June 1997, a month after the Labour government took office, energy minister John Battle launched a review into how the UK could achieve a 10 per cent target for renewable energy. The process was characterised by sluggishness. In March 1999, there were reports that Labour was backtracking on its 10 per cent pledge. Alleged conflicts between the Department of Trade and Industry, the Department of the Environment, Transport and the Regions, and the Treasury led to two different draft papers on renewables being prepared: one with a strong commitment to the 10 per cent target and one without any such commitment. Ian Taylor of Greenpeace expressed concern that delays in committing to renewable energy would deter investors in British technology:

> The DTI is supposed to be the champion of British industry but this would mean selling our firms down the river ... If this is a turf war between departments, then it is appalling ... Jobs will be lost while at the same time our environmental future will be forfeited. It's the worst of all worlds.[50]

Frustrated by the lack of meaningful action on climate change and renewables, Greenpeace UK challenged the government in December 1998 to set up a renewable energy task force.[51] Two months earlier, at the annual conference of the British Wind Energy Association, Battle had made an announcement about government consultation on offshore wind power. There was no follow-up. As we have seen, the UK has the best offshore resource in Europe for wind power, with a potential equivalent to three times the UK's current electricity usage, yet it still lies at the bottom of Europe's renewable energy league table. According to Nick Goodall, chief executive of the British Wind Energy Association, 'We are in a bizarre situation in that we have the greatest wind resource of any European country, yet one of the worst records for harnessing it'. The lack of 'joined-up government' – indeed the constant 'turf wars' between departments – has not helped. Geoffrey Lean, environment correspondent of the *Independent on Sunday*, reported:

> Treasury civil servants are mounting a determined bid to stop ministerial plans for a rapid increase in the amount of energy Britain generates from

the wind, water and the sun ... The stand-off threatens to escalate into a row between Gordon Brown, the Chancellor and Peter Mandelson, the [former] Secretary of State for Trade and Industry.[52]

In October 1998, Battle announced a record 261 new projects that had received approval to generate electricity from renewable sources. He stated that 'consumer demand for green energy was growing fast and the government wanted to do all it could to help'.[53] This proclamation of government commitment was dubious in the light of the announcement the previous month by Stephen Littlechild, the government-appointed electricity industry regulator, that meeting government manifesto targets for renewable energy was uneconomic because it would cost up to £15 billion. He said, 'It is for consideration whether the benefits of renewable energy justify incurring costs on such a scale'.[54]

While welcoming Battle's announcement of support for new renewable projects, enthusiasm in some quarters was tempered by the 'experience ... that less than half the approved schemes ever get built.' Crispin Aubrey, the editor of *Wind Directions*, the magazine of the European Wind Energy Association, also bemoaned the over-competitive structure of the UK's system of selecting successful renewable schemes from candidate proposals:

> It has tended to favour the larger players with access to cheap finance rather than community-led schemes, and has singularly failed to encourage any domestic manufacturing industry.[55]

Aubrey pointed out that the DTI, which controls the price support system for renewables, and the Department of the Environment, which controls the planning system for siting windmills, appeared to 'operate from different planets'. Aubrey suggested encouraging renewables in a different, more streamlined way, as in Germany, where renewable projects are paid a guaranteed premium price for the electricity they produce. When planning permission is obtained, building is allowed to proceed immediately. Every local authority is expected to designate certain areas as suitable for renewable development. This helps ease log jams in obtaining planning permission. As a result, there are now over 5,600 wind turbines operating in Germany compared with 850 in Britain. In one German state, Schleswig-Holstein, wind energy already supplies 12 per cent of the power and local people are involved financially in schemes 'to an extent unheard of in Britain'.[56]

Another massively under-utilised renewable resource in the UK is wave power. Over the next 20 years, it is predicted that the British wave power market could be worth £20 billion. In October 1999, Greenpeace helped launch the Wave Power Commission for Scotland to harness the country's huge wave power resource. The cross-party commission included Members of the Scottish Parliament, wave energy experts, representatives of electricity companies and delegates from the Scottish Trade Union Congress. Allan Thomson, the managing director of Inverness-based Wavegen, one of the world's leading wave power companies and an observer to the commission, contrasted the fossil fuel and renewable paths: 'Some of the tens of billions that will be invested in oil production in the Atlantic Frontier should be spent on renewable energy. That way, you'll get a yield not for 20 years but for thousands of years.' Thomson, addressing fears of job losses in the oil industry, spoke of taking 'the fantastic knowledge and technology of the oil industry and applying it to wave power'.[57] Professed or genuine fears of job losses in the oil industry as a result of shifting to renewables are unfounded; Greens and other progressives have consistently asserted – using underpinning research to back the claim – that a decentralised, renewably-driven economy would be more labour-intensive than a centralised, fossil-fuel economy.

The wave energy resource off the Western Isles in Scotland is probably the largest in Europe. If utilised with the full involvement of the local people there, it could provide secure employment and sensitively managed environmentally-friendly energy. This could help to regenerate some of the local communities which have never fully recovered from the Highland Clearances in the eighteenth and nineteenth centuries. The company Wavegen installed the first commercial-scale wave power machine, Limpet, near Islay in the inner Hebrides. Limpet became operational in November 2000.

In February 2000, the government announced its policy on renewables, after a review that had started almost three years previously. Although the target of 10 per cent of electricity generation from renewables by 2010 was reaffirmed, there was no new backing for wind, wave and solar power which could cumulatively generate 7 times the UK's electricity demand.[58] Peter Melchett, executive director of Greenpeace, expressed his disappointment:

> It seems that forces of conservatism within 10 Downing Street have blocked support for the budding industries of offshore wind, wave and solar power. In doing this the Government have broken a promise to the offshore wind industry to give them backing.[59]

One of the last functions undertaken by the House of Lords before it was reformed was to criticise the government for using the utilities review and proposed new electricity trading arrangements as a cover for inaction on renewables. The Lords warned that the UK needs 7-8 times the current renewables capacity if it is to meet the government's own target of 10 per cent of green electricity provision by 2010. It would appear that in refusing to move swiftly to a climate-friendly energy policy, New Labour's fear of alienating the powerful support of big business has once again taken precedence over environmental protection. Ministers have turned a deaf ear towards the 72 per cent of the public who would prefer the government to develop offshore renewables, rather than continue to license new oil exploration.[60]

A taxing problem?

Throughout the government's term of office, it has been deeply disappointing to many British environmentalists to see earlier signs of Labour's eco-friendly potential vanish into thin air. I was present one overcast Saturday morning in January 1997, four months before the general election, when the green wing of the Labour Party – the Socialist Environment Resources Association – gathered with other environmentalists in London. We had come to consider the prospect of an environmentally-aware Labour government coming to power. Michael Meacher, shortly to become an environment minister, and Robin Cook, the Foreign Secretary-in-waiting, both proclaimed that Labour would form the 'first truly green government in this country' by putting 'the environment at the heart of government'.

Meacher spoke passionately about a number of issues: the £3.9 billion health costs attributed to urban air pollution; greening government by setting up a strong environmental audit commission; introducing key indicators in addition to GNP on water and air quality, biodiversity, pollution, food quality; a home energy efficiency scheme to tackle the problem of 8 million fuel-poor homes in the UK. He spoke of eco-tax reform ('encourage the goods, discourage the bads') and the need to reduce carbon dioxide levels and to boost renewables. In a coy passage, Meacher stated that society was 'in a bind over transnational corporations' and conceded the need for international agreements on them. No doubt he had voluntary, rather than binding, agreements in mind. Anything else would doubtless be unacceptable to a government that values 'international competitiveness' above environmental protection.

Robin Cook, obviously well briefed by his advisers, spoke of climate change, highlighting a 30 per cent rise in average wave height in the North Atlantic over the previous 25 years. Mounting insurance claims from extreme weather events led Cook to joke that a new eco-campaign was required: 'save the insurance broker!' Biodiversity was threatened: 40,000 species had become extinct since the first Earth Summit at Rio in 1992. The list went on and on. It was apparent that Meacher and Cook were well aware of the unprecedented stress that mankind was placing on the environment. And yet the policies they proposed to deal with the crisis were simply inadequate. As the chapters of this book demonstrate – on issues such as climate, energy, trade, agriculture and genetically modified organisms – it is clear that Labour's promise to form the first truly green government was empty rhetoric.

So what is to be done on energy policy? To put it simply, governments everywhere should do much more to support renewables and at the same time restrict the use of fossil fuels. Ambitious pragmatic targets – such as obtaining 10 per cent of electricity needs in the UK from offshore wind energy alone by 2010 – would signal clearly to business that renewable energy *will* become a major player in the economy. This calls for direct intervention in energy markets, currently distorted in favour of fossil fuels. Governments could, and should, oblige energy suppliers to take specific types of renewable energy, including solar, offshore wind and wave power, which all need further investment to bring down costs. Guaranteed markets for renewables will encourage commercial developers to make a long-term commitment. 'Showcase' programmes, such as equipping roofs of major buildings with solar panels, could help to kick-start an expansion of green energy. Most importantly, instead of subsidising the nuclear and fossil fuel industries, public funds should be used to pay for the research, development and use of renewable technologies – particularly small-scale decentralised projects that allow communities to regain and retain control over their own resources. This means devolving genuine political power to communities, while also opposing the corporate agenda of free trade which leads to the private control of public and natural resources.

All of the above measures should be combined with the restriction and eventual elimination of large-scale fossil fuel combustion. Meaningful progress towards the cuts of 60-80 per cent in greenhouse gas emissions, estimated by the UN Intergovernmental Panel on Climate Change as the requirement for climate stability, will not be achieved without very significant reductions in fossil fuel use. Proposed technical fixes, such as locking up excess carbon dioxide emissions in the deep ocean, in buried sediments or in new forest plantations are, at best, uncertain and, at worst, would create additional disturbances to the complex web of life; such is the nature of technological 'solutions' to fundamental socioeconomic problems. Given the seriousness of climate change, governments should be directing industry by ending the licensing of new areas for oil and gas exploration, and by phasing in over a number of years a series of steadily reducing limits to the proportion of electricity that may be supplied from fossil fuel combustion. Introducing a major energy efficiency programme for home dwellings would save lives – 30,000 die in the UK every year because their homes are damp or cold – and create many jobs. An industrial carbon tax could raise £5 billion in the UK and used to support renewable energy schemes.[61] There is no shortage of practical and positive steps to take, but the political will has yet to be liberated from the illusions of greed, power and ignorance.

The return of nuclear power?

There are those who stubbornly claim that the need to cut greenhouse gas emissions is justification for continuing – or even expanding – the super-costly nuclear industry. Ian Fells, Professor of Energy Conversion at Newcastle University, is one notable example: 'I regard Blair's target of a 20 per cent cut [in greenhouse gas emissions] by 2010 as really heroic. It will not be achieved without nuclear power.'[62] The nuclear industry believes that 'climate change is the best friend we have had in the past 40 years'.[63] However, even using conventional economic analyses that ignore environmental and social costs, nuclear power generation is uneconomic. It is therefore not surprising that in 1997, British Energy, a privatised company operating Britain's seven advanced gas-cooled reactors and the pressurised-water reactor at Sizewell B in Suffolk, was 'railroaded by the stock market into stating it would build no more nuclear plants'.[64] By 2020, if current government policy is maintained, there will be just a handful of nuclear reactors – though still a handful too many – operating in Britain. Despite a past of massive state subsidy, guaranteed markets, debt write-off and insurance cover, Britain's nuclear industry is slowly dying, and rightfully so.

In the US, the Atomic Energy Commission (AEC) has been responsible for spending vast sums of taxpayers' money on nuclear power. According to environmentalist Steven Gorelick, government funds were used to commission the first full-scale nuclear reactor because the AEC did not believe that private industry would make the necessary huge investment in nuclear power research. Afterwards, in order to 'further spur private industry's participation in nuclear power development', the government provided funding and other assistance, but industry designed, constructed and owned the reactors. Gorelick reported that, 'US government aid to the nuclear industry has continued unabated, with almost $1 billion budgeted for nuclear power research and development in 1992, and with additional expenditures hidden in military budgets every year'.[65]

In 1976, the UK Royal Commission Report on Nuclear Power and the Environment stated that 'it would be irresponsible and morally wrong to commit future generations to the consequences of fission power on a massive scale unless it has been demonstrated beyond reasonable doubt that at least one method exists for the safe isolation of these wastes for the indefinite future'. A quarter of a century later, the failure to find 'safe' methods of disposing of radioactive waste should mean that the nuclear industry is shut down and that 'existing nuclear waste must be stored above ground where [it] can be managed, monitored and retrieved if necessary, rather than dumped where environmental contamination is inevitable'.[66]

Towards the end of 1999, it was revealed that personnel at a demonstration facility run by British Nuclear Fuels in Sellafield, Cumbria, had falsified safety data relating to fuel pellets of mixed plutonium and uranium oxide (MOX). Some of the pellets had already been shipped to Japan to be used in its nuclear power programme. The Japanese government was horrified and called a halt to further imports of the reprocessed fuel. British ministers were embarrassed and apologised profusely to the Japanese, while claiming that safety had not been breached. Then, in February 2000, the UK government's own Nuclear Installations Inspectorate released three damning reports. These covered the poor management and lack of effective inspection at Sellafield, problems surrounding the storage of high level radioactive waste on the site and BNFL's falsification of safety data for the MOX fuel sent to Japan. Tampering with safety records appeared to have been going on since 1996. Pete Roche, a Greenpeace nuclear campaigner said:

> These reports are a shocking exposé of Sellafield's plutonium business. This is a company that is dealing with one of the most hazardous materials known to mankind and they have been shown to be guilty of lax management and falsifying records.[67]

The German nuclear company PreussenElektra, the country's second largest electricity generator and a BNFL customer, responded to the crisis by switching off its nuclear reactor and removing fuel rods which it had obtained from the Sellafield plant. At the end of February, BNFL's chief executive resigned. In March, the German environment minister, Juergen Trittin, said that Germany would ban imports of plutonium fuel (MOX) from Britain until it was satisfied with Sellafield's safety standards as 'a good first step to ending Britain's plutonium trade for good.'[68] Meanwhile, Switzerland announced that it wished to end the reprocessing of its nuclear fuel at Sellafield. Calls increased for the facility to be shut down or to be limited to, as Friends of the Earth put it, 'cleaning-up and managing the nuclear legacy, both in the UK and around the world.'[69]

Nuclear power, like major fossil fuel use, forms no part of a sustainable energy portfolio. The stumbling block, as with so many other issues discussed in this book, is the corporate-led drive for expansion, which demands more energy, more resources, more customers. The concern of big business, aided by governments keen for investment, is to achieve 'sustained growth', where 'market liberalisation drives technology, competition and efficiency' in an 'uncertain world of global markets'. Large corporations are desperate to keep a tight control on technological developments in order to protect profit margins. According to one influential Shell manager:

> To reduce risk, it is essential that Shell ... is present in every major market and in every major energy technology ... We believe [that] this approach could provide opportunities for smaller firms who enter into relationships

with us. We will be looking for ways of establishing links that help us keep an eye on developments and allow us to invest at the appropriate stage.[70]

Being 'present in every major market' for a large corporation like Shell means keeping a watchful eye out for technological breakthrough wherever it may occur – inside or outside its own sphere of operations – and then stepping in to influence, or even take control of, its future direction by snapping up the company. If citizens around the world continue to acquiesce in this process, whereby corporations and governments centralise power unto themselves, then the means of energy generation – together with the other forces of globalisation discussed in this book – will continue to harm local people and environments around the planet.

Notes

1   Statement made by John Battle, during a speech concerning the government's policy on offshore wind power in 1998, quoted in Greenpeace UK, Frontier News Issue 2, 29 September, 1999.
2   Berman and O'Connor, *Who Owns the Sun?*, p. 245.
3   As we saw in Chapter 1, the imperative for growth in the capitalist economy lies, at root, in an unsustainable monetary system based on debt.
4   Quoted in *The Independent*, 8 December 1998.
5   *The Independent*, 5 May, 2000.
6   *The Independent*, 11 December 1998.
7   In the UK, Eastern were ranked highly in Friends of the Earth's 'green energy league table' (www.foe.co.uk/climatechange/bestbuy.html).
8   Douthwaite, *Short Circuit*, pp. 179-181.
9   *Ibid.*, pp. 181-182.
10 Amory Lovins, *Foreign Affairs*, October 1976, pp. 65-96.
11 Berman and O'Connor, *Who Owns the Sun?*, p. 214.
12 Gelbspan, *The Heat Is On*, pp. 179-180.
13 Friends of the Earth, 'Special Briefing Sheet: "CO2 cuts = 226,000 new jobs" ', 30 September, 1997.
14 Interview with the author, 28 October, 1997.
15 Frontier News Volume 4, Bulletin 3, Greenpeace UK, 17 November, 2000.
16 Friends of the Earth press release, 17 November, 2000.
17 *Ibid.*
18 Gelbspan, *The Heat Is On*, p. 191.
19 Schumacher Lectures, Colston Hall, Bristol, 18 October, 1997.
20 Berman and O'Connor, *Who Owns the Sun?*, p. 245.
21 Gelbspan, *The Heat Is On*, pp. 90-91.
22 *The Independent*, 9 October, 1998.
23 *The Independent*, 12 December, 2000.
24 Matthew Spencer, Greenpeace UK, personal communication, 23 November, 1999.
25 Greenpeace UK, *Frontier News*, Issue 2, 29 September, 1999.
26 *The Independent*, 5 June, 1997.
27 *The Independent*, 10 May, 1998.
28 *New Review*, The Quarterly Newsletter for the UK New and Renewable Energy Industry,

Issue 42, November 1999, www.dti.gov.uk

29   *The Independent*, 12 October, 1998.

30   *The Independent*, 25 May, 1999.

31   A view implicitly acknowledged in a fax from Dr David Welsh, Group Health Safety and Environment Manager, Centrica plc to the author, 10 December, 1998.

32   Quoted in *Greenpeace Annual Review 1997.*

33   Bates and Watkins, *The Potential for Sustainable Energy in the UK.*

34   Cited in *Greenpeace Business,* October/November 1998, p.5.

35   *Independent on Sunday,* 20 June, 1999.

36   Cited in *Breaking the Solar Impasse,* Greenpeace briefing, September, 1999, p. 11.

37   KPMG, *Solar Energy: From Perennial Promise to Competitive Alternative,* cited in Greenpeace UK, *Frontier News,* Issue 1, 22 September, 1999.

38   *Greenpeace Annual Review 1999,* p. 4.

39   *Independent on Sunday,* 20 June, 1999.

40   Cited in Greenpeace UK, *Breaking the Solar Impasse,* p. 11.

41   *Independent on Sunday,* 20 June, 1999.

42   Berman and O'Connor, *Who Owns the Sun?,* pp. 220-221.

43   Gorelick, *Small is Beautiful, Big is Subsidised,* p. 26.

44   European Wind Energy Association and the Forum for Energy and Development, 'Wind Force 10: A Blueprint To Achieve 10 per cent of the World's Electricity from Wind Power by 2020', *Financial Times* World Renewable Energy Conference, Brussels, 5 October, 1999.

45   Quoted in Greenpeace UK, *Frontier News,* Issue 1, 22 September, 1999.

46   Border Wind, 'Offshore Wind Energy – Building a New Industry for Britain'.

47   *The Independent,* 8 December, 2000.

48   Adapted from Greenpeace International, *Danish Wind Energy: An Industrial Success Story.*

49   Quoted in *ibid.*

50   *The Independent,* 23 March, 1999.

51   Greenpeace UK press release, 8 December, 1998.

52   *Independent on Sunday,* 11 October, 1998.

53   *The Independent,* 20 October, 1998.

54   *The Guardian,* 9 September, 1998.

55   *The Guardian,* 14 October, 1998.

56   *Ibid.*

57   Greenpeace UK, *Frontier News,* Issue 6, 13 October, 1999.

58   Greenpeace UK press release, 1 February, 2000.

59   *Independent on Sunday,* 26 October, 1997.

60   Survey cited in Bates and Watkins, *The Potential for Sustainable Energy in the UK.*

61   *The Independent,* 25 August, 1998.

62   *Independent on Sunday,* 26 October, 1997.

63   Balanyá *et al., Europe, Inc.,* p. 165.

64   *Independent on Sunday,* 26 October, 1997.

65   Gorelick, *Small is Beautiful, Big is Subsidised,* p. 25.

66   Greenpeace UK submission to the Royal Commission on Environmental Pollution study on energy and the environment, November 1998.

67   Greenpeace UK press release, 18 February, 2000.

68   Greenpeace UK press release, 8 March, 2000.

69   Friends of the Earth press release, 28 February, 2000.

70   'Seizing Renewable Energy Opportunities', speech by Dr John Mills, Director of Corporate Affairs Shell UK, at the Renewable Energy Conference, UK Government Office of the East Region, Cambridge, 26 February, 1998.

6

UNHEALTHY LAND, UNHEALTHY PEOPLE

Corporate enclosure versus community empowerment

The awareness that we are slowly growing into now is that the earthly wilderness that we are so complexly dependent upon is at our mercy. It has become, in a sense, our artifact because it can only survive by a human understanding and forbearance that we now must make.

Wendell Berry[1]

Let us build cities that are not too big, but spacious, with traffic flowing freely through their leafy avenues, with children playing safely in their green and flowery parks, with people living happily in bright efficient houses.... Let us balance agriculture and industry, town and country – let us do all these sensible and elementary things and then let us talk about culture.

Herbert Read[2]

Disappearing world

Towards the end of 1998, a truly shocking report was released to the public. Its conclusion was that 30 per cent of the natural world had been lost in 25 years, destroyed by human activity. That is almost impossible to absorb on first hearing and bears repeating. Almost one-third of the world's natural ecosystems – as measured by the state of forest, freshwater and marine biomes, where most of the world's biodiversity resides – have disappeared between 1970 and 1995, because of human pressure.

The study[3] was published by the World Wide Fund for Nature and revealed that the world's natural forest cover[4] had decreased by 13 per cent between 1960 and 1990, from 37 million square km to 32 million square km. Most of this loss took place in tropical regions. For example, in the Brazilian Amazon, which contains about 40 per cent of the world's tropical rainforest, the loss of forest cover up to 1996 exceeded an area the size of Spain out of an original forest area the size of Western Europe. Brazil now plans to spend £27bn spent over seven years on roads, hydroelectric dams, railways and waterways which could leave only 5 per cent of the rainforest intact by 2020.[5] According to WWF, half of the world's original forest has now been cleared to make room for agriculture and human civilisation.

The health of freshwater ecosystems such as lakes, rivers and wetlands was analysed by examining trends in the populations of over 200 fish, reptile, bird and mammal species, as well as monitoring changes in the ecological state of fresh-water lakes. During the last 30 years, about 50-60 per cent of examined freshwater species – such as the Eurasian bittern, estuarine crocodile, junin grebe and river dolphin – were in decline, 35-40 per cent remained stable and only 5-10 per cent increased. By focusing on threats from overfishing, coastal development, siltation and pollution, comparisons of two global surveys of over 90 freshwater lakes yielded a sad picture. Only 3 per cent of European cases showed an improvement. In 35 per cent there was no change, while the remaining 62 per cent of the lakes had deteriorated. The situation in Latin America was even more dire: the condition of 78 per cent of the lakes surveyed had deteriorated, 22 per cent had experienced no change, leaving no cases where there had been any improvement.

The state of the world's oceanic and coastal biodiversity also gives great cause for alarm. Analysis of over 100 marine vertebrate species – including the beluga whale, northern fur seal, jackass penguin and loggerhead turtle – shows that over the study period of 1970-1995 about 40 per cent of marine populations had declined, about 25 per cent remained stable, and 35 per cent increased. The average marine fish catch for 1990-95 was 84 million tonnes per year, double what it was in 1960, and on top of this there were at least 27 million tonnes of 'by-catch' – in other words, unwanted fish which were caught and discarded – making a minimum estimate of fish caught of more than 110 million tonnes a year. According to the UN Food and Agriculture Organization (FAO), the 'maximum sustainable potential of the oceans is between 82 and 100 million tonnes a year';[6] current fishing levels are therefore unsustainable. In 1994, the FAO declared that '60 per cent of the world's fish resources were either fully exploited or in decline'.[7] In 2000, scientists advising the European Commission warned that in some areas stocks of cod and hake were close to 'total collapse'.[8]

All in all, the WWF report made rather depressing reading. The study made a brief splash in the newspapers – with articles illustrated by pretty colour world maps depicting depleted resources and lost biodiversity – then quickly died away again. There were no calls by politicians for a commensurate response to the planetary threat posed by human industrial activity, no global Marshall Plan to tackle environmental destruction, as previously espoused by US Vice-President Al Gore,[9] no action taken to reduce the destructive 'footprint' of consumer capitalism, particularly amongst the resource-greedy rich nations of the North.

When delegates gathered at the sixteenth International Botanical Congress in St. Louis, Missouri, in August 1999, they listened to one presentation which revealed that humanity's impact on the earth has increased extinction rates to levels unseen since the demise of the dinosaurs (and many other species) in the last mass extinction, 65 million years ago. According to the speaker, Dr Peter Raven, director of the Missouri Botanical Garden, the current extinction rate is now approaching 1,000 times the background rate and may climb to 10,000 times the background rate during the next century, if present trends continue. At this rate, one-third to two-thirds of all species of plants, animals, and other organisms would be lost during the second half of the twenty-first century, a loss that would easily equal those of past extinctions.[10]

And so the evidence for massive loss of global biodiversity continues to accumulate, even as intensive agriculture, polluting industry and urbanisation continue apace.

A corporate trail of destruction

It is vital that scientific surveys – local, regional and global – are regularly undertaken of the ecological state of the planet. But unless a strong link is made between loss of biodiversity, and the specific enterprises and government policies responsible, there is generally little societal pressure for moves towards solving the crisis: greater regulation of business, coupled with more democratic land ownership. Enormous suffering is being inflicted on people around the globe, in particular the poor, because of the destruction of ecosystems by companies involved in forestry, fishing, mining and other industrial sectors.

Take forestry, for instance. John Madeley, a writer and broadcaster specialising in Third World development issues, points out that 'transnational corporations are leading actors in the axing and burning of forests'.[11] In October 1991, devastating floods in the Philippines which killed 7,000 people were attributed to deforestation. In 1997, catastrophic forest fires spread rapidly in parts of Indonesia, destroying an estimated 10 million hectares and creating dense poisonous smog in the region, including over Malaysia and Singapore. The fires occurred during an unusually long dry season brought about by the effects of the strongest El Niño since modern records began, perhaps at least partly caused by global warming. But the fires were undoubtedly precipitated by unsustainable logging practices encouraged by the regime of President Suharto who, as we saw in Chapter 3, was favoured by the West for his opening up of Indonesia to foreign investors. Suharto's forestry policies resulted in the destruction of the third largest area of tropical rainforest in the world over the last three decades. According to Frances Carr of the campaigning group Down to Earth, 'over 60 per cent of Indonesian timber is probably the result of illegal logging'.[12] The Indonesia-based Centre for International Forestry Research states that the Indonesian government has encouraged and licensed many companies to develop new industrial plantations of rubber, oil-palm and pulpwood, as well as transmigration sites. These activities require the clearing of hundreds of thousands of hectares, and fires are their cheapest option.[13]

Japanese companies have led the assault on forests in developing countries in Asia, particularly in the Philippines where forest cover has declined from 17 million hectares in 1945 to just a million hectares by 1989. Mitsubishi, one of the firms involved, is in the world's top 100 transnational corporations and has logging companies not only in the Philippines but also in Malaysia, Indonesia, Papua New Guinea, Thailand and Burma. An official inquiry into logging in Papua New Guinea declared: 'Some of these [logging] companies ... are roaming the countryside with the self-assurance of robber barons, bribing politicians and leaders, creating social disharmony and ignoring the laws in order to rip out and export the last remnants of timber.'[14]

Another logging TNC of interest is Aracruz Celulose, a Brazilian-Norwegian company and a member of the World Business Council for Sustainable Development. Aracruz owns 203,000 hectares of cultivated land in the Brazilian state of Espírito Santo, in an area of tropical rainforest that was previously inhabited by local smallholders and the Indian Tupiniquim people. The latter lost their rainforest homes so that Aracruz could clear the land for eucalyptus plantations, providing pulp to be turned into paper products. The rapid growth of eucalyptus trees consumes great volumes of groundwater, at the expense of local vegetation and local waterways. As a result, claim local groups, 176 lakes and many rivers have dried up. According to João Pedro Stedile of Brazil's Landless Workers' Movement: 'This used to be one of the best fishing areas in the country but local fisheries have been devastated. 50,000 people in the area used to eat fish every day. Now they eat fish no more.'[15] In response to company claims that its forestry methods are sustainable, a workers' group official said: 'What does Aracruz sustain? It sustains misery, it sustains the degradation of people.'[16]

As for the fishing industry, TNCs control much of the global fish stock, while wielding undue influence over the governments which ought to be regulating them. Pescanova, a Spanish-based corporation, owns one of the world's largest fishing fleets of around 140 trawlers. Pescanova has a network of around 30 companies in 18 developing countries, processes about 20 per cent of the world hake catch, and has 25,000 retail outlets. Courtesy of fishing agreements, companies like Pescanova may fish inside the 200-mile exclusive economic zones of coastal developing countries. One of these nations is Senegal which depends heavily on fish as an earner of foreign exchange to pay interest on its debt. But under an EU-Senegal agreement the livelihoods of 35,000 local fishermen are under threat. Because the EU trawlers deploy large dragnets which scoop up enormous hauls of sole and hake out at sea, there are fewer fish to swim into the 10-kilometre coastal strip which is reserved exclusively for local fishermen, who are then forced into waters further from the coast in unsuitable boats. Occasionally, the large EU trawlers run through the nets and fragile boats of the Senegalese fishermen with devastating loss of life and of fish catches.[17]

Madeley points out that since international agreements are not working to the benefit of the poor, the best option may be to follow the example of Namibia, where foreign trawlers have been regulated at national (i.e. Namibian) level. The rights of foreign fleets to fish in Namibian waters is limited to joint ventures and fish catches must be landed fresh for processing on land (rather than the practice of Europe's boats of freezing and processing catches on board). Namibia's Ministry of Fisheries believes that the policy encourages the right kind of investment, and estimates that 1,500 new jobs a year are being created in the fisheries sector. Madeley concludes, 'Taking action to control the activities of the TNCs has paid off'.[18]

Other industrial activities which directly threaten ecosystems and people's health and livelihoods, particularly in the South, include mining and fossil fuel production. For example, Shell's activities in Nigeria's oil-rich Ogoni region is opposed by the people living there, who have called upon the oil giant to stop 'the ecological war' it has been waging – including oil spills and the wasteful flaring of gas – and to clean up its mess. According to the late Ken Saro-Wiwa, former president of the Movement for the Survival of the Ogoni People (MOSOP) :

> The flaring of gas ... has destroyed wildlife, and plant life, poisoned the atmosphere and the inhabitants in the surrounding areas, and made the residents half-deaf and prone to respiratory diseases. Whenever it's raining in Ogoni, all we have is acid rain which further poisons water courses, streams, creeks and agricultural land. Acid rain gets back into the soil, and what used to be the bread basket of the delta has now become virtually infertile.[19]

Ken Saro-Wiwa, together with eight other members of MOSOP, was hanged by the Nigerian military junta on 10 November 1995, following a trial described by the British government as 'judicial murder'.[20]

British countryside in decline

Just as the loss of biodiversity around the globe has been reliably documented, so has the loss of wildlife and natural landscapes in the UK. In 1990, the Countryside Survey revealed a decade of decline in British animal and plant life.[21] This comprehensive scientific survey – now carried out at 10-year intervals, analogous to the census of the UK's human population – revealed loss of biodiversity in woods, crop fields and semi-natural pastures. The richness and variety of species in hedges, verges and stream banks fell between 1978 and 1990. The Royal Society for the Protection of Birds, the Council for the Protection of Rural England and Friends of the Earth (FoE) were among the environmental and conservation groups calling for urgent government action to halt the decline. According to agricultural expert Graham Harvey, more than 150,000 miles of hedgerow have been lost in England alone since the introduction of farming subsidies. They are still disappearing at the rate of 10,000 miles a year.[22]

Intensive farming, road construction, 'greenfield' house building, and other harmful practices are all to blame. But in the 1990s a number of greener government policies began to take effect, notably in agricultural support where farmers were paid to look after wildlife on their land. One example of such a policy was the use of a grant system that encouraged farmers to leave pesticide-free strips around field edges, thus creating 'conservation headlands'. This allowed wildflowers to make a comeback. Other positive developments included a net increase in the number of ponds and an increase in broadleaved woodland planting, both supporting large and varied amounts of wildlife. Consequently, the most recent national countryside census in 2000 revealed a modicum of good news: the decline of the British countryside appeared to have been halted in a number of areas, although the state of the environment had stabilised 'at a lower level than before'.[23] In the same month, Friends of the Earth warned that we are still 'facing a biodiversity crisis because business interests and intensive farming are being put before positive action for our biodiversity resources'.[24]

Indeed, the overall evidence strongly suggests that the roll call of extinct British species is getting longer and longer. WWF warned of considerable and rapid species loss in a devastating report in 1998 titled *Doomsday for Wildlife*. Using government wildlife figures and extrapolating current trends, WWF warned that the skylark, grey partridge and marsh fritillary (a butterfly) would disappear from the British landscape within 20 years. Other species, such as the high brown fritillary (another butterfly) and the pipistrelle bat may become extinct even sooner. A British bee, the short-haired bumble bee, is almost certainly already extinct. The WWF warned 'that the moves towards extinction are expected to accelerate over the next 20 years, with the effects of climate change, growing development pressures and the continued threat of the European Union's Common Agriculture

Policy' (CAP).[25] Agricultural support is estimated to have cost European consumers £48 billion in 1990, with taxpayers contributing an additional £27 billion. £46 billion was transferred to farmers who then spent much of it on fertilisers, pesticides 'and the general destruction of the countryside'. Graham Harvey concludes: 'In essence the CAP takes cash from the most disadvantaged members of the community and puts it into the pockets of the wealthiest.'[26]

Groups such as WWF and FoE have called upon government to provide added protection for the disappearing habitats which wildlife depends upon. The existing legislation, in particular the 1981 Wildlife and Countryside Act, failed to protect the natural heritage in the face of fierce forces promoting destructive development. This natural heritage includes Britain's 50-year-old network of Sites of Special Scientific Interest (SSSIs), comprising around 6,500 areas of wood-land, meadow, mountain, heathland, bog and river valley that have been designated as important for their flora, fauna or geological features. According to English Nature, 45 per cent of SSSIs are in an 'unfavourable condition' and over 300 of them suffer significant damage in every year.[27] FoE reported that 'bad farming practice has caused over a thousand incidents of damage to over 650 SSSIs, in just six years'.[28]

Green groups have been pushing for tough new wildlife laws to provide proper safeguards for SSSIs. Although Environment Minister Michael Meacher acknowledged the need for greater protection, a government consultation paper, 'SSSIs, Better Protection and Management', was criticised heavily by FoE for failing to tackle the issue of SSSI peatlands being destroyed for profit. According to the pressure group, Britain's largest lowland peatlands – Thorne and Hatfield Moors in South Yorkshire – are still being damaged by Levingtons (a UK company owned by Scotts, a large US corporation), who strip peat from the sites to sell in bags of compost. The consultation paper made no mention of the issue despite the long-running campaign to save these sites, strong feeling from local people, MPs and local authorities, and the view of government wildlife adviser English Nature that peat extraction should end on the sites.[29]

The government later offered a glimmer of hope when it proposed that the four main peatlands suffering from extraction – Thorne Moor and Hatfield Moor in Yorkshire, and Wedholme Flow and Bolton Fell in Cumbria – would become Special Areas of Conservation Interest under the EU Habitats Directive. Changing their classification would give local authorities the power to review and possibly remove the extraction licences for these areas. The bad news, however, is that this process could take as long as a year, and in the meantime the peatlands 'could be mined to virtual extinction'.[30]

One government proposal for protecting SSSIs that few would disagree with is to scrap the present skewed system under which some landowners receive large sums of public money merely to refrain from destroying the landscape. The replacement scheme would instead reward positive conservation work. Sadly, the call by some environmental economists and campaigners to encourage efficient, sustainable land use by introducing a tax on the site-value of land is simply not on New Labour's agenda.[31] Neither is the wider issue of reforming the system of land ownership to ensure environmental protection and social justice for the benefit of local communities, despite heartening examples of community 'buy-outs' in Scotland such as at Knoydart, North Assynt and the island of Eigg. It remains to be seen whether the Scottish Parliament will introduce land reform legislation which truly assists local communities at the risk of upsetting the current crop of wealthy landowners. Given that the social, economic and environmental credentials of New Labour – the senior partner in the Scottish governmental alliance – are patchy, to say the least, there does not appear to be much scope for hope.

Failure of leadership

In March 2000, following immense public pressure, a new countryside and rights of way bill was published. One proposed measure would allow English Nature and the Countryside Council for Wales to refuse permission for activities which threaten SSSIs. Another would ensure that work is undertaken to combat neglect of sites. The bill also provides greater public access to the countryside, despite considerable opposition from many wealthy landowners. While welcoming the new initiative, FoE drew attention to the government's 'flagging environmental reputation' and vowed to maintain pressure on the government to strengthen the bill's measures for protecting wildlife sites.[32] Such pressure had some success. A later amendment provided a lifeline to threatened species such as the red squirrel, water vole and early gentian. Moreover, a new section was introduced before the bill became law which would make 'all Government departments play their part in biodiversity conservation'.[33]

It remains to be seen whether such a fine objective will be attained. The fact is that Labour has failed to live up even to the modest promise of its 1994 environmental manifesto, *In Trust for Tomorrow*. A prime example is the poor performance of the Environment Agency (EA) – the 'pollution watchdog' in England and Wales.[34] In a scathing report published in May 2000, the all-party House of Commons environment committee found that the EA had failed to meet its statutory duty to protect the public and the countryside from pollution. The report castigated the agency for its 'failure of leadership' and lack of a 'cogent ethos and strategy'.[35]

In its first year of operation, the largest fine imposed by the courts for a case brought by the EA was only £175,000. The culprit was wealthy Severn Trent

Water which had polluted a Welsh river, killing 35,000 fish – its forty-second pollution offence since privatisation in 1989. Even the agency's chief executive, Ed Gallagher, admitted the puny nature of the punishment, pointing out that the court's imposition of the penalty was 'the equivalent of a £15 fine on someone earning £30,000 a year'.[36] The 'polluter pays' principle was clearly being diluted to the point of ridicule. Campaigning groups deplored the 'cosy relationship' shared by the agency and industry, which had led to the EA's apparent reluctance to come down hard on business for clear misdemeanours. The following year, Gallagher admitted that the 'going rate' for fines for chemical pollutants averaged just £2,000 per tonne of pollution. Meanwhile, Lord De Ramsey, then chairman of the agency and former head of the Country Landowners' Association, came under attack for selling some of his farmland for housing and allowing the testing, on other parts of his land, of genetically modified crops.[37]

In March 1999, when the EA released its latest 'league table' of Britain's worst polluting companies, some of the usual suspects made an appearance: ICI Chemicals, Shell UK and British Nuclear Fuels. ICI topped the list mainly because of a £300,000 fine imposed on it for a single incident of polluting ground water with almost 150 tonnes of chloroform in April 1997. However, the average fine for an offence was under £2,800 and the agency called for the courts to impose much larger penalties. Moreover, the agency has claimed that it is unable to pursue many cases of industrial pollution because it is hampered by limited resources of staff and funding. This is surely an indication of the lack of governmental resolve to tackle polluting industry. How else are we to understand the following episode?

In November 1998, the EA brought a court case against Petrus Oil, a small oil company. The dispute centred on oil company pipes which agency officials had visited on a number of occasions to investigate complaints of foul smells coming from the plant. However, when the agency launched a belated attempt to prosecute the firm, a judge threw out the case saying that the agency had taken so long to initiate the claim that they had effectively 'acquiesced' in the pipe's existence! At one stage, the agency even faced the humiliating prospect of having to pay Petrus Oil £155,000. At the time of writing, the dispute has become subject to a public enquiry. This inept and farcical episode seems a tragically apt symbol of the government's role in environmental 'protection'.

Perhaps one of the most outlandish proposals to use land by a private company in recent years was the reported scheme to store nuclear waste in one of the most scenic and unspoilt parts of Britain. In October 1998, Omega Pacific – even the name suggests the company's globalised nature – announced that it was considering using underground tunnels in a secluded valley in west Wales to store intermediate and low grade waste for an 'unnamed third party'.[38] Such secretive dealings highlight the urgent need for new legislation 'which would give people information on all health-threatening pollution in their area'.[39] The Access to Environmental Information Bill – modelled on existing legislation in the United States – is being promoted by FoE to cover releases from all factories (not just the large factories which are obliged to report to the Environment Agency), rubbish dumps, traffic and 'other pollution sources'. Although FoE's campaign focuses on factory emissions, it is clear that 'other pollution sources' ought to include nuclear dumps.

Genuine environmental protection and the need for democratic renewal are intimately entwined, and increasingly recognised as such even by mainstream institutions. The European Commission wishes to enshrine the 'right to a healthy environment, and the duty to ensure it' in the provisions of the Treaty of Union. The European Parliament also wants the 'right to know' written into the treaty 'to ensure openness in the political process and institutions of the European Union'. At the UN, negotiation on an Economic Commission for Europe Convention has addressed the question of access to environmental information. However, the idea of a fundamental right 'to live in a healthy environment' raised by Belgium was opposed by three countries, including the UK.[40] With British government opposition to such an elementary principle, there is clearly some way to go in ensuring basic environmental rights for all citizens – rights which would protect local communities against the type of damaging proposed large-scale development that we will encounter in the case study below.

A bay too far: when globalisation really hits home

The modern-day story of Southampton's docks encapsulates the ever-increasing conflict between the corporate demand for economic growth on the one hand, and environmental protection coupled with people's quality of life on the other.

Associated British Ports, the large company which operates many of the ports around Britain's coastline, regards Southampton as the 'jewel in the crown', ripe for expansion to cater for the new breed of large container ships which criss-cross the world's oceans. Half of the UK's trade with the Far East goes through Southampton. In 1998, the docks handled 850,000 container units and more than 35 million tonnes of cargo. Over 500,000 new cars pass over the quayside every year – around 70 per cent of them for export. The port's position as number one in cruise shipping was assured in 1997 with the renewal of contracts with cruise companies Cunard and P&O. Andrew Kent, ABP's regional manager, said: 'The port continues to thrive and we are very excited about future expansion.'[41]

An important plank in this major expansion is an ambitious proposal to build a huge new container terminal. The terminal would be built just outside the city of Southampton in the so-called 'Waterside area' at Dibden Bay, opposite the current port. The Waterside area lies between the New Forest and Southampton Water. Dibden Bay is a 'strategic gap' between the settlements of Hythe and Marchwood. It provides an open vista from Southampton, a wildlife corridor to the New Forest from the Waterside, and one of the few remaining undeveloped areas on Southampton Water.

Dibden Bay's 240 hectares of open grazing marsh and mudflats form part of an internationally important wildlife haven notable for its diversity and number of birds. The bay forms part of the Solent and Southampton Water Special Protection Area (SPA) under the European Union Birds Directive, and is a Wetland of International Importance under the Ramsar Convention. Hythe to Calshot Marshes, which includes the bay, has been declared a Site of Special Scientific Interest (SSSI) because it includes extensive areas of saltmarsh and mudflats, supports a high number of rare grasses, and provides feeding and roosting sites for migratory and over-wintering waders and other birds. More than 1 per cent of the global population of dark-bellied Brent geese frequent the area, as well as large numbers of teal, widgeon, ringed plover, black-tailed godwit and many other birds. The grassland behind the shore is not part of the SPA or the SSSI, but does support rare plants, insects and wintering birds, and is a local authority-designated Site of Importance for Nature Conservation. The multitude of designations for environmental protection does not end there. Part of the site is also included in the candidate Solent and Isle of Wight Maritime Special Area of Conservation under the EU Habitats Directive.[42] The container terminal would adjoin the New Forest, one of the most important heathlands in the UK and home to many rare plants, birds and animals. The area is of international significance for its woodlarks, Dartford warblers and nightjars. The New Forest, once William the Conqueror's hunting preserve and now one of England's biggest tourist attractions, was even shortlisted by the British government for consideration as a World Heritage site.

In the summer of 1997, ABP unveiled their ambitious plans for Southampton port expansion at the first meeting of the Dibden Forum, a carefully selected audience supposedly 'representing local community, environmental and business interests'. The total area proposed for development is 325 hectares (ha), including over 2 kilometres of quayside, 150 ha of hardstanding for containers, 50 ha for a rail marshalling yard with 12 tracks, 40 ha of support services and administration, and 90 ha of intertidal and seabed dredging. The construction phase would last 10 years and, when complete, would involve 24-hours-a-day, 365-days-per-year operation (including continuous noise and light pollution), 6,100 vehicle movements per day, an estimated 52 per cent increase on 1995 traffic flows on local roads by 2011, increased contamination and pollution from spills and leaks, and total loss of foreshore mudflats, grazing marsh and the strategic gap between Southampton and neighbouring communities on the western side.

Despite all of this, ABP promised that port expansion offered 'real environmental improvements'.[43] In an interview and 2-page spread putting forward ABP's case in the local newspaper, Captain Jimmy Chestnutt, ABP's deputy port manager in Southampton, explained: 'We intend to build ... a specially created tidal creek which will be a great addition to the environment and replace bird feeding grounds, at present being eroded, with new ones.' He continued, 'The port [authority] has put environmental responsibilities at the heart of its proposals'.[44] On the other hand, the Royal Society for the Protection of Birds which, along with English Nature, had been consulted by ABP, were not convinced that ABP would 'improve' the environment, having already warned that the piecemeal planning approach to port expansion represented 'the very real risk of death by a thousand cuts for the wildlife sites'.[45] According to RSPB senior conservation officer Chris Corrigan, 'Changing the mud flats is still a very new science and we do not know if it will work'.[46] Indeed, a similar case at Felixstowe, where a new wildlife site was created, did not provide a home for the same types of birds.[47]

A major focus of concern for local residents would be the inevitable increase in port-related traffic congestion and pollution. ABP admit that two-thirds of containers would come by road or rail rather than via sea routes, the preferred government option. Port access to Dibden Bay would increase pressure on the local trunk road which is already snarled-up at peak times. As a sweetener, ABP offered at one stage to contribute to Hampshire County Council's existing plans to upgrade the road, although this offer now appears to have been quietly dropped. It remains an open question how the council will square Dibden Bay development with its obligations under the Road Traffic Reduction Act (Local Targets), which requires local authorities to limit – then reverse – the growth in local road traffic levels. ABP responded: 'We've studied the traffic implications for five years and we're proposing light rail developments and other environmentally sensitive solutions.'[48]

Environmental concerns for Dibden Bay and the surrounding area may ultimately be outweighed by the alleged dependence of the regional – and national – economy on Southampton's port. ABP claimed: 'The continuing success of the Port of Southampton means we're nearing the time when Dibden Bay will be needed to support the growth in the UK's international trade'. Company management contended on the basis of 'independent economic studies' that 'more than 10,000 jobs are directly related to port business' and that the new port 'would create 3,000 new jobs for Hampshire'. [49]

According to Paul Vickers, chairman of the local residents' group, which opposes port expansion, the figure of 10,000 jobs related to the port is 'misleading'. Half that number relates to local employers operating within the port authority area – such as Esso, shipbuilding company Vospers and the military port. The remaining 5,000 jobs in the port itself 'include car workers, Martini factory workers, car component, cruise, grain and fruit workers. None of these have any relation to the container port.' Vickers added, 'We have it in a letter from P&O that the Southampton Container Terminal supports only 500 full-time jobs.'[50] As for the 3000 new jobs allegedly on offer, Vickers pointed out that over one-third of these would be one-off construction jobs. As for the rest, 'The number of new full time jobs could be debated endlessly'.[51] In fact, the spectre of increasing port automation and increasing efficiency in port operations loomed large, casting doubt on the large numbers of jobs ABP offered. Ironically, at around the same time, ABP quietly announced 150 company job losses at their other ports around the country. The insecurity of dock-related employment, and the extent to which workers' rights will be trampled upon when corporate profit is threatened, has been amply demonstrated by the story of the Liverpool dockers as documented, for example, by John Pilger in *Hidden Agendas*.[52]

ABP argues that without the Dibden Bay scheme, the port of Southampton will decline and jobs will be lost. International trade would bypass the city and the UK as a whole. 'If container vessels were forced into [mainland] European ports,' say ABP, 'the extra cost of shipping would result in increased prices in the high street and more expensive exports. Current trade may be taken away, and jobs, too.'[53] ABP wishes to see Southampton develop as a 'hub port', receiving cargo from deep sea ships for onward shipment on feeder vessels to a number of smaller ports. The local residents' group has researched ABP's stated aim towards increased trans-shipment and remains sceptical: '75-80 per cent of the containers on ships entering or leaving the English Channel are related to mainland Europe because of its larger economy, and consequently more than one call is made at Continental ports. It is illogical to believe that containers are going to be landed in Southampton for shipment across to the Continent.'[54]

ABP is supported in its plans for Dibden Bay port development by Southampton's Labour-led city council and the city's Labour MPs, but not by the politicians who represent the people in and around the New Forest and the Waterside area; in other words, the communities most likely to be directly affected by port expansion. Local residents, who have amassed a wealth of factually-based arguments opposing ABP's position, question the need for expansion when the company had until recently been selling and leasing much of their land. There are suspicions that ABP would like to shift some of its existing port activity to Dibden Bay, freeing up land elsewhere to sell to property developers, as it has done in the past, and as it is now proposing to do again.[55] A spokesman for ABP responded: 'Some years ago our parent company sold some land for development that was not suitable for port use. The port is busier than ever now. Everything we have is being used as intensively as possible. We urgently need more land.'[56] But there is evidence that Southampton's port is being used inefficiently. Dr Caroline Lucas, Green MEP for the south-east, wrote to Margot Wallström, the European Commissioner for the Environment, asking her to intervene to protect Dibden Bay because of its EU-protected status, and enclosed industry figures showing that 'the existing port is being used at a level of efficiency far below that which is normal for the industry'.[57] Local campaigners also point out that there is sufficient spare capacity at alternative locations in the UK: 'Felixstowe and Thamesport both have spare capacity available or coming on stream, equivalent to Southampton's current throughput.'[58] The possibility of developing an alternative location at the former Shell Haven refinery site within the Port of London was summarily rejected by ABP's group chief executive when it was suggested by Dr Julian Lewis, a Conservative New Forest MP. The battle lines appear to have been set for a long drawn-out public enquiry starting in autumn 2001.

ABP's argument that port expansion has to go ahead on the edge of the New Forest is one which local residents are in a strong position to counter. Slowly but surely, people are becoming aware that economic globalisation is not an abstract phenomenon, but is a process which hits home if left unchecked. The heartening news is that people are prepared to learn about the issues, to see that preservation of biodiversity, local communities and quality of life are interdependent, and to defend these interests with vigour and, one hopes, some success.

Farming a dying countryside

One of the principal threats to biodiversity is the industrialisation of agriculture, often resulting in landscapes covered with sweeping monocultures of chemically-intensive crop production. This has devastating effects on wildlife. Graham Harvey directly links these effects with economic globalisation: 'Are we really prepared to strip away what's left of our hedges and woods, our wild birds and mammals, in order that a handful of farming companies can sell their wheat to China as cheaply as Kansas or Manitoba can?'.[59]

As well as a ravaged countryside, another defining feature of modern farming methods, according to campaigning group Compassion in World Farming (CIWF), is 'intensive husbandry systems [which] frustrate animals' behavioural needs and often lead to serious physical disorders and pain'.[60] For example, battery-farm chickens are typically kept five to a cage, unable to walk around, build a nest or even spread their wings. They often suffer broken bones in the cramped conditions. Pig rearing is little better: most pigs never see the light of day nor have access to fresh air, and are packed together in barren, concrete-floored pens.

One of the most distressing examples of cruelty to farm animals is the selective breeding for faster or larger growth, which 'has led to painful leg problems in chickens and degenerative hip disorders in turkeys and to cows carrying such huge udders that their back legs are forced outwards, causing lameness'. According to John Webster, Professor of Animal Husbandry at the University of Bristol, 'the chronic pain suffered by millions of broiler chickens [reared for their meat] must constitute the most severe example of man's inhumanity to another sentient creature'. CIWF summarises with an understatement: 'It is difficult to give general approval to any system of husbandry that relies on painful mutilations to sustain the system'. [61]

The large-scale inhumane treatment of farm animals, and the increasing loss of wildlife and countryside, is at odds with some farmers' oft-repeated claim to be 'stewards of the countryside'. However, the farmer is often a victim of enormous pressures to be 'competitive' in an increasingly globalised economy (although many farmers do not see it that way and are, in fact, enthusiastic about globalisation). The result is often lower environmental standards and more chemical inputs into the land.[62] Bankruptcies and suicides are alarmingly high in agricultural communities. Moreover, countryside workers sometimes fall prey to the chemical products that they use. A report sponsored by the British government found that nearly a fifth of Britain's sheep farmers may have suffered nerve damage from using highly toxic sheep dips.[63]

In September 1998, the National Farmers' Union in the UK released a report, *Landscape in Peril*, which indicated that financial hardship in the lowland farming industry was actually putting the British countryside and wildlife at risk. Farmers of lowland cattle and sheep had such reduced incomes that 'they could no longer afford basic environmental management, such as hedge maintenance and tree-planting. Some were going out of business, and grassland that needed grazing to keep its wildlife value was being abandoned, while others were under extreme pressure to plough up grassland and plant crops'.[64] The NFU report was backed by English Nature, the RSPB and the Wildlife Trusts.[65]

Many threats to British biodiversity are a direct result of globalisation impinging on the domestic agricultural sector. This may even worsen if agricultural markets are forced open in ongoing negotiations at the World Trade Organisation. The pressure for British agricultural products to compete in world markets has already led to unsustainable, intensive and unecological practices. The BSE-afflicted beef industry, followed by a massive outbreak of foot and mouth disease, have been the highest profile cases to date. We consider, in particular, the 'madness' of BSE, in which the 'British government betrayed the British people', in more detail below.[66] Suffice it to say here that the British beef industry, heavily dependent on international sales, suffered crippling losses when a beef export ban was imposed by the EU in March 1996. The ban was formally lifted in July 1999, after British exporters had lost £1 billion and UK taxpayers had shelled out £3 billion.

Locking agriculture into the international trading system has exacerbated farmers' vulnerability to changes in interest rates and the value of sterling – weaknesses endemic not just in the farming industry but in many others in today's globally integrated economy. On 28 August, 1998, *The Independent* had a cover story with a headline that said it all: 'Farming hit by worst crisis since the Thirties'. According to the report, 'an unprecedented coming together of adverse economic factors' – such as the rise in the value of the pound and the collapse of the Russian economy – meant that for almost every agricultural commodity, the price farmers were receiving for their product was less than the cost of its production. The main exception was wheat, which was still in profit thanks to EU subsidies. The effect of the 'adverse economic factors' on farm animals was severe. Livestock farmers, the hardest hit of all, found that because of market collapses and the end of government subsidies, they were left with a million ewes and 600,000 dairy calves – unwanted by the market and therefore with no value. Rather than pay slaughterhouses to dispose of them, some farmers abandoned livestock in public places or with animal charities.[67]

Nick Brown, the Minister of Agriculture, responded uneasily to the depth of the crisis by saying that there was no 'easy solution' and 'that there was a limit to what the Government could do': an unsurprising position for a minister in a government which is confusingly both enthusiastic and fatalistic about economic globalisation.[68] At the same time, notwithstanding passing references to 'market collapses' and 'adverse economic factors', there was a gaping hole in the media debate on the agricultural crisis – namely, its systemic roots in the drive for increasing globalisation. Closely tied to the agriculture industry is the food industry – which is one sector where consumers can really exert their collective muscle in the resistance to corporate takeover.

Mounting food scares

Industry's unhealthily close relationship with government has rarely been exposed in such an obvious manner as at the Labour Party annual conference in the autumn of 1998. Big business money pervaded the event, right down to the delegate badges sponsored by the supermarket Somerfields. But the corporate hold on the business of government really came to the fore when the food company Nestlé – which had a stall at the conference – asked the organisers to rip down posters which cast its baby milk policy in a bad light.[69] The posters depicted an Indian woman nursing twins, one of whom was bottle fed and later died of gastroenteritis. The children's organisation Unicef and the pressure group

Baby Milk Action had wanted to draw attention to Nestlé's massive promotion of its baby products in the Third World, which had bullied mothers away from breast feeding and into bottle feeding. However, Nestlé claimed the poster 'broke conference rules about displaying publicity in appropriate areas' and conference organisers caved in and removed the offending material.

While the above incident may be of little import in itself, it is symptomatic of the collapse of the traditional role of government as defenders of public health and food safety. In recent years there has been an alarming succession of food scares, which has gone hand in hand with the increasing intensification of agriculture. One of the first major food scares to impact on the British consumer in modern times was when Edwina Currie, then a junior health minister, stated candidly and correctly in December 1988 that most eggs produced in the country were infected with salmonella – an announcement which led ultimately to her political demise. Next, ready-cooked poultry and soft cheeses were found to be the source of a listeria outbreak in 1989. Then it was botulism lurking in yoghurt. After that, in 1993, high levels of the naturally-occurring toxin patulin were found in apple juice. Two years later, the government warned shoppers to peel carrots before eating them because of the discovery of high levels of organophosphates arising from chemical agriculture.

In May 1996, parents were horrified when leading brands of baby milk were found to contain phthalates, so-called hormone-disrupting 'gender bender' chemicals, although the European Commission later claimed that 'there was no danger to babies'. Then a major outbreak of E. coli 157 occurred when a butcher in the Scottish town of Wishaw supplied contaminated meat for a party, leading to the deaths of 20 mostly elderly people. The government ordered an inquiry which led belatedly to the setting up of a Food Standards Agency.

But the largest food scare in the UK has been over beef, in particular the link between bovine spongiform encephalopathy (BSE) in cattle and variant Creutzfeldt-Jakob disease (vCJD) in humans. The BSE epidemic occurred as a result of intensive farming practices, specifically the recycling of animal protein in meat and bonemeal for cattle feed. In other words, the remains of individual diseased cattle were recycled as feed for healthy animals. People later caught vCJD from eating infected beef. The high incidence of young victims has been linked to eating beefburgers. In 1990, John Gummer, then Minister of Agriculture, displayed his support for the British beef industry when he infamously fed his 6-year-old daughter a beefburger at an agricultural fair in front of an assembled throng of press photographers.

A £16m enquiry, chaired by Lord Phillips, concluded in October 2000 that 'the public were misled with constant government reassurances over the safety of beef despite growing fears that public health was in danger'. More than 80 people have died to date, almost all of them young. The Phillips report criticised 26 ministers, civil servants and advisers for their poor handling – in fact worsening – of the crisis. As *The Independent* put it: a 'catalogue of errors and misjudgements occurred in practically every sphere of government that dealt with the [BSE] crisis'.[70]

BSE was first investigated by government veterinary scientists in 1985 following reports of a strange new disease in cattle on dairy farms. There was an embargo on passing information in the first six months after the BSE epidemic was identified and it was not until 1988 before the government set up a working party to examine the epidemic. The working party eventually recommended the compulsory slaughter and incineration or burial of cattle showing disease symptoms. By 1993, there were 100,000 confirmed cases of BSE-infected cattle. In 1994, a number of teenagers fell ill, apparently from vCJD, with the Conservative government denying any link to BSE. In 1995, 19-year-old Stephen Churchill died – the first-known victim of vCJD. There were two other known deaths from the disease that year. Finally, on 20 March, 1996, Stephen Dorrell, then Secretary of State for Health, publicly admitted that, after all, there most probably *was* a link between BSE and vCJD. As a result, the EU banned British beef – a £500 million industry – and, shortly after Labour came to power in 1997, Jack Cunningham, the new Minister of Agriculture, banned the sale of beef on the bone.

As Britain battled within the EU to have the ban on British beef exports lifted, there came yet another twist in the BSE scandal. Scientists highlighted the risk of BSE occurring not just in cows, but in sheep. Professor Jeffrey Almond, a member of the government's Spongiform Encephalopathy Advisory Committee (Seac) warned on BBC Radio 4's *Farming Today* that 'BSE-infected material was fed to sheep in the 1980s; that it is possible to transmit BSE to sheep experimentally; and that BSE may go undetected in sheep because its symptoms are similar to scrapie, a natural disease of sheep'.[71]

The Labour government reacted to this latest food scare by undertaking a rebuttal campaign in which government press officers were issued with a set of questions and answers, and instructions not to deviate from it when fielding any press enquiries. The central question of whether 'the national flock' had actually been infected with BSE went unanswered. Seac had already recommended the removal of sheep brains from the human food chain in 1996, followed by bans on spinal cords, spleen and mechanically recovered sheep meat in 1997. But detecting BSE in animals is difficult because there is no simple test for it. In the case of sheep, it is doubly difficult because of its similarity to scrapie. By September 1998, only nine sheep in the national flock of 20 million had been tested and found to be clear of BSE. As Professor Almond said, 'Having found zero out of nine, what confidence can we attach to the statement "BSE is not present in sheep"? The answer is "very little"'.[72] The Phillips report concluded that we may never know for certain how and why BSE first appeared. Only time will tell what the final human toll will be, but it will 'probably be in the hundreds'.[73]

Food scares have now become such a common feature of today's industrial economies that there is paradoxically a risk of complacency; the consumer is in danger of switching off with every new warning. But still the food scares come along. In November 1998, routine tests on supermarket cans of tomatoes revealed dangerously high levels of tin. Affected batches were removed from shelves and customers who might have bought contaminated cans were urged to contact their retailer. This prompted Jeff Rooker, the UK Food Safety Minister, to praise the food industry for taking a 'responsible attitude'.[74] Early in the summer of 1999 came news that cancer-causing dioxin had entered the food chain through the use of contaminated animal feed by Belgian farmers. It turned out that the Belgian government had sat on the problem for two months before informing consumers.

Meanwhile, the British government was setting up its new 'independent' Food Standards Agency, which it promised would lead to tighter controls on food safety and greater openness about food production. The new agency reports to the Department of Health rather than the Ministry of Agriculture, Fisheries and Food, which had been seen as placing the interests of the food industry above those of consumers. Initially, a levy of £90 was going to be imposed on every restaurant, supermarket and shop, regardless of size or turnover, to help finance the new agency. But vehement protests from small businesses forced a government retreat and a banded system was proposed instead, involving escalating charges according to floor space. Professor Sir John Krebs, former head of the Natural Environment Research Council, was appointed to head the FSA with a £96,000 annual salary and a four-day week. While at NERC, Krebs had undertaken a study of badgers that had led to a controversial government cull to see whether the animals spread TB to cattle. As an academic with no experience of the consumer world or food industry, Krebs' selection as FSA chief was greeted with dismay by critics. The Consumers' Association said that the government should have appointed a 'strong, credible, consumer chair'. Tim Lang, professor of food policy at Thames Valley University, called Krebs' appointment 'bizarre'.[75]

One crisis after another

In 2001, Britain was in the midst of yet another agricultural nightmare. A widespread outbreak of foot and mouth disease amongst livestock led to the slaughter of more than two million animals. Carcasses were incinerated in giant pyres or dumped in mass graves. Many areas of countryside were declared out of bounds in a desperate attempt to contain the spread of the disease. Consequent losses to the tourist industry were predicted to top £5bn. There was little evidence that the government was in control of the situation – indeed, indecision, delays and inefficiency were in abundance. With foot and mouth disease predicted by epidemiologists to peak in early May, Tony Blair decided to delay elections which had been set for May 3.

Although it was not clear at that stage what the original source of the outbreak was, it was certainly clear that long-distance transportation of live animals had contributed to the rapid spread of the disease. Having first been identified in the UK, the disease spread to other European countries and led to a ban on all meat and animal exports from the UK. Caroline Lucas, a British Green MEP, warned in a Green Party press release on 3 March 2001: 'Globalisation, the free-market, increased trade and unsustainable food production methods have caused problems like this to be far more widespread than they should be. Agriculture is now organised in a way that makes transmission of the disease very easy now that we have a global food distribution system'.

As the Greens have pointed out, the transport of live animals over long distances is cruel, unnecessary and ought to be banned. Food should be consumed much closer to where it is produced, decreasing the spread of infection and also reducing lorry traffic on the roads.

Dr Lucas added, 'The big supermarkets, who control much of the food business, are constantly demanding cheaper produce. But this leads to corners being cut, as we have seen with BSE and now again with foot and mouth. Our food must be produced in a much more sustainable way'.

Foot and mouth, just like BSE before it, demonstrated that we should end industrial agriculture. Instead, agriculture needs local, sustainable solutions based on the needs of farmers, consumers and the environment, rather than big business and further globalisation.

Going organic

Until the BSE scandal shook the country, the official British government line appeared to have been that all food scares have been the result of a lack of consumer information, and resultant deepening suspicion of officialdom. However, Sheila McKechnie, director of the Consumers' Association, poured scorn on the notion that the more we know about how our food is produced, the more reassured we will be. On the contrary, as consumers learn more about the way animals are factory-farmed and slaughtered before ending up on the dinner plate, and about the increasing technological and chemical input into agriculture, the more likely they are to demand healthy alternatives. According to McKechnie, the 'food industry has an unshakeable belief in whizz-bang techniques to conjure up the impossible – food that is safe and nutritious but also cheap enough to beat the global competition'. But consumers are justifiably sceptical of 'technical solutions'. Instead, 'the evidence is that we want less, not more, technological input. This is what's driving demand for organic food and why it is currently outstripping supply'.[76]

Peter Segger, an ardent proponent of organic agriculture in the UK, suggested in 1997 that organic growth rates could exceed 30 per cent in many countries, taking total turnover from $11 billion to around $100 billion by the year 2006. Organic produce could capture more than 15 per cent of the market in some countries.[77] In Austria, 18,000 farmers converted to organic agriculture in just four years, involving 10 per cent of total farmland. Germany, Denmark, Sweden and the Netherlands have also witnessed an expansion in organic farming, with government assistance.

The British organic market was worth around £260 million annually in 1998, double what it was in 1995. In 2000, it was predicted that annual organic sales would reach £546m and that annual sales would exceed £1bn by 2002.[78] But, astonishingly, Britain is still importing a huge 70 per cent of the organic produce sold, some from as far afield as Israel. The domestic organic movement is at risk of stalling. A major stumbling block is the higher prices of its products, at an average of 70 per cent more than those of 'conventional' products which have been kept artificially low by massive EU subsidies, courtesy of the countryside-crippling Common Agricultural Policy. Of the UK's 150,000 farms, just 0.5 per cent are organic. In early 1998, the government attempted to kickstart renewed growth in farm conversions by increasing its Organic Aid Scheme by 80 per cent – a rise that still kept support below the EU average.[79] The large supermarkets – with an eye to consumer trends – increased lines of expensive organic produce on their shelves. One year later, continued pressure on the UK government led it to release an extra £6 million in grants to assist conversion to organic farming, offering up to £450 a hectare over 5 years. Nick Brown, the Agriculture Minister, proclaimed the initiative to be a sign of the government's 'serious commitment' to pesticide-free farming. But the Soil Association, promoters of organic agriculture and administrators of the scheme, pointed out that the money would only be just enough to help the backlog of farmers already waiting to convert, and that it would do little to put more organic produce on shop shelves: 'the government is so out of touch ... we could have predicted the inadequacy of the budget.'[80]

At the end of 1999, Nick Brown announced yet another package, this time promising that an average of £230 million a year would be allocated for the following seven years to be spent on protecting landscapes and wildlife, and encouraging farmers to diversify land use and convert to organic agriculture. While welcoming a trebling of the budget for environmental protection, green activist and *Guardian* columnist George Monbiot warned that under the scheme small farms would not receive their fair share. The amount proposed was just a fraction of the sum of money spent subsidising damaging agricultural practices promoted by the European Union's CAP: 'The British taxpayer will now be spending £230 million a year on protecting the farm environment, and some £5bn on destroying it.' Even after Brown's latest offer of support, the money allocated to organic farming is just one-seventh of the subsidy required to achieve the Soil Association's modest target of 30 per cent organic production by 2010. As Monbiot warned, 'Most alarmingly, the whole package still relies on the big farmers' repeatedly broken promise of self-regulation. There is nothing to prevent a landowner from destroying a habitat the taxpayer has spent a fortune to restore, the moment the price of sugar beet rises'.[81]

A genuine boost to environmental sustainability has been the large increase in Soil Association-promoted vegetable box schemes and in farmers' markets. Both of these link growers and shoppers in local regions, thereby cutting the long-distance transportation of goods and promoting local economies. A good example is the pilot scheme in Bath which typically sees 40 sellers and 4,000 customers at city centre Saturday markets.[82] Trade is restricted to producers based within a 30-40 mile radius. Similar markets are planned, or are already operating, in Canterbury, Huddersfield, Glastonbury, Oxford and Salisbury. In the United States, 2,000 new farmers' markets have been set up in cities, run by growers in the urban fringes of New York, Chicago, Washington and San Francisco. According to author and filmmaker Herbert Girardet, a requirement for a 'sustainable city' is reduced dependence on imported food and more urban food growing. In the UK today, there are hundreds of thousands of allotments being used for growing vegetables. Girardet makes an impassioned and cogent plea for urban planners and administrators to overturn their prejudices about such sites being 'messy' and instead actively promote allotments while protecting them from destructive building development.[83]

In the UK, box schemes have grown from just two in 1992 to over 400 in 1997, supplying over 50,000 households a week with fresh, healthy produce. Most schemes are certified organic and most are working at full capacity – there are simply not enough schemes to keep up with the huge demand. Customers like the fact that they know where their food is coming from, and that they are supporting local producers. New partnerships are also being forged between growers and consumers in schemes known as community-supported agriculture (CSA). In CSA, locals give a farmer interest-free capital, sharing the risks as well as the seasonal produce of the agricultural enterprise. Scheme members often get to know the farmer, as well as each other, and have an enhanced interest and a direct role in how the food on their plates is produced, sometimes to the extent of actually helping out on the farm, particularly at harvest time.[84]

Lifting the lid on corporate food

Despite such promising signs of genuine sustainability, the viability of local-scale food initiatives is under severe threat from the stranglehold of corporate food manufacturers, large supermarkets and fast food chains such as McDonald's. But just occasionally, things do not go the way the corporate giants would like. After the longest-running trial in English legal history, a High Court judge ruled in June 1997 that two anarchist campaigners, Helen Steel and Dave Morris, were correct to state in a controversial leaflet that McDonald's paid their employees low wages, were responsible for cruelty to some animals and exploited children in their advertising.

Although the judge in the 'McLibel Trial' declared that other statements made in the anarchists' leaflet were false – such as McDonald's being responsible for starvation in the Third World and destruction of rainforests – the trial was a dreadful loss of face for McDonald's, whose corporate practices had been prised open to unprecedented public scrutiny. The company had to pay £10 million in costs for this scrutiny that had inflicted immense harm on their cosy, family-friendly image. Although the multinational giant was awarded £60,000 damages against Steel and Morris, it seemed reluctant to pursue the two defendants for payment. Two years later, when an appeal judge reduced the cost of damages to £40,000, the judge upheld additional accusations by Morris and Steel that a diet of McDonald's products was linked to a risk of heart disease and that McDonald's employees 'do badly in terms of pay and conditions'.[85] The fast-food giant was further embarrassed in a separate development when it was revealed that child labourers in China worked from 7am to midnight, packaging cuddly toys sold with McDonald's meals in Hong Kong.[86]

The McLibel case was an important event, not merely because of the media hype it generated, or the books, videos and TV dramatisation on Channel 4. As columnist Suzanne Moore explained:

> The McLibel trial illustrated what capitalism is actually like, its ruthlessness, its efficiency, its ability to transform itself. Words like capitalism and glob-alisation conjure images of giant machines that can never be stopped, that go on working whoever is in charge, that endlessly regenerate themselves. The McLibel Two reminded me of something else altogether – the power of human agency, the ability of little people to jam up the works, to sabo-tage the bosses, to just say no.[87]

It is not just in the fast-food industry where there is a corporate stranglehold; even basic foodstuffs are made available to us courtesy of a diminishing number of giant businesses. Today, just five transnational corporations in each food industry control 90 per cent of the world exports of corn, wheat, coffee, tea and pineapples.[88] Given that we all have to eat, it may well be that the food industry will be one of the first economic sectors to feel a sustained citizens' backlash against corporate might. The spotlight of public interest cannot be far off: What kind of life is led by the farmers – or peasants – who produce the food that ends up on my plate? What happened to the land it came from? How much chemical input was required? What are the social and environmental impacts of transporting the products such great distances around the world? Why are the products not available locally and from an organic source? Even asking such questions reveals the unsustainable, deeply unjust way in which food is produced, distributed and sold. The crux of the matter that civil society still has to grasp is that not only can 'little people' say no to economic globalisation, but that they can go further and say yes to a more sustainable future, by wresting control back from the corporations, institutions and politicians who have surreptitiously usurped it. As the next chapter demonstrates, the public have already rebelled against the corporate force-feeding of consumers with genetically modified foods.

Notes

1   Wendell Berry, US writer and farmer, from the essay 'Preserving Wildness', in *Standing on Earth*, p. 218.

2   Herbert Read (1893-1968), British poet, critic and anarchist, cited by Howard Zinn in *The Zinn Reader*, p. 654.

3   Lon, *Living Planet Report 1998*.

4   As the report explains: 'Plantations, which make up large tracts of current forest area, neither support the same levels of biodiversity nor perform the same ecological functions as old-growth forest.'

5   *The Guardian*, 20 January, 2001.

6   Quoted in Lon, *Living Planet Report 1998*, p. 6.

7   *Ibid*, p. 8.

8   *The Independent*, 18 November, 2000.

9   Gore, *Earth in the Balance*, pp. 295-360.

10 Report at http://ens.lycos.com/ens/aug99/1999L-08-02-06.html

11 Madeley, *Big Business, Poor Peoples*, p. 71.

12 *The Guardian*, 11 August, 1999.

13 Quoted in Madeley, *Big Business, Poor Peoples*, p. 73.

14 Quoted in *ibid*, p. 74.

15 Quoted in *ibid*, p. 76.

16 Quoted in *ibid*, p. 77.

17 Quoted in *ibid*, p. 83.

18 *Ibid*, p. 86.

19 Quoted in *ibid.*, p. 122.

20 Quoted in Rowell, *Green Backlash*, p. 1.

21 *The Independent*, 18 November, 1993.

22 Harvey, *The Killing of the Countryside*, p. 7.

23 *The Independent,* 30 November 2000.

24 Friends of the Earth press release, 22 November, 2000.

25   *The Independent,* 14 December 1998.
26   Harvey, *The Killing of the Countryside,* p. 13.
27   Personal communication from Matt Phillips, senior wildlife campaigner, Friends of the Earth, 3 August, 1999.
28   Friends of the Earth press release, 21 February, 2000.
29   Friends of the Earth press release, 21 December, 1998.
30   SchNEWS, issue no. 273, 1 September, 2000.
31   See, for example, Robertson, *Future Wealth*, pp. 104-105; Robertson, *Transforming Economic Life*, pp. 43-44; and The Land is Ours website: www.oneworld.org/tlio. TLIO take their inspiration from the Diggers who, at the end of the English Civil War in 1649, proclaimed the right to rent-free land for all. The modern-day campaigners assert that, 'If we are to have a socially just and ecologically sustainable future, we must have a say in the decisions which our society makes about land use, its ownership and value'.
32   Friends of the Earth press release, 3 March, 2000.
33   Friends of the Earth press release, 22 November, 2000.
34   The Environment Agency covers England and Wales only. In Scotland, the equivalent body is the Scottish Environmental Protection Agency. It is interesting to note the use of the word 'protection' north of the border.
35   *The Independent,* 20 May, 2000.
36   *The Independent,* 17 September, 1997.
37   *The Independent,* 3 September, 1998.
38   *The Independent,* 9 October, 1998.
39   Friends of the Earth press release, 8 February, 1999.
40   McLaren *et al., Tomorrow's World,* p. 305.
41   *Southern Daily Echo,* 23 February, 1999.
42   Residents Against Dibden Bay Port website at: http://members.aol.com/dibdenbay/index.html; Friends of the Earth (South East), Dibden Bay briefing sheet, May 1999; and Friends of the Earth website at www.foe.co.uk/wildplaces
43   Associated British Ports, 'Dibden Update', Issue 2, July 1997.
44   *Southern Daily Echo,* 9 July, 1997.
45   RSPB briefing note, November 1996.
46   *Southampton Advertiser,* 10 July, 1997.
47   Friends of the Earth (South East), Dibden Bay briefing sheet, May 1999.
48   *The Guardian,* 24 January, 2001.
49   *Southern Daily Echo,* 1 January, 1999.
50   Paul Vickers, personal communication, 22 January, 2001. Information also available at: http://members.aol.com/dibdenbay/Detr/detr.html#3
51   http://members.aol.com/dibdenbay/Detr/detr.html#3
52   Pilger, *Hidden Agendas,* pp. 334-358.
53   *Southern Daily Echo,* 9 July, 1997.
54   http://members.aol.com/dibdenbay/Detr/detr.html#5
55   *Southern Daily Echo,* 4 January, 2001.
56   *The Guardian,* 24 January, 2001.
57   Letter from Dr Caroline Lucas MEP to Margot Wallström, European Commissioner for the Environment, 26 September, 2000.
58   See website of Residents Against Dibden Bay Port: http://members.aol.com/dibdenbay/index.html
59   Harvey, *The Killing of the Countryside,* p. 17.
60   Compassion in World Farming website: www.ciwf.co.uk

61   *Ibid.*
62   Personal communication from Matt Phillips, senior wildlife campaigner, Friends of the Earth, 3 August, 1999.
63   Cited in *The Independent,* 2 July, 1999.
64   Unlike the problem of 'under-grazing' in lowland areas, upland areas typically suffer from over-grazing.
65   *The Independent*, 19 September, 1998.
66   *The Observer*, 29 October, 2000.
67   *The Independent,* 28 August, 1999.
68   *Ibid.*
69   *The Independent*, 3 October, 1998.
70   *The Independent*, 27 October, 2000.
71   *The Independent*, 8 September, 1998.
72   *Ibid.*
73   *The Independent*, 27 October, 2000.
74   *The Independent*, 21 November, 1998.
75   *The Independent*, 2 September, 2000.
76   *The Guardian*, 10 February, 1999.
77   Cited in *Triodosnews*, Summer/Autumn 1998, p.3.
78   *The Independent*, 2 September, 2000.
79   *The Independent*, 10 September, 1998.
80   *The Independent,* 11 April, 1999.
81   *The Guardian,* 9 December, 1999.
82   *The Independent*, 20 October, 1997.
83   Girardet, *Creating Sustainable Cities.*
84   Further details and examples of community-supported agriculture can be found in Douthwaite, *Short Circuit*, pp. 283-309 and Schwarz, *Living Lightly*, Chapter 6.
85   *The Independent*, 1 April, 1999.
86   *Independent on Sunday*, 3 September, 2000.
87   *The Independent*, 20 June, 1997.
88   Barry Coates, 'WDM in Action' newsletter, winter 1999, World Development Movement, London.

7

GLOBAL GENETICS

Another chink in globalisation's armour

The large agrochemical companies will soon be in a position to dictate the future of the food industry. And they know just how they want our food to be produced – in ways which will maximise their own profits. That means using gene technology which they have patented and can control, despite the risk of irreversible global consequences for the rest of us.

Soil Association[1]

The rich countries and their corporations have already taken most of the Third World's natural resources, minerals, trees and soils, as raw materials for their industries. Now that these resources are almost gone, they want to take away the Third World's rich and diverse biological materials, seeds and genetic resources.

Mohamed Idris, a coordinator of the Third World Network in Malaysia[2]

Genetic Snowball

In early 1999, two women from the direct action group GenetiX Snowball, who were awaiting trial after uprooting genetically modified maize from a field in Devon, were told in a dramatic about-turn that all charges against them had been dropped. One of the women's lawyers later claimed, 'The last thing the Crown wanted was to see a jury . . . acquit people who took direct action against genetically modified organisms'.[3] At the same time, a panicky government was flummoxed by the overwhelming weight of public opinion against the free-trade promoted influx of GM crops and foodstuffs into the UK, as well as a domestic programme of GM crop growing.

But around the globe, citizen opposition is growing against the corporate quest for profit masquerading as altruism, with its business propaganda that society needs biotechnology and all its attendant risks of genetic pollution in order to feed the world's growing population. At the beginning of the twenty-first century, a small number of transnational corporations – Novartis, DuPont, Zeneca, Monsanto and a handful of others – are on the verge of controlling the food chain. However, consumer resistance to the genetic modification of foods may turn out to be one of the defining moments in citizen opposition to the 'unstoppable' forces of globalisation. As *The Guardian* put it:

> The gulf between industry and consumer is still very wide. The industry views the consumer as befuddled by the issues or gripped by romanticism about a previous golden age of food production. It talks about letting market forces rule, free from the nannying interference of big government, but has done nothing to prevent Monsanto turning the market-place upside down by introducing genetically modified soya into food despite wholesale opposition. This is nannying to be sure, corporate-style, force-feeding consumers with genetically modified foods many don't want.[4]

Media attention in the UK focused on Monsanto which deliberately placed itself in the public eye with a £1 million advertising campaign in the summer of 1998. The US conglomerate, based near St Louis in Missouri, has made acquisitions enabling it to shape every step in the food process, from the seed planted by the farmer to the way the product is finally delivered to the shopper. The company's size, global presence and influence are enormous. Monsanto was worth $35 billion in 1998, an astonishing sixfold rise in five years.[5] In spring 1998, the company announced an attempted $4 billion buy-out of Delta and Pine Land, a company which had developed 'terminator technology' and patented it together with the US Department of Agriculture (USDA). This technology genetically corrupts seeds, so that seed saved from a crop will not germinate and cannot be used to produce the next crop, a system which literally goes against the grain of sustainable agriculture. By pushing its terminator products into markets in the developing South, Monsanto, the world's second biggest seed company, would be able to capture a dependent customer base of vulnerable farmers and emerge as a global monopoly which would threaten worldwide food security. It was a chilling progression from the warning issued in 1993 by the USDA of a shrinking domestic market for American-produced food. New markets were needed and moves were duly made to forcibly open them up by free trade rules. South Asia was highlighted as a major 'growth opportunity', representing a potential two-thirds share of the global market by 2000.[6] Terminator technology is perhaps the most invidious means by which US 'market penetration' in the South could yet be achieved.

Indian activist Vandana Shiva points out how, by virtue of terminator technology, the engineered seed is converted from a renewable resource – one able to reproduce itself – into a non-renewable resource. Moreover, the engineered seed is only able to produce a crop with the aid of purchased chemical inputs. The ecological cycle of the crop is thus ruptured: 'It is this shift from ecological processes of production through regeneration to technological processes of non-regenerative production that underlies the dispossession of farmers and the drastic reduction of biological diversity in agriculture.' Shiva concludes that such a shift 'is at the root of the creation of poverty and unsustainability in agriculture'.[7]

But then, in October 1999, Monsanto chairman Robert Shapiro made a surprising pledge in an open letter: 'we are making a public commitment not to commercialize sterile seed technologies, such as the one dubbed "Terminator".'[8] The Rural Advancement Foundation International (RAFI), a non-profit organisation based in Winnipeg, Canada, applauded the public pressure that had apparently forced Monsanto to reject the terminator technology, following a similar move by AstraZeneca, a UK-based biotech company. Pat Mooney, executive director of RAFI, praised the civil society organizations, farmers, scientists, and governments who had waged highly effective campaigns during the previous 18 months. 'The public unanimously rejected Terminator', said Mooney, 'because it's bad for farmers, food security, and the environment'.[9]

However, Monsanto did not rule out the development of other 'gene protection' technologies. Although the company said it was not currently investing resources to develop such technologies, it did 'not rule out their future development and use for gene protection or their possible agronomic benefits'.[10] Amid fears that the company was simply dropping the technology until the public could be won over at a later date, Greenpeace challenged Monsanto to sell the pressure group its terminator patents for £1, saying that nobody would ever trust a biotech company not to use an invention it owns: 'If they were really committed to not using it, they could sell it to us. This changes nothing. The shadow is still there.'[11] Abandoning, or shelving, terminator technology took place just as Monsanto seemed in full retreat from a massive wave of negative public reaction to genetically modified organisms (GMOs).[12] The company even took to participating in conciliatory talks with its fiercest critics, such as Greenpeace and the Soil Association. It was a significant change of demeanour from outright arrogance to apparent humility on the part of the biotech corporations. However, RAFI warned that terminator technology is just one type of 'traitor' technology in which certain beneficial or undesirable traits in seeds can be turned on or off when the farmer adds the right proprietary chemical, such as a herbicide or fertiliser. For example, biotech companies could engineer a negative trait, such as inhibition to good crop yields, which needs to be turned off. Farmers could be induced into buying 'upgrades' to produce better crops. Although the technology is still in the laboratory, RAFI warned that, 'In less than 10 years, 12,000 years of farmer-saved seed and community plant breeding could be irreversibly brought to an end ... chemically-dependent seeds will more likely lead to bioserfdom'.[13] However, a report by a committee of senior British government advisors argued that 'such technology has great potential to protect the environment and stop the creation of cross-breed crops'. Friends of the Earth retorted that such advice was 'naïve' and 'dangerous'.[14]

Around this time, GM markets were shrinking and investors appeared to be losing confidence in the biotech industry. Life sciences companies such as AstraZeneca and Novartis were reportedly considering disposing of their genetic engineering operations after years of large investments but few financial returns. In August 1999, Europe's biggest bank, Deutsche Bank, circulated a report to investors recommending that they sell their shares in GM companies. Washington-based analysts with the Bank, Frank Mitsch and Jennifer Mitchell, stated that it was nine months since they had first voiced concerns that the biotech industry 'was going the way of the nuclear industry ... but we count ourselves surprised at how rapidly this forecast appears to be playing out'. The Bank warned that 'it appears the food companies, retailers, grain processors and governments are sending a signal to the seed producers that "we are not ready for GMOs" '.[15]

Before its entry into GM technology, Monsanto had already gained notoriety as a chemical company for its product Agent Orange, which was used by the US in its invasion of Vietnam to decimate jungle areas, thus reducing ground cover for Vietnamese troops. Use of the chemical in Vietnam led to dioxin contamination up to 1,000 times higher than the concentration found in domestic herbicides. The product has been linked to various cancers and serious skin and liver disorders. It is estimated that the number of children with dioxin-related deformities born in Vietnam since the 1960s is 500,000.[16] Environmentalists were also already well aware of Monsanto's dismal pollution record relating to its manufacture of polychlorinated biphenyls[17] – which have caused catastrophic deaths of marine mammals and are linked to reproductive disorders in humans – and its genetic technology of recombinant bovine growth hormone (also known as bovine somatotropin) to stimulate cows to produce more milk than they would naturally.[18]

The pesticide connection

Early warnings about Monsanto's impending stranglehold on agriculture and food production arose from its designing of Roundup Ready soya which had been engineered to produce an enzyme to make it immune to the company's own Roundup herbicide. Farmers were offered a joint package: they could happily spray their fields of GM soya with copious quantities of Roundup herbicide, killing off the weeds but leaving the crops intact. Since the crops are immune to the herbicide, it is likely that *more* herbicide is used than would normally be the case (where farmers need to be careful to target the weeds alone, while diligently avoiding the crops). Monsanto's proud boast that GM technology reduces the use of agrochemicals such as herbicide is therefore difficult to substantiate. But the danger does not end there. Weeds will inevitably develop resistance to Roundup, necessitating ever more applications of the herbicide. According to Margaret Mellon, of the US-based Union of Concerned Scientists, '... pretty soon, farmers will again have lots of weeds and even fewer weed control options'.[19]

Luke Anderson, a writer and campaigner on genetic engineering, also highlights the danger to wildlife if large areas are swept with Roundup, as 'the increased use of herbicides will kill the weeds which support the insects and produce the seeds fed on by worms. This could be the final blow for such bird species as the skylark, corn bunting and linnet, already in decline due to industrialised farming practices'[20] (see also Chapter 6). There are yet more risks. The US Fish and Wildlife Service has identified 74 endangered plant species potentially threatened by excessive use of glyphosate, the principal constituent of Roundup. Glyphosate can kill fish in concentrations as low as 10 parts per million. It stunts the growth of earthworms or kills them, and it is toxic to many of the beneficial mycorrhizal fungi which help plants absorb nutrients from the soil. It is also the third most commonly reported cause of pesticide-related illness among farm workers in California, the only state which produces such statistics.[21]

Not only does Monsanto earn large sums of money from farmers because of 'technology fees', but the technology sometimes fails to match Monsanto's claims of enhanced yields. In 1996, farmers in the United States planted a genetically engineered cotton variety from Monsanto called 'Bollgard'. The cotton had been modified using DNA from the soil microbe *Bacillus thurengesis* (Bt) to produce proteins poisonous to the bollworm, a cotton pest. The farmers paid Monsanto a 'technology fee' of $79 per hectare in addition to the price of seed. But the technology failed spectacularly: the bollworm infestation of the genetically engineered crop was up to 50 times the level that typically triggers spraying.[22]

Additional evidence that GM crops do not necessarily produce better yields, or permit significantly lower use of pesticides, was contained in a study published by the US Department of Agriculture.[23] The conclusions were based on the analysis of commercial crop results for 1997 and 1998 in regions where both traditional and GM varieties of cotton, maize and soya were being sown. The US report gave added impetus to calls from English Nature, who advise the British government on wildlife matters, to assess the ecological effects of GM crops in the UK before allowing any commercial use. Even if there had been a reduction in pesticide use, that could have disguised more significant changes. Brian

Johnson of English Nature explained why: 'the herbicides used with GM crops are broad-spectrum – they kill everything. If you change from using a lot of something with a mild effect to less of something with a dramatic effect, that is not necessarily good.[24] Adrian Bebb, a campaigner with Friends of the Earth, welcomed the US study saying that 'it undermines the propaganda pumped out about the biotech industry'.[25]

And then there is the potential risk to human health. In April 1999, the EU overruled a request from the UK government to ban GM maize containing antibiotic-resistant genes.[26] The British government had sought such a ban following advice from its Advisory Committee on Novel Foods and Processes that there was a risk that resistance to antibiotics could be passed on from animal feed – the GM maize – to bacteria in human stomachs. Resistance to antibiotics is building up in humans and animals because of its overuse in medicine and animal feed. Luke Anderson notes that in the UK, where in some hospitals strains of the common pathogen *Staphylococcus aureus* are resistant to almost all known antibiotics, antibiotic-resistant bacteria kill more people every year than road accidents.[27] The EU accepted that there was a risk that antibiotic resistance could be passed to humans, but they 'considered that this was not significant enough to warrant the material being banned from use in animal feed'. [28]

Free trade rules OK?

The controversial issue of genetic engineering has a longer history than the recent explosion of media interest would suggest. Pressure groups such as Greenpeace had been warning of the dangers for almost a decade, and attracting little media attention, when, in 1997, came strong hints of a trade war between the US and the EU over GM crops. Responding to immense consumer concern, the EU proposed segregating and labelling genetically engineered food. But the United States government vehemently opposed any segregation or labelling. US Trade Representative Charlene Barchefsky estimated that the EU proposal would threaten $4-5 billion in annual US agricultural exports. In June 1997, she gave a stern warning to EU leaders that they could expect 'at the minimum' punitive action through the WTO if they allowed European concerns to disrupt US agricultural trade.[29]

In May 1998, Codex Alimentarius, the UN body responsible for establishing international rules on food, rejected consumer demands for segregation of GM and non-GM ingredients and for comprehensive labelling, and recommended instead 'a much more limited labelling regime that suited the food and genetic engineering industries'.[30] Julian Edwards, Director General of Consumers International, representing 235 consumer organisations in 109 countries, stated:

One of the ironies of this issue is the contrast between the enthusiasm of food producers to claim that their biologically engineered products are different and unique when they seek to patent them and their similar enthusiasm for claiming that they are just the same as other foods when asked to label them.[31]

Following sustained pressure from consumer groups and environmentalists, the European Commission introduced a limited labelling scheme – despite threats of a trade war with the US – covering GM soya and maize. However, soya and maize derivatives which are used in most processed food in Europe, including soya oil, lecithin and corn (maize) syrup, were excluded from the labelling scheme, to the dismay of pressure groups.

Even the limited EU proposal was vociferously opposed by US agricultural companies. American farmers, who export about a quarter of their soya crop to Europe, were afraid that they would be forced to segregate the modified crop from the non-modified variety, at least for the European market, and that they would have to be harvested, transported, stored and shipped in separate and clearly labelled streams. Not only would this raise costs to producers, but they feared that consumers would steer clear of the labelled modified foodstuffs. The response of US business groupings such as the American Soybean Association was to state that segregation was 'impossible' and to co-opt the US Department of Agriculture to threaten to obtain a damning judgement from the WTO, namely that Europe's labelling plans were an impediment to free trade and therefore illegal. A senior British government adviser on GM food later admitted that Britain had 'missed a trick' in allowing the importing of GM crops from the US. Professor Derek Burke, chair of the Advisory Committee on Novel Foods and Processes, admitted that it should have been anticipated that US farmers would mix GM and non-GM crops and export them together in bulk, in the knowledge that any ban would contravene free trade agreements.

The British government's limited response to increasing public opposition to GM food was to introduce labelling of such produce when served by cafés and restaurants. This was criticised by public interest groups as inadequate, hasty and unenforceable. The legislation was introduced in March 1999, with caterers being given until September 1999 to tell customers whether or not they were serving GM food. The law came into immediate effect, however, for retailers such as supermarkets. And so, rather than apply a labelling policy 'upstream', at the producers' end – which would undoubtedly incur the wrath of the World Trade Organisation as 'hindering free trade' – the labelling policy was applied 'downstream', leaving retailers and restaurateurs with the problem of finding out from their food suppliers exactly which items, if any, had GM ingredients. The

Ministry of Agriculture, Fisheries and Food only sent out guidance on how the law would operate more than half-way through the 6-month notice period. Not only had the government failed to tackle unfair free trade rules, but it had dumped responsibility for enforcing the new labelling law onto local authorities which complained – understandably – that they would not have sufficient trading standards officers to check whether restaurants and cafés were labelling correctly their meals.[32]

More twists in the tale were to follow. In October 1999, the EU agreed that food marked 'GM free' may actually contain up to 1 per cent genetically modified ingredients. Another flaw in labelling schemes was highlighted when a British newspaper reported that Monsanto used genetic engineering to produce the common food sweetener aspartame. GM bacteria are used during the manufacturing process, but because there is no modified DNA in the finished product, the use of genetic engineering does not show up in tests. Consumer groups argued that there was no guarantee that aspartame made using genetic engineering could not be imported from the US into the UK, and that further testing for toxic side effects should be carried out.[33]

The fundamental mismatch between WTO-promoted 'free' trade and public concern is hardly ever mentioned in mainstream reporting. One exception was a report by *The Independent*'s environment correspondent who noted in 1997, when GM food technology started to hit the headlines, that recent events 'showed how global free trade could bypass Britain and the EU's laws and licensing system for the introduction of genetically modified foods.'[34] However, as we saw in Chapter 3, such reporting is rarely expanded upon, nor are deeper questions raised. Which other laws protecting the environment, health and labour standards are being overridden by 'free' trade? Who are the powerful corporations and state politicians behind such developments? Why are they pushing GM technology instead of organic agriculture? How can it all be turned around for the benefit of people and the environment?

The battle for public opinion

In the summer of 1998, Monsanto ran a £1 million advertising campaign in the UK with the slogan 'Food, Health, Hope' in an attempt to persuade British consumers to swallow GM technology. The company's ads hid its profit imperative behind a façade of concern for feeding the world's hungry and ever-expanding human population. Genetic engineering, with its alleged promise of growing crops in drought-stricken regions, enhanced yields and pest-resistant properties, could supposedly help save the world. The fact that, according to some estimates, the world already produces one and a half times the amount of food that is needed,[35] and that the rate of increase in cereal production is greater than that in population,[36] did not appear in Monsanto's ads. Nor did the ads identify the real causes of food insecurity – that food is produced unsustainably and that it is unevenly distributed; the politics and economics of greed are to blame, not lack of technology. Monsanto's advertising campaign was criticised by the British Advertising Standards Authority for making 'wrong, unproven, misleading and confusing' claims.[37]

Monsanto's image, and that of the biotech industry as a whole, took yet another knock when the company was fined in 1999 for 'genetic pollution' following the escape of GM pollen from an oilseed rape trial site in Lincolnshire. A licensing condition of the site was to keep a 6-metre-wide pollen barrier of non-GM crops around the modified oilseed rape to prevent modified pollen mixing with conventional plants in the area.[38] A government inspection found that the pollen barrier had been cut back in some areas to just 2 metres to allow roadway access and to improve the 'look' of the site. The resultant fine of just £17,000 was lambasted as 'pathetic' by Friends of the Earth.

As the British government struggled throughout the summer of 1999 to keep on top of the GM issue, Jeff Rooker, the Food Safety Minister, claimed that there was a 'robust' regulatory system on GM crops and food in place, and that consumer protection was the government's top priority. But within a few months the government was forced into an embarrassing retreat when the Ministry of Agriculture, Fisheries and Food published a report providing evidence of transgenic pollution from GM crops to neighbouring fields, a risk which organic farmers had already been complaining about bitterly. The report, commissioned from the John Innes Centre in Norwich, concluded that contamination of organic plants could not be 'entirely eliminated'. Research by the Soil Association, which certifies organic produce in the UK, had already shown that more than 80 per cent of rape seed pollen is carried by bees and that bees can travel more than 3 miles, while wind can carry it much further. However, the government rejected environmentalists' call for 6-mile buffer zones as 'impractical'.[39]

The Pusztai affair

A significant development in the GM debate in Britain centred on the scientific research of Arpad Pusztai, and the treatment meted out to him by the scientific and political establishments. Pusztai, based at the Rowett Research Institute in Aberdeen, conducted research which showed changes in the guts of rats fed on GM potatoes. Before the work had been published in a peer-reviewed scientific journal, Pusztai briefly mentioned the results, with his institute's permission, on a television programme. His results appeared to contradict the government's line that GM foods were safe and the media gave extensive coverage to the story. The Rowett Institute suspended his experimental work, sealed his computers and confiscated his data. Sir Robert May, the government's Chief Scientific Adviser, accused Pusztai of violating 'every canon of scientific rectitude', while the Royal Society said his work was 'flawed in many aspects of design, execution and analysis'. Jack Cunningham – the Cabinet 'enforcer' who was directly responsible for the government's inept handling of public opposition to GM food – gloated that Pusztai's research had been 'comprehensively discredited'. Several months later, following a minor heart attack, Pusztai had his work published in *The Lancet*, Britain's top medical journal. According to a *Guardian* report, publication in the journal went ahead despite a threatening telephone call made to Richard Horton, *The Lancet*'s editor, by Peter Lachmann, the former vice president and biological secretary of the Royal Society and president of the Academy of Medical Sciences.[40] Lachmann allegedly told Horton that if he published Pusztai's paper that this would 'have implications for his personal position' as editor.[41] Horton published the paper regardless. Friends of the Earth commented, 'Scientific concerns about the safety of GM foods are clearly real. Jack Cunningham, Sir Robert May and all the other politicians, officials and scientists who tried to rubbish Dr Pusztai and his work owe him a sincere and public apology'.[42]

The government's frustration, irritation and, indeed, panic over the whole GM issue came to the fore despite, or perhaps because of, some rather desperate spin-doctoring. Tony Blair blamed the media for whipping up public 'hysteria' over GM foods, claiming that reporting was 'skewed' against the biotech industry,[43] perhaps in an attempt to divert attention from his own government's close links with the industry. It is noteworthy that, just days before Blair's outburst, a confidential letter from the Cabinet Office, leaked to Friends of the Earth, showed the extent of the government's PR offensive in support of genetically-modified food.[44] The letter revealed the existence of a 'Biotechnology Presentation Group' to spin government policy to the media. Ministers belonging to this group were Jack Cunningham, Tessa Jowell (Health), Jeff Rooker (Agriculture) and Michael Meacher (Environment). The note of their meeting showed government attempts to 'identify an "independent" scientist to appear on the [influential BBC Radio 4] *Today* Programme' to refute the findings of a Christian Aid report on the damaging impact of GM foods in the Third World. There was also a decision to revise a key paper from the Chief Medical Officer and Chief Scientific Adviser on health and environmental risks from GM food to make it more 'intelligible' to the lay reader. But ministers needed 'to guard against the charge that the Government was seeking to influence the findings of the paper'. Charles Secrett, FoE's executive director, noted afterwards: 'the Government is not interested in a genuine debate on GM food. It wants to spin GM food down our throats whether we like it or not.'[45]

Resisting the US bully

The extent to which politicians have defended the interests of the biotech corporations is noteworthy. Monsanto, in particular, makes use of friends in high places. US President Bill Clinton allegedly leant on British Prime Minister Tony Blair to allow GM crops from US companies such as Monsanto into Britain. Al Gore, the supposedly ecologically-aware Vice President, was part of the lobbying process to permit the sowing of GM crops in France. Monsanto was one of five companies that spearheaded Clinton's welfare to work programme and was praised by the President in his State of the Nation address in 1997.[46] Luke Anderson reports that New Zealand was also placed under pressure by the United States not to interfere with free trade in GM products. The US was unhappy with New Zealand's intention to test and label GM food, and warned that such a move 'could impact negatively on the bilateral trade relationship and potentially end any chance of a New Zealand-United States Free Trade Agreement'.[47]

In the US, the introduction of GM products essentially took place by stealth. The level of debate there had, until around 1999, been much lower than in the UK and elsewhere in Europe. The Food and Drug Administration does not stipulate that GM products have to be labelled. In February 1999, US opinion appeared to be strongly behind the technology: in a survey by the International Food Information Council, '62 per cent of those questioned said that they would be more likely to buy vegetables that had been genetically engineered to taste better or fresher'.[48] However, there are now signs of rising unease amongst US consumers as a result of the backlash against GM foods in Europe. Ironically, by the end of Monsanto's UK advertising campaign alerting consumers to the presence of GM products on supermarket shelves, the proportion of the British population opposing such technology had actually risen. No wonder Monsanto was castigated by its biotech peers for bringing the industry into disrepute. In the United States, domestic consumer resistance to GM technology, coupled with importers' resistance abroad, eventually forced a tightening in rules governing GM food in 2000. It is likely that the decision of major corporations, including McDonald's, not to buy GM products was a major factor in persuading US food producers to modify their stance. US companies are now required to submit detailed research results and information on new GM products to the US Food and Drug Administration. This had previously only been a voluntary requirement. However, the rules stopped short of compulsory labelling of GM products. As the Union of Concerned Scientists pointed out, there was still 'insufficient monitoring of the long-term health and environmental implications of GM food'.[49]

In the countries of the South, Monsanto has been under strong citizen pressure too. The Grameen Bank, a 'microcredit' association famed for its programme of small loans to poor farmers, suddenly withdrew from a joint venture with the biotech company after protests from environmentalists. Opponents had feared that Monsanto would exploit the Grameen Bank's extensive network of farmer borrowers to introduce GM seeds and agrochemicals in Bangladesh.[50] In India, the WTO clause on trade-related intellectual property rights (TRIPs), has created considerable disquiet. (TRIPs are a protective measure initiated by corporations and were pushed into the WTO by an industry coalition which included Monsanto, Du Pont and General Motors). In July 1993, farmers in the Indian state of Karnataka burnt down a building belonging to the seeds company Cargill, because they feared that the TRIPs provision could make it illegal for them to replant seeds that had been used for hundreds of years, without paying royalties to patent holders. In October 1993, over 3 million Indian farmers came to the state capital Bangalore to demonstrate against the WTO. Development specialist John Madeley reported that farmers were also angry at what they believed to be the misleading advertisements of Cargill for hybrid sunflower seed. Many farmers claimed that these seeds produced only a fraction of the advertised yield and that the hybrid crops were not fit to eat.[51] Irate Indian farmers also burnt fields of GM crops in a 'Cremate Monsanto' campaign.

The ties that bind government and industry

In the US, a 'revolving door' policy between Monsanto and relevant federal regulatory bodies – in particular the Food and Drug Administration (FDA) – has been operating for years. Key government personnel have either held office at Monsanto, or are destined to do so on retiring from government. Marcia Hale, a former assistant to President Clinton on intergovernmental relations, took up a job coordinating public affairs and corporate strategy for Monsanto in the UK. Mickey Cantor, a former US Trade Representative and Secretary of Commerce and the person responsible for initiating action at the WTO against the EU ban on beef hormones, later joined Monsanto's board of directors. Robert Shapiro, Monsanto's chairman, was the chair of President Clinton's Advisory Committee for Trade Policy and Negotiations. When the FDA was drawing up guidelines for deciding whether GM foods should be labelled, one of the key players was Michael Taylor, a former lawyer for Monsanto. There are many other examples to demonstrate that, as the St. Louis *Post-Dispatch* put it, 'where Monsanto seeks to sow, the US government clears the ground'.[52] But getting the government on the corporate side involves much more than the exchange of personnel. According to environmentalist Steven Gorelick, the development of biotechnology in the United States would not have been possible 'without vast direct and indirect subsidies as well as a Patent Office willing to ensure that new life forms are patentable – and therefore profitable'. Gorelick noted too that the President's

Council on Competitiveness Biotechnology Working Group, which promotes US biotechnology in the global marketplace, 'sits *above* all the regulatory agencies on the government flowchart'. The conclusion must be 'that the US government is far more interested in promoting biotech than regulating it'.[53]

So, not only has the precautionary principle been cast aside, with the public taking the risk of the GM revolution going wrong, but the taxpayer is subsidising, directly or indirectly, the enormous costs of research. Examples in the US include a $62 million arrangement between Monsanto and Washington University, Hoescht's $70 million deal with Harvard, and Ciba-Geigy's $20 million payoff to the University of California at San Diego. Such deals, noted Gorelick, 'effectively turn those institutions into appendages of the corporations that fund them'. The companies get exclusive licenses and patent rights, a sneak preview of research results and access to the labs themselves. The corporations end up 'paying only a fraction of the cost of research'.[54]

In the UK the story is similar. The government gives companies 100 per cent write-off against tax for research costs, and 25 per cent write-off per year for ancillary costs. Huge amounts of direct public grant aid are channelled into research institutes where genetic engineering is under development. Generous tax breaks are offered over extended periods of time, and monopoly profits are guaranteed as companies sell consumers the products that have been publicly subsidised every step of the way. According to Alan Simpson, Labour MP for Nottingham South: 'This is even before we put a cost to the voluntary contributions which come from the public in the form of their family history, medical records, blood and tissue samples, all given freely as part of the research effort.'[55]

In the UK, as in the US, the boundaries between government and industry are blurred. Lord De Ramsey, the former head of the Environment Agency, allowed the use of his land for the testing of GM crops. In 1998, Friends of the Earth shone a spotlight on the government's Advisory Committee on Releases into the Environment (Acre), exposing 8 of its 13 members for having links with the biotech industry, 6 of whom were actually paid by organisations allowed by the committee to grow genetically engineered crops.[56] Michael Meacher, Environment Minister, responded by announcing 'sweeping changes'. By this he meant the appointment of three ecologists or biodiversity experts to Acre.[57] Several months later, in a long-awaited report on government policy on GM technology, the Commons Environmental Audit Select Committee called for members of the public to be appointed to 'powerful government bodies overseeing genetically modified crops ... the addition of lay people would ensure that ethical concerns were added to the normal scientific advice given to ministers'. Just what would be done with such 'ethical concerns' was not spelt out. And so when the new Agriculture and Environment Biotechnology Advisory Commission was set up a year later, FoE warned that if it 'is to be more than just another PR exercise it needs to grasp the nettle ... and call on the Government to abandon its GM trials'.[58] The Select Committee's report also revealingly called for 'an end to cabinet splits over GM issues.'[59] Jack Cunningham has since left the Cabinet and returned to the back benches.

For some pressure groups, the nature of the closeness of business and government was personified by Lord Sainsbury of Turville, the Science Minister who had been recruited from his family supermarket business. He adopted a non-impartial role in promoting biotech interests within government. The press reported that Sainsbury had made a major investment in Paradigm Genetics, a US biotech firm, a few weeks before becoming a minister.[60] The US company later teamed up with Bayer, the German pharmaceutical and chemical company, in a deal which earned it around £26 million. It was reported that Paradigm would receive additional fees from Bayer if its herbicide-resistant crops were to be grown commercially. Sainsbury, although not directly involved in licensing GM products, was at the time on the Cabinet committee with responsibility for biotechnology. As Science Minister, he is also in overall charge of all the government-funded Research Councils, including the Biotechnology and Biological Science Research Council.

Sainsbury's direct involvement in the biotech industry arose through his investments in two firms – Innotech and Diatech. The Gatsby Foundation, Sainsbury's charity, had put more than £2 million a year into the study of plant science since 1990, most of which had been spent on a Norwich laboratory developing GM crops based at the John Innes Centre, itself the biggest genetic research centre in Europe. Sainsbury's response to criticism was to state that his investment interests had been placed in a trust as soon as he became a minister and, farcically, that he would leave the room during biotech Cabinet committee meetings, chaired by 'enforcer' Cunningham, if his financial interests and his governmental role risked coming into conflict. Calls for his resignation made by opposition politicians and environmental pressure groups went unheeded.

Still the farce continued. Labour's close links with big biotech business resulted in egg on the government's face after it emerged that a food company run by one of Tony Blair's favourite businessmen had decided to phase out GM ingredients. Northern Foods, chaired by the Labour peer Lord Hoskins, reportedly decided to do so in the wake of public concern.[61] Hoskins, chairman of the government's Better Regulation Task Force, is a large donor to the Labour Party and one of Blair's most trusted business advisers. His company's decision came at a particularly embarrassing time for Blair and his ministers, who had repeatedly stressed that GM products were safe. Northern Foods had not gone public on its new non-GM policy because it was not the 'culture' of the company to boast of its activities.

The government's enthusiasm for facilitating commercial applications of GM crops through its promotion of 'farm-scale' field trials is another measure of its pro-business approach. Activists responded by uprooting plants at various test sites, including Lynge in Norfolk, where Peter Melchett, the Executive Director of Greenpeace UK, and 27 other campaigners were arrested. Environmentalists were divided on non-violent direct action, with Friends of the Earth not supporting damage to farmers' property. Greenpeace, GenetiX Snowball and others countered that the government and industry had not responded to public concerns over the planting of GM crops and that peaceful intervention was therefore both acceptable and necessary. Doug Parr, campaign director for Greenpeace, explained further: 'Open-air release is a potentially irreversible act of pollution and could eliminate organic agriculture. Pollution is not acceptable simply because we cannot measure it.'[62] On 20 September 2000, a jury decided that the 28 Greenpeace activists had not broken the law. The Criminal Damage Law, 1971, allows for property to be damaged if this is undertaken to protect other property. The jury accepted Greenpeace's defence that the maize was uprooted so that its pollen could not 'genetically pollute' crops in neighbouring fields. After the verdict, a government spokesperson was at pains to point out that 'the crop trials will continue... our top priority is to protect the environment and human health.'[63]

A year earlier, in November 1999, the government had announced a voluntary moratorium on commercial GM crop planting until 2002, while maintaining its commitment to field trials of GM crops. Environmentalists criticised the decision and called it a 'political holding operation' until the government could try to win round public support. Greenpeace campaigner Sarah North warned: 'the so-called 'trials' will actually mean more GM crops in the ground than ever before, more risk of GM contamination and the possibility of these trial crops reaching the food chain via animal feed.'[64] Friends of the Earth accused the government of promoting 'discredited' trials on 'a massively increased scale' and pointed out that 'winter oilseed rape is still being grown at over 20 locations throughout the UK – including three farm scale trials – without any legal consent'. Moreover, by granting commercial licenses to the biotech industry, 'companies will have full legal permission to proceed with commercialisation of GM crops whatever the outcome of the trials or the concerns of the public'.[65] Despite overwhelming public opposition to GM crops and food, the government is bending over backwards to promote growth in the biotech industry. There is no clear separation between government, which is charged with regulating crop and food technology for the protection of consumers and the environment, and industry, which is pushing GM technology in its ceaseless drive for profits.

Biopiracy

Biotech interests even extend to patents on life itself. One of the outcomes of the 1992 Earth Summit in Rio de Janeiro was the Convention on Biological Diversity, which has twin aims: conserving biodiversity and ensuring the fair share of benefits arising from the use of biodiversity. Such a convention needs to be strong to resist the threat of resource expropriation in the South by corporations based in the North. As biologist Mae-Wan Ho of the Open University in the UK notes, the private industries of the North are increasingly using countries of the South 'as reservoirs of biological and genetic resources to develop new crops, drugs, biopesticides, oils and cosmetics'. The expansion in biotechnology has led to a new class of patent claims by rich corporations on genetic and intellectual resources that belong by right to communities in the South. These 'patents on life' include plant varieties cultivated and, continues Ho, used 'by indigenous communities for thousands of years, as well as genes and cell lines obtained under false pretext from indigenous peoples themselves'.[66]

One example of the usurping of products and processes derived from indigenous knowledge of plants is that of the neem tree in India. The neem, *Azadirachta indica*, has been used for centuries in India as a medicine and biopesticide. Vandana Shiva warns that:

> Today, this heritage is being stolen under the guise of IPRs [intellectual property rights]. For centuries, the Western world ignored the neem tree and its properties: the practices of Indian peasants and doctors were not deemed worthy of attention by the majority of British, French and Portuguese colonists.[67]

The Indian Patents Act of 1970 forbids the patenting of inventions relating to agricultural and horticultural processes. In 1996, India's parliament rejected a bid to change the law, thus defending the farmers' traditional ability to innovate and adapt their own plant varieties, and protecting their accumulated biodiversity material and skill.[68]

But transnational corporations have already applied for 40 patents on Indian crops and species as a result of the agreement on trade-related intellectual property rights administered by the WTO. In 1995, the US-based company W. R. Grace took out a US patent on neem-based pesticides. By the company's own estimates, the global market for this product was expected to reach $50 million by 2000. But in May of that year the corporation's attempt to patent the product in Europe was blocked by the European Patent Office (EPO) in a major victory for a global coalition of environmental groups.

However Grace has already established a base in India with at least an additional three neem-related patents. Shiva reports that the company has tried to persuade several Indian companies to stop manufacturing value-added neem products and to switch instead to providing the raw material to Grace. Other patent-holding enterprises are likely to join Grace in India. *Nature* reported that the EPO had received 51 patent applications for 'inventions' based on the neem tree alone, and had so far granted 11. Around 90 patents exploiting the tree had been granted worldwide.[69] According to the journal *Science*, 'Squeezing bucks out of the neem ought to be relatively easy'.[70]

This corporate annexation of the natural resources of the South, sanctioned by WTO free trade rules, has been christened 'biopiracy' by campaigners. Biopiracy even extends to potentially owning the DNA sequence for the human species itself. The Human Genome Diversity Project – a 10-year, $3 billion project to identify the elements and sequence of all the genes in the human genome – has been described by critics as 'business disguised as science' and 'the commodification of the sacred'.[71] Shiva warns that allowing biopiracy to take place is to accept a system of corporate planetary control and, ultimately, the destruction of biodiversity: 'Can the planet afford to have biodiversity swallowed up as raw material for a globally-organized corporate culture which produces only uniformity?'[72]

The corporate moulding of a GM-friendly Europe

The European Union's Life Patents Directive is a prime example of the EU's less than stringent standards in environmental protection, human health and animal welfare. The key issue of this directive is not the ethics or limits of biotechnology, as might be thought, but the establishment of the private ownership of the genetic vocabulary of life on Earth. In the 1990s, with a spate of mergers and takeovers in the biotech and pharmaceutical industries, the corporate pressure for market expansion and the creation of new markets intensified enormously. The business argument was that investment in costly research to find new drugs and cures could only be justified if patents could be taken out on the stuff of life itself. Backstage business lobbying at the EU for a patents directive was part of a bigger picture of corporate fixing of the rules to create a deregulated Europe. One of the most influential lobby groups in Brussels is the European Roundtable of Industrialists (ERT), comprising the chief executives of Europe's forty-five biggest multinationals, including Bayer, BP, DaimlerChrysler, Ericsson, Nestlé, Shell, Solvay and Unilever. The ERT has been meeting since the early 1980s 'in a project', wrote Alan Simpson MP, 'aimed at writing the script of European legislation which would construct twenty-first-century Europe as a corporate fiefdom. Deregulated markets may have been part of their script, but so too was the patenting of genes'.[73]

The ERT has been influential in shaping a corporate-friendly EU, but there are also lobby groups devoted specifically to boosting the biotechnology industry. The most important of these is EuropaBio, an umbrella organisation of virtually all the major players such as Bayer, Novartis, Monsanto Europe, Nestlé, Rhône-Poulenc, Solvay and Unilever – unsurprisingly, there is considerable overlap with the ERT. According to the multinational public relations firm Burson-Marsteller, which was responsible for setting up the infamous Global Climate Coalition (see Chapter 4), EuropaBio has an 'indispensable direct role in the [EU] policy-making process'. When public opposition to GM food rose to fever pitch, Burson-Marsteller advised the industry not to participate in public debates. Instead, advised the PR firm, it should be left to 'those charged with public trust in this area – politicians and regulators – to assure the public that biotech products are safe'.[74] It is another example of governments being used as tools by corporate interests.

The 1993 Delors White Paper on Growth, Competitiveness and Employment was a major boost for biotechnology. Then Commission president Jacques Delors praised biotechnology as 'one of the most promising and crucial technologies for sustainable development in the next century'.[75] This claim did not spring from nowhere, but followed years of vigorous corporate lobbying in the form of numerous glossy reports and high-level meetings of industry managers with EU officials. In 1998, the industry enjoyed a stunning victory in winning European Parliament approval for the Life Patents directive, after a similar proposal had been defeated in 1995. But it was hardly surprising given the huge efforts made by biotech lobbyists in Brussels. The pharmaceutical company SmithKline Beecham spent £20 million on a pro-directive campaign. Corporations manipulated various groups representing patients – 'no patents, no cures' was the rallying cry – to do their bidding. (These public interest groups have since 'clarified their positions on the patenting of genes', with a shift away from full support for the biotech industry.) The International Chamber of Commerce even pressurised the drafters of the directive, issuing detailed comments on specific clauses and going as far as suggesting new text. Lobbyists for the European chemical industry had argued that the EU's patenting system had to become more business-friendly, in order to compete with US corporations. Just as representatives of the fossil fuel industry have raised the spectre of lost jobs in the face of perceived threats, so have chemical lobbyists, with claims that up to 2 million jobs would be at risk if the industry did not get a Life Patents directive to its liking. It did, though the directive has since been challenged in the European Court of Justice.[76]

Countering ecological violence

The social forces surrounding biotechnology are a microcosm of the battle of global deregulation versus public and environmental protection. As we sleepwalk our way into an era of corporate feudalism, multinational companies are steering the development of a world which they can dominate, with the approval of national governments – and largely at public expense. In particular, Alan Simpson MP rightly sees the explosion of biotechnology through issuing patents as 'anti-research, anti-science and anti-democratic'. We have now broken the tradition of research 'being done in pursuit of a cure, not a fortune'. Until recently, agricultural knowledge and medical breakthroughs were part of the global commons. Patenting has distorted all of this: 'We are now invited to accept that unless patents are obtained, all medical and agricultural research will cease.'[77]

This is a corporate threat that must be revealed as plain and simple blackmail of the public. As we saw in Chapter 1, the corporate push for deregulated markets – through intense lobbying of 'business-friendly' governments and multinational institutions like the WTO – is the inevitable product of an unsustainable economic system which demands continual growth. Biotech companies are desperately trying to create opportunities to sell new products in new markets, to the extent that they are now attempting literally to privatise the planet for their own ends. Non-governmental organisations from around the globe attempted to oppose such planetary privatisation by demanding a strong biosafety protocol which would impose a moratorium on the international trade in genetically modified organisms, until their health, environmental and social impacts could be rigorously assessed. As we saw earlier, the protocol springs from the 1992 Rio Biodiversity Convention. In February 1999, talks on the protocol collapsed when the United States, who are not even a party to the protocol and so are ineligible to sign a final agreement, insisted on the exclusion from the regulations of all commodity crops, accounting for more than 90 per cent of genetically modified organisms presently traded. According to Greenpeace, 'outside the last day's session, delegates from two EU countries stated that US President Bill Clinton had actually personally called their governments the previous night, in an effort to pressure them to agree to weak standards'.[78] Once again, President Clinton was doing Monsanto's bidding, just as he had done allegedly with Tony Blair, a few months previously.

However, at the following year's biosafety talks in Montreal, soon after the impressive display of citizen opposition at Seattle's WTO meeting, agreement was reached on new rules to regulate international trade in GM crops and food. Despite continued US opposition, key decisions included acknowledgement that GM food and crops are fundamentally different to those conventionally bred; a requirement for advance agreement on the import of GM seeds; and allowing countries to follow the 'precautionary principle' and ban GM crops if they have safety concerns.[79]

Many commentators have remarked that genetic engineering, and public opposition to it, will be one of the major societal issues in the new millennium. As

John Vidal, environment editor of *The Guardian*, put it:

What we are witnessing is one of the greatest revolts against a new technology in history, dwarfing the European protests against Shell over Brent Spar and Nigeria. Whether this revolt will be judged by history as a triumph of new democracy and a significant step in the reining in of corporate power, or as a backward response to inevitable 'progress', it proposes a new relationship between politicians, corporations and consumers.[80]

To ensure a sustainable future, the new relationship needs to swing in favour of people and the planet. At present, as Shiva eloquently points out, diversity in cultures is under attack from globalisation which thrives on 'monocultures'; in other words, uniformity in agricultural practices, environmental conditions and cultural needs. Shiva says simply, 'global control of raw materials and markets makes monocultures necessary'.[81]

Economic globalisation has undermined the ability of local communities to grow their own food, to eat healthily, to self-organise and to prosper in harmony with other communities and the environment at large. Monocultures can only exist through ecological violence inflicted by centralised control and coercion – violence directed against communities and environmental resources. The solution lies in the alternative of local democracy, decentralisation and self-organisation, thus allowing people to develop according to their own needs, structures and priorities, not by artificial 'needs' foisted upon them by centralised and largely unaccountable political and corporate structures. The struggle to regain control over what we eat, to protect our local biodiversity and to reject the privatised exploitation of the very stuff of life is at the heart of public opposition to the forces of economic globalisation, and the driving force for the democratic development of progressive alternatives.

Notes

1   Soil Association leaflet, *Look what the Gene Dictators are growing just for you*, 1998.
2   Quoted in Curtis, *The Ambiguities of Power,* p. 235.
3   *The Guardian*, 29 March, 1999.
4   *The Guardian*, 10 February, 1999.
5   *Independent on Sunday*, 16 August, 1998.
6   Cited by Dr. Mae-Wan Ho of the Open University, Triodos Bank meeting, Westminster Central Hall, London, 27 March, 1999.
7   Shiva, *Biopiracy*, p. 54.
8   Open letter to Rockefeller Foundation president Gordon Conway, quoted at Environmental News Service: http://ens.lycos.com/ens/oct99/1999L-10-06-02.html
9   http://ens.lycos.com/ens/oct99/1999L-10-06-02.html
10   *Ibid.*
11   *The Guardian*, 6 October, 1999.

12   On December 19, 1999 Monsanto announced that it planned to merge with drug industry giant Pharmacia & Upjohn to create a new company, named Pharmacia, with combined annual sales of $17 billion. 20 per cent of Monsanto's agrochemicals division are to be sold off on completion of the merger.

13   Quoted in Hugh Warwick, *The Ecologist*, Vol. 30, No. 3, p. 50.

14   A report by the sub-group on Best Practice in GM Crop Design, part of the Advisory Committee on Releases into the Environment, reported in *The Independent*, 14 October, 2000.

15   *The Guardian,* 25 August, 1999.

16   Hugh Warwick, *The Ecologist*, Vol. 28, No. 5, pp. 264-265.

17   Joseph E. Cummings, *The Ecologist*, Vol. 28, No. 5, pp. 262-263.

18   Paul Kingsnorth, *The Ecologist*, Vol. 28, No. 5, pp. 266-269.

19   Quoted in Anderson, *Genetic Engineering, Food and Our Environment*, pp. 25-26.

20   *Ibid.,,* p. 27.

21   *Ibid.,,* pp. 24-25.

22   Shiva, *Biopiracy*, pp. 41-42.

23   Cited in *The Independent,* 8 July, 1999.

24   *Ibid.*

25   *Ibid.*

26   Genes which code for antibiotic-resistance are commonly used as 'marker genes'. This allows scientists to identify which plant cells have taken up DNA which has been transferred from another species. See Anderson, *Genetic Engineering, Food and Our Environment* for further details.

27   Anderson, *Genetic Engineering, Food and Our Environment,* p. 20.

28   *The Guardian,* 27 April, 1999.

29   Anderson, *Genetic Engineering, Food and Our Environment,* p. 101.

30   *Ibid.,* p. 100.

31   *Ibid.,* p. 100.

32   *Independent on Sunday*, 1 August, 1999.

33   *Independent on Sunday,* 20 June, 1999.

34   *The Independent*, 11 March, 1997.

35   World Health Organisation figure, cited by Alan Simpson, Labour MP for Nottingham South, *The Food Programme*, BBC Radio 4, 8 February, 1999.

36   Cereal production is increasing by 2.2 per cent per year, while the human population is rising by just 1.7 per cent per year. Figures from the Institute of Science in Society, cited by Dr. Mae-Wan Ho of the Open University, Triodos Bank meeting, Westminster Central Hall, London, 27 March, 1999.

37   *The Observer*, 28 February, 1999.

38   Concerns about the current 50-metre safety zones in Britain have been raised by the European Commission who said that they should be doubled to 100 metres to prevent cross-contamination with natural plants. Anti-GM campaigners said that this is 'too little, too late' (*Scotland on Sunday*, 21 January, 2001).

39   *The Independent*, 17 June, 1999.

40   *The Guardian,* 1 November, 1999.

41   *Ibid.*

42   Friends of the Earth press release, 4 October, 1999.

43   *The Independent*, 28 May, 1999.

44   Friends of the Earth press release, 19 May, 1999.

45   *Ibid.*

46   *Independent on Sunday*, September 6, 1998.

47   Anderson, *Genetic Engineering, Food and Our Environment,* p. 102.
48   *The Guardian,* 20 February, 1999.
49   *The Independent,* 4 May, 2000.
50   *The Ecologist,* Vol. 28, No. 5, p.3 .
51   Madeley, *Big Business, Poor Peoples,* pp. 31-32.
52   *The Guardian,* 20 February, 1999.
53   *The Ecologist,* Vol. 28, No. 5, p.283.
54   Gorelick, *Small is Beautiful, Big is Subsidised,* p. 33.
55   Alan Simpson, GenetiX Snowball, Newsletter Issue 1, February 1999.
56   *The Guardian,* 9 July, 1998.
57   *The Independent,* 15 February, 1999.
58   Friends of the Earth press release, 5 June, 2000.
59   *The Independent,* 14 May, 1999.
60   *The Independent,* 18 February, 1999.
61   *The Independent,* 7 May, 1999.
62   *The Times,* 23 August, 1999.
63   *The Independent,* 21 September, 2000.
64   Greenpeace UK press release, 5 November, 1999.
65   Friends of the Earth press release, 5 November, 1999.
66   Mae-Wan Ho, *The Ecologist,* Vol. 28, No. 3, p. 182.
67   Shiva, *Biopiracy,* p. 73.
68   Madeley, *Big Business, Poor Peoples,* p. 31.
69   *Nature,* vol. 405, pp. 266-267.
70   R. Stone, *Science,* 28 February, 1992.
71   See, for example, Baumann *et al., The Life Industry.*
72   Shiva, *Biopiracy,* p. 127.
73   *Resurgence,* May/June 1998, p. 13.
74   Quoted in Balanyá *et al., Europe, Inc.,* p. 82.
75   *Ibid.,* p. 81.
76   *Ibid.,* ch. 9.
77   *Resurgence,* May/June 1998, p. 13.
78   Greenpeace International, press release, 24 February, 1999.
79   *Earth Matters,* Spring 2000, p. 8.
80   *The Guardian,* 19 March, 1999.
81   Shiva, *Biopiracy,* p. 103.

8

FORCES FOR CHANGE

Diversity in adversity

As awareness of the interconnected nature of our problems grows, so does a sense that we can change things. People feel empowered and motivated when they realise that reversing globalisation will solve a whole range of environmental, social and personal problems.

Helena Norberg-Hodge[1]

The challenge before public interest activists now is to develop institutions, mechanisms and rules to rein in the corporate activity that has been plundering the planet under the banner of economic globalization.

Robert Weismann[2]

The regrouping of radicals

This book started off by saying that, until recently, corporate and political elites appeared able to organise world affairs to suit themselves, with little public opposition or even awareness of what was happening. A 'new world order' had been decreed after the 'collapse of communism' at the end of the 1980s. Economic globalisation and 'free trade' stepped up a gear. Dissidents were, as ever, marginalised by the mass media. Although there has not yet been a reining in of the state-corporate forces that are privatising the planet, there is now a growing sense amongst the public of what is going on, and a growing willingness to question it, to protest against it and to campaign for alternatives.

There is no single watershed that marks this subtle shift of power, but there are a number of significant developments which should be highlighted. The World Trade Organisation ministerial meeting in Seattle in 1999 is one. It ended in political embarrassment for the hosts when the talks collapsed, following colourful, educated and largely peaceful protest by around 50,000 people from all walks of life. Protests continued the following year at major meetings of the International Monetary Fund and World Bank in Washington DC in April and Prague in September. Citizen opposition to the failed Multilateral Agreement on Investment was a landmark – although perhaps temporary – victory against the forces of global capital. Public condemnation of the way genetic engineering has been rammed down our throats, and a growing desire for sustainable food, are heartening. The Jubilee 2000 campaign to cancel debt for the poorest of the poor countries in the South is a beacon of hope. Another telling example is the effect of public pressure on Western politicians, who were essentially forced to come to the aid of the East Timorese in 1999 after the post-referendum violence by militias who were in league with the Indonesian army (itself supported for years by the West). The contrast with the West's indifference to – even active involvement in – the 1975 Indonesian takeover of East Timor (see Chapter 3) is striking.

All of these issues around which people have mobilised share at least one common feature – the art of coalition building. While corporate and political interests figure out ways to sweet-talk, bludgeon or simply circumvent the public to get their own way, various – sometimes widely disparate – pressure groups fighting for radical change are exploiting the power of working together in a shared cause. It is becoming increasingly common to see clergy organising with debt campaigners, trade unionists siding with environmentalists, and conservationists co-operating with land rights reformers.

The overarching goal here is the transfer of political and economic power from corporations, investors and their government allies to locally-based, participative communities. Of course, these communities may well strive towards strong regional, national and international links in a benign, mutually-supporting form of globalisation, courtesy of the ongoing revolution in communications technology. But 'localisation', the title of a recent book by Colin Hines, will be the key process. Because, as residents, schoolchildren, students, employees or employers, we all have a particular interest in the environmental, economic and social conditions of our neighbourhoods where we are based: how clean the air, water and land are; the provision of decent, affordable homes for all; the quality and accessibility of schools, hospitals, shops, leisure facilities and other services; the safety of our streets; and so on. In other words, in our local environments we are all 'stakeholders' – a word quickly appropriated and just as quickly dropped by New Labour, perhaps fearing a conflict of interest between protecting the public good and promoting corporate goals.

So where does this leave us? Susan George, writer and campaigner, is blunt: 'we must try to put down transnational tyranny before it puts us down.'[3] Helena Norberg-Hodge, director of the International Society for Ecology and Culture, succinctly points the way to 'turning the globalisation tide' through the twin processes of renewal and resistance:

> Renewal comes from the ground up; it is a process of pulling power downwards from the international level to the national to the local. It is about rejuvenating local economies, repairing the local environment, reinvigorating small-scale businesses, and breathing life back into communities.[4]

But renewal, whilst a necessary step, is not sufficient. Such initiatives will be continually trampled underfoot while economic centralisation is allowed to proceed courtesy of institutions such as the World Bank, the International Monetary Fund and the World Trade Organisation, even if there is evidence of a greater willingness on their part to listen to campaigners because of the sheer force and success of civil dissent. Local, small-scale and people-friendly economies have to be protected against the destabilising, divisive and destructive nature of global free trade and transnational capital flows. This leads to the counterpart of renewal in a two-pronged attack on globalisation – the process of resistance. Norberg-Hodge explains it thus:

> Resistance means countering and challenging current notions of 'development' and progress through international information exchanges and public education campaigns. It means restricting corporations and resisting their entry into countries and communities; it means protecting our jobs, our communities and the natural world from the volatility of a runaway global economy.[5]

Renewal is a long-term process. Resistance, on the other hand, is an immediate necessity, and must be focused, efficient and highly internationalised – indeed, a global phenomenon. And therein lies the irony. The demise of economic globalisation will be enabled by advances in globe-encircling information technology, which will allow activists to share news, insights and developments and bring these into the public domain rapidly via faxes, e-mail and the internet. This could be the lever that brings public pressure to bear upon transnational interests, and reins in their power. As we saw in Chapter 1, this phenomenon came to the fore, perhaps for the first time, in public resistance to the MAI. Though this was a defensive victory, in that it halted, or delayed, the continuing attack of corporate power on democracy, Noam Chomsky countered that nonetheless, 'popular victories should be heartening', adding that:

> One should attend carefully to the fear and desperation of the powerful. They understand very well the potential reach of the 'ultimate weapon', [grassroots mobilisation] and only hope that those who seek a more free and just world will not gain the same understanding, and put it effectively to use.[6]

The globalisation of economic and political power, with its attendant global-isation of technological and cultural forces, contains the seeds of its own destruction.

A green Europe as catalyst?

In the mid-1990s, the Green Party in England and Wales debated – with heated words on both sides – whether the European Union was inherently undemocratic, corporate-biased and unsustainable, or had the potential to raise environmental, social and health standards across national borders and oppose the hegemony of global free trade. In the end, those Greens who argued for remaining inside the EU and reforming it from within won out over those who wanted to see the UK withdraw.

In June 1999, with the introduction of proportional representation, British Greens made a historic breakthrough in the elections to the European Parliament, gaining two new MEPs. The Green Group in the European Parliament (GGEP) obtained their best results ever, increasing its number of MEPs from 27 to 38 and becoming the fourth strongest group in the new Parliament. According to Magda Aelvoet, president of the GGEP: 'These elections have confirmed the Greens as one of the leading political forces in the European Union. The Green [MEPs] ... come now from eleven countries in the EU, up from eight.'[7]

But the enlarged group of Green MEPs had their work cut out for them in dealing, for example, with the damaging effects of the Common Agricultural Policy. Another factor impacting adversely on the quality of the European environment is the allocation of billions of euros of taxpayers' money on constructing transport routes across the continent – the so-called Trans-European Networks (TENs) – at the behest of powerful corporate lobbying groups in Brussels, such as the European Roundtable of Industrialists (see previous chapter).[8] Despite widespread popular support for strong EU action to protect the environment and considerable legislative effort, a Green party study concluded that 'the EU consistently prioritises trade and economic growth over environmental protection' and that 'EU environmental policy is patchy, overly technocratic and suffers from a democratic deficit'.[9]

As we saw in Chapter 1, campaigners such as Colin Hines have argued that a 'protect the local, globally' plan can bring about a transformation that leads to genuine sustainable development: more self-reliance (without resorting to complete self-sufficiency), rather than countries straining to become 'internationally competitive' and hitting the poorest in the process. At first sight it may seem paradoxical to suggest that the EU could play an important role in a shift from globalisation to localisation. But it may require such a large economic bloc to oppose the powerful corporate interests represented by groupings such as the

World Trade Organisation, the European Roundtable of Industrialists, and the International Monetary Fund. European MEPs, as well as other elected representatives, ought to be working together with environmental and social movements to demand radical changes to trade and currency regulations. The point is that both 'top-down' and 'bottom-up' approaches will be required; one does not exclude the other – indeed they will likely be complementary.

The globalisation of resistance

Around the world there are many strong grassroots movements for social justice which are not often reported in the mass media. In Brazil, for example, the rural landless workers' movement (the MST) has been instrumental in opposing years of neoliberal policies at home, particularly 'agricultural modernisation'. Such policies have subsidised and promoted agro-business and large-scale export-oriented farms, while displacing massive numbers of small farmers and rural workers from the countryside. The federal government agency in charge of land distribution has settled less than 7 per cent of the landless rural families – 331,276 out of 4 million – and the majority of these were the result of MST-organised land occupations. After a demonstration attracted 100,000 people in Brasilia in 1996, the government attempted to neuter the MST by offering a limited quota of land deals in exchange for demobilising the movement. Instead, the land occupation strategy intensified, based on co-operation between church organisations, trade unions, human rights activists, political parties and local groups. However, government allies at state and local level, together with landlords, retaliated with restrictive judicial processes and violent methods to stem the rising appeal of the MST. This culminated in April 1996 with a massacre at Eldorado de Carajas in the state of Para, when 19 landless workers were killed by military police who had been ordered by the state governor to repress a peaceful protest march. Consequently, public opinion strengthened behind the landless movement and the government was put on the defensive, although it continued its World Bank-promoted 'market agrarian reform'. The MST has since increased its efforts to form coalitions at the national level to challenge the government directly, while continuing to organise locally and occupy uncultivated estates in the countryside. According to James Petras, a specialist on Latin America, President Cardoso of Brazil has appealed to foreign capital while pursuing public cutbacks and the control of labour, leading to ever greater repression. The pressure to compete in the global economy has meant that Cardoso 'has become deeply enmeshed in the web of traditional oligarchic politics: foreign giveaways, landlord alliances, regressive social policies, and military repression'. But Petras is cautiously optimistic that there are 'great opportunities' for the MST to capitalise on their popular support.[10]

Broad-based grassroots mobilisation is also a feature of the Zapatista rebellion that was launched on 1 January, 1994 – the day that the North American Free Trade Agreement came into force – in the deprived southern Mexican state of Chiapas. Of 3.5 million people in the state, 1.5 million lack access to medical care, and 54 per cent of the population are malnourished. In Mexico, 79 per cent of households have running water; but in Chiapas, just 58 per cent. In Mexico, 88 per cent of households have access to electricity; in Chiapas, 67 per cent. 72 per cent of children do not complete the first year of primary school.[11] Massive numbers of people in Chiapas and elsewhere in the country are suffering at the hands of the Mexican government's neoliberal policies which have led to the loss of land rights, livelihoods and even lives. As in the poor rural regions of Brazil, the people of Chiapas have organised themselves in response to the threats posed by economic globalisation. According to analyst Harry Cleaver of the University of Texas in Austin, the Zapatista rebellion is of particular importance because it quickly achieved a high profile around the world – in large part because of skilful use of the internet by the Zapatistas – and because it 'aimed at finding new and more effective ways of interlinking both opposition to capitalism and mutual aid in the elaboration of alternatives'.[12] The uprising has involved many indigenous peoples with interrelated languages and cultures. The Zapatistas have developed a system of autonomous communities based on inclusive village assemblies. Women, in particular, have organised peaceful resistance to the 70,000-strong occupation army of Mexican troops. The Zapatistas are demanding fundamental constitutional reforms to redress the inequitable balance of power held by the government and its supporters, while offering their own experiences of successful community self-organising as one, but not the only, example of an alternative to the modern state.

Protest: the new globalisation

Meanwhile, transnational corporations are being increasingly targeted by campaigners because of abusive corporate practices in vulnerable communities around the world. In 1999, the giant international mining conglomerate Rio Tinto was ambushed by protestors at the company's annual meeting in London. Activists in suits and ties infiltrated the meeting, making it difficult for the chairman to pick out shareholders with straightforward questions on the company's financial performance. Instead, awkward questions on the company's environmental and labour record were raised by campaigners from Friends of the Earth and the World Development Movement, miners' representatives from the company's Australian operations, trade unionists, and tribespeople from Irian Jaya. When one questioner declared that she had a question about US mining operations, the chairman visibly breathed a sigh of relief, only to be grilled on Rio Tinto's approach to the Western Shoshone tribe over land rights in Nevada.[13]

Civil protest, it has been noted by several commentators, is becoming the new globalisation. During the worldwide protest campaign against the Multilateral Agreement on Investment, Maoris marched against the threat to their traditions posed by the MAI in New Zealand; thousands of people protested in Seoul, South Korea, against crippling programmes of structural adjustment; and at the Pacific Rim summit in Malaysia, anti-government demonstrators demanded people's rights in favour of the deregulated globalisation dumped upon them by the Asia-Pacific Economic Co-operation forum. With the defeat of the MAI, there was a new spring in the step of activists. On 18 June, 1999, a 'carnival of resistance' took place in over 40 countries against financial institutions around the world. A diverse network of groups dubbed J18 planned their protest to coincide with the G8 summit of the world's richest nations in Cologne, Germany. Resistance, J18 proclaimed, was as transnational as capital. A 1.5 million-strong union of garment workers in Bangladesh launched a day of action, Canadian postal workers stopped the mail in Toronto and in Uruguay mock banks allowed the poor to 'deposit' their misery and unemployment.[14] In the financial centre of London an initially peaceful protest was marred when police and a number of violent demonstrators clashed, leaving 46 people in hospital. Mainstream media coverage generally gave short shrift to the reasons for the protests, or its international dimensions, focusing instead on the 'riots' that occurred: '4,000 marchers turned from peaceful protest to riot when the demonstration was hi-jacked by anarchists, intent on organised violence, who targeted unprotected police'.[15] The tabloid *Daily Star* was typically more pithy: 'Booze-fuelled hardcore anarchists turn anti-capitalist protest into orgy of violence.'[16] The biased mass media reporting of the global June 18 events, and similar days of protest since, is a classic demonstration of Herman and Chomsky's propaganda model in action (see Chapter 3). Demonstrators and bystanders complained, however, of heavy-handed police tactics. One protester told BBC Radio 4's *Today* programme: 'Police in full riot gear and looking extremely offensive charged at the demonstrators and started attacking them.'[17] Assistant Commissioner James Hart of the city police warned: 'We may, if conditions call for it, be more assertive next time; we'll come in harder, at significant risk to innocent members of the public, peaceful protesters and police officers.' Or, as the alternative weekly newspaper *SchNEWS* suggested, 'maybe they'll just ban dissent altogether'.[18]

The J18 protest was followed by the N30 day of action to mark the first day – November 30 – of the World Trade Organisation ministerial meeting in Seattle. When the WTO delegates gathered there to hold talks to further trade liberalisation, they were met by up to 50,000 protesters, from steel workers to Indian peasants, from international church representatives to French farmers. The round of WTO talks was designed to bring yet more economic sectors into the organisation's domain, including investment, health care, education, competition policy and government procurement. A version of the discredited MAI was even given a dusting down and resurrected. Ahead of the Seattle meeting, over a thousand organisations from 87 countries signed a statement opposing the so-called Millennium Round of talks and any further liberalisation, stating: 'In the past five years, the WTO has contributed to the concentration of wealth in the hands of the rich few; increasing poverty for the majority of the world's population; and unsustainable patterns of production and consumption.'[19] Seattle saw the strengthening of links between industrial workers and environmentalists, two groups traditionally wary of each other. Journalist Andrew Rowell reported one steel worker consultant saying that: 'Because labour and environmentalists are both strong constituencies that have to be listened to, the idea that they are singing the same song is really scary to a lot of policy makers.'[20]

The Seattle authorities were unable to cope with the mass protest – which was almost exclusively conducted peacefully and with good humour – and resorted to heavy riot 'robocop' police tactics. Tear gas and rubber bullets were used by the police, sometimes in an apparent attempt to provoke a violent response from the peaceful protesters. Local residents and meeting delegates complained bitterly of being gassed and roundly condemned the police actions. British environment minister Michael Meacher, who was present in Seattle, broke diplomatic convention and publicly criticised the police for their behaviour.[21] Worldwide television and press coverage, even though it did not fully portray the heavy-handed police tactics, cast Seattle and the United States in a very poor light. The Seattle police chief announced his resignation a few days after the WTO meeting. The talks themselves had actually ended without agreement, following accusations from many emboldened delegates from developing countries that, despite rhetoric from the Americans and Europeans about listening to them this time round, nothing had changed. The WTO remained essentially a forum for US-EU dialogue. However, even that was a failure, with serious disputes about agricultural subsidies, for example, left unresolved.

In India, where there is considerable citizen action against the forces of globalisation, a 'Declaration of the Indian People Against the WTO' was launched.[22] The 10 million-strong Karnataka State Farmers' Association (KRRS) played a role in destroying Kentucky Fried Chicken outlets in India, occupied offices of seed company Cargill, and burned fields of Monsanto's GM crops. The KRRS organised an 'Intercontinental Caravan' of Indian farmers and others to tour the world in 1999, alerting the public to the dangers of globalisation.[23] Its prominent role in the J18 protests formed part of this strategy. Whilst on tour, 37 of the farmers stormed into the London offices of the biotech-supporting Nuffield Council demanding an end to GM crops, then later joined an illegal occupation of a Monsanto GM test site. Ajmer Lakshowal, president of the Punjabi farmers' union, said:

> The G8, the multinationals and the World Trade Organisation are going to put more burden on us. We have been struggling against that for the last 10 years. We had not dreamt that the poor people of Europe would join us. To put an end to the oppression of one person by another you have to be strong, you have to use force and you have to fight back. It is bad to do crime but it is worse to put up with their crime.[24]

Farmer occupation of offices and GM test sites, even if illegal, amounts to no more than non-violent direct action, despite the use of words such as 'force' and 'fighting back'. It is simply the exertion of the historical democratic right that people possess to express their dissent by peaceful means. This is the same philosophy that underpinned the success of the anti-roads movement in Britain, derailing a 5-year £22 billion road construction programme. The same resistance has fuelled other campaigns against destructive roads such as the Trans-Amazonian highway in Brazil, and schemes in Venezuela, Indonesia and other countries where indigenous people have protested against the destruction of their land, livelihoods and cultures. The writer Paul Kingsnorth has tracked these and other 'Heads of Hydra' of global protest.[25] Kingsnorth and others link the need for economic and environmental renewal with the issue of ownership and control of the land itself. As Kingsnorth puts it, 'land is increasingly being expropriated for large-scale projects that power the onward movement of the global market'. Apart from road building, examples include enormous dams such as the Narmada project in India; deforestation in the Amazon region, Indonesia and Malaysia; and the struggles by native peoples of Kenya and Tanzania to retain their land rights against the onslaught of mass tourism.[26]

The role of education and 'subvertising'

As well as co-operation between grassroots groups with a common aim, education is one of the crucial elements of a resistance and renewal strategy which is necessary to overturn the orthodoxy of more economic growth, more deregulation, and more globalisation. The Seattle meeting, for instance, was preceded by a 'Teach-In' hosted by the International Forum on Globalisation to highlight the failures of the current economic model – in particular, the role of the WTO – and to propose sustainable alternatives. David Orr, an educator and writer, argues strongly that the Western educational model needs to be radically reformed if future citizens are going to be able to recognise and respond effectively to the threats and opportunities posed by the world today and tomorrow:

The generation now being educated will have to do many vital things that we, the present generation, have been unwilling to do: prevent climate change; protect biological diversity; reverse forest destruction; stabilise the world's population; reduce levels of consumption. They must rebuild the economy in order to tackle the power of giant corporations and unelected global institutions. And they must do all of this while addressing worsening social and racial inequalities. No generation has ever faced a more daunting agenda.[27]

Not only should school, college and university education be reformed to address this daunting agenda, but challenging the stranglehold of corporate advertising – which aims to educate the public into becoming voracious consumers and passive citizens – is vital. Kalle Lasn, a former documentary filmmaker, and Bill Schmalz, a cinematographer, set up the Vancouver-based Media Foundation to generate 'subvertising'. This uses the style of familiar big advertisers but subverts their message, flinging consumer capitalism back in its collective face. One example – a spoof of a famous Marlborough poster depicting two smoking cowboys on horseback heading into a glorious sunset – carries the slogan: 'I miss my lung, Bob.'

The Media Foundation publishes *Adbusters,* a magazine which is now published in 24 countries across five continents. *Adbusters* is a masthead for what Lasn calls 'culture jamming': confronting the corporate consumer culture head on, and – by declaring it 'uncool' – undermining it.[28] But Lasn takes the argument beyond the witty, subversive and ironic nature of culture jamming. His underlying message is deadly serious:

> When a corporation like General Electric, Exxon, Union Carbide or Philip Morris breaks the law, causes an environmental catastrophe or other-wise undermines the public interest, the usual result is that nothing very much happens. The corporation may be forced to pay a fine, revamp its safety procedures, face a boycott. At worst – and this is very rare – it is forced into bankruptcy.[29]

The solution, Lasn suggests, is to rewrite corporate rules so that every share-holder assumes partial liability for mishaps. Rather than buying shares in companies with dubious environmental, health or labour records, people would be able to choose enterprises which make a positive contribution to people and the planet. Not only that, but shareholders would be forced to take responsibility for their investments. The rules also have to be rewritten to ensure that companies which misbehave are brought to heel. This would be done in such a way that 'a company caught repeatedly and wilfully dumping toxic wastes, damaging water-sheds, violating anti-pollution laws, harming employees, customers or the people living near its factories, engaging in price fixing, defrauding its customers, or keeping vital information secret, automatically has its charter revoked, its assets sold off and the money funnelled into a superfund for its victims'.[30]

Public pressure *can* bring about such seemingly momentous changes. The reversal of Shell's dumping of the Brent Spar, the collapse of the Multilateral Agreement on Investment, massive demonstrations at Seattle, Washington and Prague, and the public's rejection of GM foods are harbingers of the coming globalisation of civil protest.

The criminalisation of dissent

In August 1998, activists who had gathered in Geneva for a meeting sponsored by People's Global Action (PGA) were briefly arrested, following house raids by police. Seven computers, over a hundred diskettes, address books and a large amount of documentation were confiscated.[31] The PGA, a network of 100 grass-roots organisations from around the world, was formed after a conference in February 1998. Members include people from the Zapatista movement in southern Mexico, the Nigerian Movement for the Survival of the Ogoni People, Play Fair Europe! and the Indian Karnataka State Farmers' Association. It was formed to oppose the destructive globalising forces unleashed by the WTO and other undemocratic corporate power structures.[32]

Incidents in which activists are abused or harassed by the forces of 'law and order' are on the increase, facilitated by ever-more repressive statutes. In the last two decades, civil protest – 'Britain's oldest democratic tradition', in the words of *Guardian* columnist and environmentalist George Monbiot – has become ever more criminalised. Margaret Thatcher's authoritarian union laws of the early 1980s were followed in 1986 by the Public Order Act, which restricted the right to demonstrate. Then along came the 1992 Trade Union Act which made it an offence to carry 'insulting' banners. The 1994 Criminal Justice Act allowed the police to break up almost any public protest. The 1996 Security Service Act and 1997 Police Act included in their definition of serious crime 'conduct by a large number of persons in pursuit of a common purpose'. As Monbiot says, 'peaceful protesters were thus exposed to state-endorsing bugging, burglary and arbitrary searches'.[33]

It doesn't end there. At the end of 1998, the National Public Order Intelligence Unit was set up to track green activists and public demonstrations in Britain. Based at Scotland Yard, the unit planned to use information from Special Branch officers, MI5 and other sources to compile profiles of protesters and organisations considered to be potentially troublesome. As if that wasn't enough, in early 1999 Her Majesty's Inspector of Constabulary issued a report – *Keeping the Peace: Policing Disorder* – which suggested that new legislation should be introduced to prevent the 'fortification process' of green campaigners and anti-road protesters constructing 'battlefield bunkers' and acting in a 'quasi terrorist mode'.[34] Later that year, the Home Secretary Jack Straw announced sweeping new anti-terrorist proposals which would lump together IRA terrorists and environmentalists who ripped up GM crops. John Wadham, director of the civil rights group, Liberty, warned that it would create a 'two-tier criminal justice system, where those who commit crimes with a political motive have fewer rights and safeguards than those who commit crime for personal gain, malice or revenge'.[35]

All of these political and legal developments are steadily eroding the right that people in a democracy ought to have to express dissent or even simply to debate issues of fundamental importance. Such attacks on freedom of expression are taking place just when the power of local self-determination is seeping away from communities to corporate headquarters; in other words, when the need for protest has arguably never been greater. By remaining uncritical or silent on this erosion of inclusive democracy, the mainstream media – with a few notable exceptions – have colluded in an insidious process which, with the complicity or even active assistance of governments, is transferring power from the hands of citizens to the clutches of private corporations. As Monbiot says, 'Britain is embarking on a massive new adventure in enclosure ... the transformation of things that once belonged to all of us into exclusive private property'. In the introduction to this book, we referred to the historical processes of enclosure and clearances in which land rights were removed from the common people and concentrated in the hands of the wealthy. New laws were brought in to prevent ordinary people from contesting the seizure of their property. Today, such enclosure has extended to the global arena. In some sectors, such as food and agriculture, a few powerful institutions are destroying, or absorbing, small businesses. Genetic material is being registered as private property, and international investors and businesses 'are insisting that even anticipated profits should be regarded worldwide as inalienable possessions'.[36]

And it is happening mostly by stealth – unless you can get your hands on 'radical', 'alternative' or 'underground' news sources. It certainly remains largely unreported by the same media-owning corporate forces that stand to gain most from the 'liberalisation' in global markets, or whose hegemony would be threatened by grassroots challenges to the established order.

Business as usual?

There are activists on the 'soft' or self-proclaimed 'pragmatic' wing of the green movement who argue that environmentalists ought to work with business, at least those companies which have the potential to transform themselves into 'promoters' of sustainable development. Amory Lovins, the green energy advocate who founded the innovative Rocky Mountain Institute in Colorado, has been called a 'prophet and midwife' for what he terms 'natural capitalism': business enterprises which will value and preserve scarce natural resources if it is made profitable to do so. Natural capitalism is a theme which has appealed to successive US governments and corporations, largely because it does not entail a radical restructuring of the way society is organised. Lovins is one of the recipients of the Right Livelihood Foundation's awards – the 'Alternative Nobel Prizes'.

Tony Juniper, FoE's director of policy and campaigns, argues that 'environmentalists [should] oppose the excesses of big business tooth and nail' but should also 'work with the better companies even if it means compromise'.[37] He points to UK government regulations requiring occupational pension funds to define their ethical and environmental policies and to set out how they are to be implemented: 'it could be the first step in making social and environmental performance hit the bottom line of companies like BP-Amoco, BA and Rio Tinto.' Juniper provides the example of the energy sector where – as we saw in Chapter 4 – a few fossil fuel giants have made moves into renewables. 'BP-Amoco still needs pushing, but it is a company with whom dialogue has been shown to be productive.' Ironically, in the very same magazine in which Juniper presents his case for 'supping with the devil', Caspar Henderson reports that BP's 'solar investments have actually declined to less than 0.1 per cent of the overall company portfolio.' So much for productive dialogue. As Henderson warns: 'He who sups with the devil should be careful that he doesn't end up working full time in Hell's kitchen!'[38]

There *are* heartening examples of business enterprises introducing genuinely ethical and environmental policies: Solar Century (supplying solar electricity to household consumers), the Triodos Bank and organic producers. The problem is that these companies are rarely the big players dictating the direction of the global economy, a direction which has seen gains for an elite few, but losses for many more. The underlying disturbing story is that economic globalisation would not have been possible without governments making huge public subsidies available to private interests. Or, as Steven Gorelick puts it ironically in the title of his excellent 1999 report, *Small is Beautiful, Big is Subsidised*. For example, each of the 400 or so airports in the United States has received large sums of public money. Airports pay no corporation taxes, receive federal money for capital improvements and can borrow at low rates: all the better to promote long-distance travel and trade. Communications networks such as British Telecom, Japan's Nippon Telephone and Telegraph and Telefonica de Espana, crucial to the global economy, were often built up with government support before being privatised. Noam Chomsky has frequently highlighted the fact that the private sector, such as the aviation and computing industries, 'has relied on advanced technology that is readily transferred from military [i.e. publicly funded] to commercial use'.[39] As we saw in Chapter 4, fossil fuels and nuclear energy have received massive state support, to the detriment of small-scale renewable energy projects. Publicly funded road networks and large-scale infrastructure projects – dams, bridges and ports, for example – are growing to promote 'international competitiveness' and free trade. Large corporations tap into publicly funded scientific research to convert academic research results into commercial products, processes and services. Citizen dismay and outrage at such use of taxes, leading to social and environmental collapse, would surely be enormous if the message could be brought more forcibly into the public arena. This will undoubtedly form a core task for campaigners opposing economic globalisation and building democratic alternatives.

'Liberalisation' = corporate protectionism

At root must be the realisation that people have the power to change things. The present destructive course of economic globalisation can only be maintained as long as we are prepared to accept it and – worst of all – subsidise it with our own taxes. We are living in a welfare state, but one in which international investors and transnational corporations receive the handouts from the public purse. As Chomsky frequently points out, current structures are based on 'socialism for the rich and capitalism for the poor'. But we *can* build an alternative system – even if the first step is as simple as demanding fresh, local, sustainably-produced food. By forging anew the links between local producers and local consumers, an array of business-friendly props will simultaneously be exposed to public scrutiny: the destructive nature of long-distance transport, the massive subsidies paid to large-scale chemical agriculture, the corporate stranglehold of the food chain, the sustained poverty of agricultural workers in the South, and so on. The quest for good food may be one of the most rewarding – and certainly the most delicious – results of the war against globalisation.

If we want to see genuine sustainable development, it will mean not just *opposing* the WTO but *dismantling* all the large centralised state and corporate entities that are currently wreaking havoc on people and the planet. In the words of Susan George, 'it is fruitless to ask [transnational corporations] to do a little less harm: we have to oppose what they *are*'.[40] Most greens and other progressives would probably agree that it would be for the benefit of all to encourage – and even work with – the kind of locally-based small and medium-scale enterprise that demonstrates the capacity for ecological development and social justice. But to many environmentalists and leftists, the large corporations by their very nature are undemocratic, wielding far too much unaccountable power, and will have to be fought every step of the way if there is going to be a genuinely green future. Proposed measures to achieve such a future include limits on company size to prevent unfair competition, community reinvestment obligations, subsidies to promote local economies, tight regulation of company taxation and capital flows, and strict adherence to high standards of environmental, health and labour protection.

In response to immense public concern about economic globalisation, supporters of free trade institutions such as the WTO have pleaded that *more* liberalisation is require to help the South, in particular. Charlotte Denny, an economics correspondent at *The Guardian*, put it this way:

> The concerns of poor countries have gone largely unnoticed in the western media, crowded out by a coalition of western consumer and environmental lobbyists who are opposed to the very existence of the WTO. The third world's calls for market access and for the west to stop dumping the products of its subsidy-bloated farming sector on their economies are falling on deaf ears.[41]

Clare Short, the UK's International Development Secretary, called for the WTO Millennium Round to give priority to poor country development and even castigated public interest groups for jeopardising this. She argued that, 'the interests of the poor are unlikely to be centre stage in the next round [of WTO talks] if their natural allies – the development NGOs and the Western trade unions – are arguing that there shouldn't be a trade round at all'.[42] Or, as Mike Moore, WTO director-general, put it, 'The people who march[ed] in Seattle [were] marching against opportunities for poor countries to sell their products and services . . . the countries that have been more open have better human rights, better living standards and more commerce'.[43] Moore, of course, believes that liberalisation should be expanded to include yet more economic sectors. Speaking in response to concerns from South-based campaigners about the existing wide range of sectors already administered by the WTO, Moore responded impassively, 'I will not influence the developed countries against new issues'. He pointed out that the world economy is not standing still, providing the example of electronic commerce which, only a few years previously, was not a major medium. He agreed however that developing countries were facing problems trying to absorb policy changes: 'There are real problems of implementation for developing countries and we should focus on this.'[44]

Rubens Ricupero, secretary-general of the United Nations Conference on Trade and Development, makes the telling point that: 'Most developing countries have liberalised much more quickly in the last few years than developed countries, which have liberalised at a slow pace.'[45] Ricupero's comment about the relative pace of liberalisation in the North and South is an unwitting admission of the economic strategy of powerful corporate elites, namely: prising open untapped resources and markets in the South, while furiously resisting any attempt to counter their own protectionist measures. These measures include forming business alliances, corporate lobbying of politicians, and subsidising private enterprise at public expense (e.g. the fossil fuel and biotech industries). It is simply not plausible that TNCs and their political allies have poverty alleviation or environmental protection – rather than the opportunity for expansion of private profit – as core objectives. Nor can we argue with reference to the facts that both objectives – public-planetary wellbeing and private-corporate earnings – are even compatible. For the historical record points strongly to the following conclusion: that 'liberalisation' creates more losers than winners, and that the biggest winners tend to be the biggest companies and investors, while the biggest losers are those already at the bottom of the pile: the poor. To grant yet more opportunities for corporate growth to the elite would be akin to arming a serial killer with an impressive armoury of hi-tech weapons.

Protest or apathy?

This is all very well, you may think, but surely the vast majority of the public are just not interested in being 'radical'? Most people are struggling to scrape together a living, or are content – or resigned – to work long hours, collapsing in front of the television at the end of the day, perhaps after having finally managed to put the children to bed. When less than 30 per cent of the British electorate bother to vote in local council elections year after year, and only 23 per cent in the Euro elections of 1999, is there any realistic prospect of mass public interest in – never mind protest *against* – the forces that currently shape the way we lead our lives? This is an important question and one that is difficult to answer. However, it must be said that low voter turnouts are a sign that most of the public feels little or no connection with the politics spun to them by politicians and the media. This does not overly concern powerful politicians despite occasional rhetoric to the contrary, far less the privileged private interests who appear quite content to see low levels of grassroots involvement in electoral politics so as 'to protect the minority of the opulent against the majority', in the words of James Madison, the eighteenth century father of the American constitution.[46]

It is certainly true that it is difficult to bring to the public's attention the argument that all of today's major societal problems – poverty, homelessness, pollution, and so on – are interlinked and symptomatic of fundamental problems in capitalism. As we saw in Chapter 3, mainstream media channels – generally shaped by powerful corporate or state interests – carry swaths of mindless 'entertainment' which inhibit meaningful public debate about the unsustainable nature of the rich North's way of life. As for the tired old notion that 'the public gets what the public wants', it is worth recalling the views expressed by the 1962 Pilkington Report on the media:

...to give the public what it wants is a misleading phrase... it has the appearance of an appeal to democratic principle, but the appearance is deceptive. It is in fact patronizing and arrogant, in that it claims to know what the public is but defines it as no more than the mass audience, and it claims to know what it wants, but limits its choice to the average of experience.[47]

And so, in today's media climate of 'manufactured consent', changing the destructive course of economic globalisation is going to be the toughest task ever faced by campaigners of any persuasion.

But historical examples abound of seemingly hopeless attempts to achieve measures of social justice and environmental protection: the abolition of slavery in the United States; organising trade unions to protect workers' rights; the suffragette movement, giving women the right to vote; dramatically reducing urban air pollution by the passing of the 1956 Clean Air Act in Britain; the rise of the peace, women's and black movements in the 1960s; and the phasing out of CFCs which are destroying the ozone layer. Despite the hype of the West's political leaders and other promoters of planetary privatisation, globalisation is neither inevitable nor irreversible. But proving them wrong will involve much more civil activism than has been visible to date. Such activism will not necessarily entail higher turnouts at election time – in fact, much of the public will undoubtedly remain unmoved, indeed, repelled by the manoeuvring of vote-greedy politicians – but will certainly hinge on a greater level of participation in pressure groups, consumer boycotts, and direct action on the streets, in corporate headquarters and on the steps of government buildings. This is not to say that electing progressive politicians is unimportant. There is hope in this quarter from the growing presence of Greens in the European Parliament and governments around Europe, for example.

If transnational capitalism can indeed be likened to a cancerous growth, as David Korten and others have claimed, then it cannot help itself – it has to be stopped. Powerful investors, the heads of TNCs and world leaders will not do this on our behalf. They have to be made to stop – now. Throughout this book, we have encountered sustainable alternatives to economic globalisation based on the work of countless activists and campaigners and the knowledge of local communities everywhere. There is no one single obvious prescription, solution or methodology; we will be flying by the seat of our pants. As economist Robin Hahnel says, the bottom line is that 'what we are fighting for is merely the substitution of the human agenda for the corporate agenda'.[48] It is more vital to build a broad-based social movement than to have the correct 'model of alternative living' worked out in advance or even to have the right 'set of demands'. Organising opposition to economic globalisation is the first priority, because it must be stopped. But the success of each community fighting for its survival or activist group fighting for its own interests is crucially dependent on building links between them all. It is significant that global corporations and investors, worried about the rising grassroots movement, are now stepping up their attempt to drive a wedge between different groups in the 'anti-globalisation' camp – environmentalists in the North and development campaigners in the South, for example. Different 'constituencies' of activists must become aware that their own success is intimately connected to the successes of all the other constituencies that are resisting economic globalisation. Hahnel calls it the 'Lilliput strategy': each constituency does its level best to tie its own string to contain the 'Gulliver' of global capital, fully aware of 'how weak and vulnerable that single string is without the added strength of tens of thousands of similar strings'. The best hope lies in building a bottom-up movement based on grassroots organisations, trade unions, independent institutes and coalitions.[49]

'The worst of times and the best of times'

If it all sounds somewhat tenuous and ill-defined, that's because it is – so far. The progressive American writer Ted Glick says that, 'It is the worst of times, and it is the best of times'. The worst of times, because of massive injustice, poverty and environmental deterioration. 'Yet, it is the best of times because there are signs of hope, people organising and acting to change those conditions'.[50] Such encouraging signs will only occasionally, if sporadically, emerge in the mainstream media, for reasons that we discussed earlier in the book. It would not do, of course, to paint a true picture of the extent and depth of the overlapping progressive movements – based on concern for human rights and the environment – which both challenge the status quo and propose other ways of living. Nor are issues of genuine popular concern discussed substantively and consistently in the media or by politicians. As Chomsky says, 'the general population, as polls make very clear, is strongly opposed to most of what's going on, but the issues don't arise in [elections]'. This is the stark reality of life in 'democratic' societies today. If citizens get uppity and rip up GM crops, demand an end to the arms trade or oppose oppressive police legislation – even when such protest is completely non-violent – it becomes a 'crisis of democracy' for elite politicians, corporate chiefs and their apologists in the media. [51]

There does not have to be – nor *can* there be – a detailed road map of 'how to get from here to there'. Nor should we heed those who say to people struggling for radical change that 'there is no alternative' (to dredge up Margaret Thatcher's infamous phrase once again) or that 'your view is utopian/unworkable/impractical'. Such remarks typically emanate from those who benefit from the current inequitable system of global capitalism, or those whose imagination and freedom have been bludgeoned by the propaganda system that supports, and is an intrinsic part of, that same system. Small-scale initiatives in sustainable living – communities of people 'living lightly', mainly in the rich North – are welcome and worthwhile, but will always remain marginal unless the issue of power in society is addressed and rectified. How else are the billions of people in the world, particularly in the South, going to have the resources and freedom to lift themselves out of poverty and oppression?

Susan George compares the present situation with the pre-revolutionary days of France and the United States in the mid-eighteenth century:

> They too were groping, not entirely sure how to get out from under an absolutist monarchy and move to a national democracy; to change their status from subjects to citizens. They didn't have a perfect blueprint (no one ever has) and finally they had to fight.[52]

The difference between then and now, I hope, is that the ongoing struggle will be non-violent. It will certainly be necessary. The prize is the planet itself.

Notes

1   *The Ecologist*, Vol. 29, No. 3, p. 200.
2   Email summary from the Institute of Public Accuracy, Washington, DC, December 6, 1999.
3   George, *The Lugano Report,* p. 184.
4   Helena Norberg-Hodge, *The Ecologist*, Vol. 29, No. 3, p. 200.
5   *Ibid.*, p. 200.
6   Noam Chomsky, 'Hordes of Vigilantes & Popular Elements Defeat MAI, for now', www.zmag.org/hordes_of_vigilantes.htm
7   Press release from the Green Group in the European Parliament, Brussels, 14 June, 1999.
8   See Balanyá *et al., Europe, Inc.*, ch. 8.
9   Woodin, *Protecting Our Future*, p.3.
10 James Petras, *Z Magazine*, March 2000, pp. 32-36.
11 Justin Podur, www.zmag.org/chiapas1/rebessay.htm
12 Harry Cleaver, www.eco.utexas.edu/Homepages/Faculty/Cleaver/lessons.html
13 *The Independent*, May 13, 1999.
14 *The Big Issue,* June 7-13, 1999, p. 10.
15 *Independent on Sunday,* 20 June, 1999.
16 Quoted in *SchNEWS,* 25 June, 1999.
17 Quoted in *Independent on Sunday*, 20 June, 1999.
18 *SchNEWS,* 25 June, 1999.
19 *The Guardian*, 6 October, 1999.
20 *Ibid.*
21 *Independent on Sunday*, 5 December, 1999.
22 See www.agp.org/agp/en/PGAInfos/980516india.html
23 Website of European coordination office: http://stad.dsl.nl/~caravan
24 Quoted in *The Big Issue,* June 7-13, 1999, p. 11.
25 Paul Kingsnorth, *The Ecologist,* Vol. 29, No. 3, pp. 203-4.
26 Monbiot, *No Man's Land.*

27   David Orr, *The Ecologist,* Vol. 29, No. 3, pp. 232.

28   Polly Ghazi, *Resurgence*, May/June 1999, pp. 46-48.

29   Kalle Lasn, *The Ecologist*, Vol. 29, No. 3, p. 221.

30   *Ibid.,* p. 221.

31   uk-anti-maif e-mail conference, 6 October, 1998.

32   Katharine Ainger, *New Internationalist*, November 1998, p. 28.

33   *The Guardian*, 19 November, 1998.

34   *The Independent*, 19 March, 1999.

35   *The Guardian,* 7 December, 1999.

36   *The Guardian*, 19 November, 1998.

37   *Earth Matters*, Issue 43, Summer 1999, pp. 10-12.

38   Personal communication, 24 August, 1999.

39   Chomsky, *Powers and Prospects*, p. 122.

40   George, *The Lugano Report,* p. 183.

41   *The Guardian,* 17 November, 1999.

42   *Ibid.*

43   *Financial Times,* 3 September, 1999.

44   G77 Meeting in Marrakech, 14-16 September, 1999, reported by Martin Khor, Third World Network.

45   *Ibid.*

46   Quoted in Chomsky, *Powers and Prospects*, p. 117.

47   Curran and Seaton, *Power Without Responsibility*, p. 178.

48   Hahnel, *Panic Rules!*, p. 102.

49   *Ibid.,* p. 103.

50   Ted Glick, *Z Magazine,* February 2000, p. 15.

51   Noam Chomsky, speech given at Kiva Auditorium, Albuquerque, New Mexico, February 26, 2000, www.zmag.org/chomskyalbaq.htm

52   George, *The Lugano Report,* p. 183.

BIBLIOGRAPHY AND FURTHER READING

Achbar, Mark (ed.), *Manufacturing Consent: Noam Chomsky and the Media* (Black Rose Books, Montréal, 1994).

Albert, Michael, *Thinking Forward: Learning to Conceptualize Economic Vision* (Arbeiter Ring, Winnipeg, 1997).

Armstrong, Alan D., *To Restrain the Red Horse: The Urgent Need for Radical Economic Reform* (Towerhouse Publishing, Dunoon, 1996).

Arnove, Anthony (ed.), *Iraq Under Siege: The Deadly Impact of Sanctions and War* (Pluto Press, London, 2000).

Athanasiou, Tom, *Slow Reckoning: The Ecology of a Divided Planet* (Secker and Warburg, London, 1996).

Balanyá, Belén, Ann Doherty, Olivier Hoedeman, Adam Ma'anit and Erik Wesselius, *Europe, Inc.: Regional and Global Restructuring and the Rise of Global Power* (Pluto Press, London, 2000).

Bates, Clive and Persephone Watkins, The Potential for Sustainable Energy in the UK: A survey of recent literature for Greenpeace UK (International Institute for Energy Conservation, London, 1997).

Baumann, Miges, Janet Bell, Floriane Koechlin and Michel Pimbert, *The Life Industry: Biodiversity, people and profits* (Intermediate Technology Publications, London, 1996).

Beder, Sharon, *Global Spin: The Corporate Assault on Environmentalism* (Green Books, Totnes, 1997).

Berman, Daniel M. and John T. O'Connor, *Who Owns the Sun? People, Politics and the Struggle for a Solar Economy* (Chelsea Green, White River Junction, 1996).

Berry, Wendell, *Standing on Earth – Selected Essays* (Golgonooza Press, Ipswich, 1991).

Bodley, John, *Victims of Progress* (Mayfield Publishing, Palo Alto, 1982).

Bookchin, Murray, *The Ecology of Freedom: The Emergence and Dissolution of Hierarchy* (Black Rose Books, Montréal, 1995).

Border Wind, *Offshore Wind Energy – Building a New Industry for Britain* (Border Wind, Hexham, 1998).

Boyle, David, *Funny Money: In Search of Alternative Cash* (HarperCollins, London, 1999).

Cato, Molly Scott and Miriam Kennett, *Green Economics: Beyond Supply and Demand to Meeting People's Needs* (Green Audit, Aberystwyth, 1999).

Chomsky, Noam, *Deterring Democracy* (Hill and Wang, New York, 1992).

Chomsky, Noam, *A New Generation Draws the Line: Kosovo, East Timor and the Standards of the West* (Verso, London, 2000).

Chomsky, Noam, *The New Military Humanism: Lessons from Kosovo* (Pluto Press, London, 1999).

Chomsky, Noam, *Powers and Prospects: Reflections on Human Nature and the Social Order* (Pluto Press, London, 1996).

Chomsky, Noam, *Rogue States: The Rule of Force in World Affairs* (Pluto Press, London, 2000).

Chomsky, Noam, *Turning the Tide: US Intervention in Central America and the Struggle for Peace* (Pluto Press, London, 1985).

Chomsky, Noam, *World Orders, Old and New* (Pluto Press, London, 1997).

Cohen, Nick, *Cruel Britannia: Reports on the Sinister and the Preposterous* (Verso, London, 2000).

Connelly, James and Graham Smith, *Politics and the Environment: From Theory to Practice* (Routledge, London, 1999).

Coyle, Diane, *The Weightless World* (Capstone, London, 1997).

Cramb, Auslan, *Who Owns Scotland Now? The Use and Abuse of Private Land* (Mainstream Publishing, Edinburgh, 1996).

Curran, James and Jean Seaton, *Power without Responsibility: The Press and Broadcasting in Britain*, fifth edition (Routledge, London, 1997).

Curtis, Mark, *The Ambiguities of Power: British Foreign Policy Since 1945* (Zed Books, London, 1995).

Curtis, Mark, *The Great Deception* (Pluto Press, London, 1998).

Douthwaite, Richard, *Short Circuit: Strengthening Local Economics for Security in an Unstable World* (Green Books, Totnes, 1996).

Douthwaite, Richard, *The Growth Illusion: How Economic Growth Has Enriched the Few, Impoverished the Many, and Endangered the Planet,* updated edition (Green Books, Totnes, 1999).

Edwards, David, *The Compassionate Revolution: Radical Politics and Buddhism*, (Green Books, Totnes, 1998).

Edwards, David, *Free to be Human: Intellectual Self-Defence in an Age of Illusions* (Green Books, Totnes, 1995).

Girardet, Herbert, *Creating Sustainable Cities*, Schumacher Briefing No. 2 (Green Books, Totnes, 1999).

Gelbspan, Ross, *The Heat Is On: The Climate Crisis, The Cover-Up, The Prescription* (Perseus Books, Reading, 1998).

George, Susan, *How The Other Half Dies: The Real Reasons for World Hunger* (Penguin, London, 1991).

George, Susan, *The Lugano Report: On Preserving Capitalism in the Twenty-first Century* (Pluto Press, London, 1999).

Goldman, Michael (ed.), *Privatizing Nature: Political Struggles for the Global Commons*

(Pluto Press, London, 1998).

Gore, Al, *Earth in the Balance* (Plume, New York, 1993).

Gorelick, Steven (principal author), *Small is Beautiful, Big is Subsidised* (The International Society for Ecology and Culture, Dartington, 1998).

Greenpeace International, *Danish Wind Energy: An Industrial Success Story* (Greenpeace International, Amsterdam, 1998).

Hahnel, Robin, *Panic Rules! Everything You Need to Know About the Global Economy* (South End Press, Cambridge MA, 1999).

Hare, Bill, *Fossil Fuels and Climate Protection: The Carbon Logic* (Greenpeace International, Amsterdam, 1997).

Harvey, Graham, *The Killing of the Countryside* (Jonathan Cape, London, 1997).

Henderson, Hazel, *The Politics of the Solar Age: Alternatives to Economics* (Knowledge Systems, Indianapolis, 1988).

Herman, Edward S., *The Real Terror Network: Terrorism in Fact and Fiction* (South End Press, Boston, 1982).

Herman, Edward S. and Noam Chomsky, *Manufacturing Consent: The Political Economy of the Mass Media* (Pantheon, New York, 1988).

Hilary, John, *Globalisation and Employment – New Opportunities, Real Threats*, Panos Briefing No. 33, May 1999.

Hines, Colin, *Localization: A Global Manifesto* (Earthscan, London, 2000).

Hunter, James, *A Dance Called America: The Scottish Highlands, the United States and Canada* (Mainstream Publishing, Edinburgh, 1994).

Hunter, James, *On the Other Side of Sorrow: Nature and People in the Scottish Highlands* (Mainstream Publishing, Edinburgh, 1995).

Hutton, Will, *The State We're In* (Vintage, London, 1996).

Hutchinson, Frances, *What Everybody Really Wants to Know About Money* (Jon Carpenter, Charlbury, 1998).

IPCC, *Climate Change 1995. The Science of Climate Change. Contribution of Working Group I to the Second Assessment Report of the Intergovernmental Panel on Climate Change* (Cambridge University Press, Cambridge, 1996).

Jacobs, Michael, *The Politics of the Real World: Meeting the New Century* (Earthscan, London, 1996).

Knudtson, Peter and David Suzuki, *Wisdom of the Elders* (Stoddart, Toronto, 1993).

Korten, David C., *When Corporations Rule the World* (Earthscan, London, 1996).

Korten, David C., *The Post-Corporate World* (WorldView Publications, Oxford, 1999).

Lambert, Jean, *No Change? No Chance! The Politics of Choosing Green* (Jon Carpenter, Charlbury, 1997).

Lang, Tim and Colin Hines, *The New Protectionism* (Earthscan, London, 1993).

Leggett, Jeremy, *The Carbon War: Dispatches from the End of the Oil Century* (Allen Lane, London, 1999).

Lon, Jonathan (ed.), *Living Planet Report 1998 – Overconsumption is driving the rapid decline of the world's natural environments* (World Wide Fund for Nature International, Gland, Switzerland, 1998).

Lovelock, James, *Gaia: A New Look at Life on Earth* (Oxford University Press, Oxford, 1979).

McChesney, Robert W., *Rich Media, Poor Democracy: Communication Politics in Dubious Times* (The New Press, New York, 2000)

Mackenzie, R.F., *A Search for Scotland* (Fontana, London, 1991).

McKibben, Bill, *The End of Nature* (Penguin, London, 1990).

McLaren, Duncan, Simon Bullock and Nusrat Yousuf, *Tomorrow's World* (Earthscan, London, 1998).

Mander, Jerry and Edward Goldsmith, *The Case Against the Global Economy: And for a Turn Toward the Local* (Sierra Club Books, San Francisco, 1996).

Meyer, Aubrey, *Contraction and Convergence: a Global Framework to Cope with Climate Change*, Schumacher Briefing No. 5 (Green Books, Totnes, 2000).

Monbiot, George, *Captive State: The Corporate Takeover of Britain* (Macmillan, London, 2000)

Monbiot, George, *No Man's Land: An Investigative Journey Through Kenya and Tanzania* (Picador, London, 1994).

Ormerod, Paul, *The Death of Economics* (Faber and Faber, London, 1994).

Parkin, Sara, *Green Futures* (Fount, London, 1991).

Pilger, John, *Distant Voices* (Vintage, London, 1994).

Pilger, John, *Hidden Agendas* (Vintage, London, 1998).

Rai, Milan, *Chomsky's Politics* (Verso, London, 1995).

Rifkin, Jeremy, *The End of Work: The Decline of the Global Labor Force and the Dawn of the Post-Market Era* (G.P. Putnam's Sons, New York, 1995).

Robertson, James, *Future Wealth* (Cassell, London, 1989).

Robertson, James, *Transforming Economic Life: A Millennial Challenge*, Schumacher Briefing No. 1 (Green Books, Totnes, 1998).

Rowbotham, Michael, *The Grip of Death: A study of Modern Money, Debt Slavery and Destructive Economics* (Jon Carpenter, Charlbury, 1998).

Schumacher, E.F., *Small is Beautiful: A Study of Economics as if People Mattered* (Abacus, London, 1973).

Schumacher, E.F., *A Guide for the Perplexed* (Abacus, London, 1977).

Schwarz, Walter and Dorothy, *Living Lightly: Travels in Post-Consumer Society* (Jon Carpenter, Charlbury, 1998).

Shell International, *Profits and Principles – does there have to be a choice? The Shell Report – 1998*, (London, 1998).

Shiva, Vandana, *Biopiracy: the Plunder of Nature of Knowledge* (Green Books, Totnes, 1998).

Smith, Adam, *Wealth of Nations* (Penguin, London, 1986).

UN Development Programme, *Human Development Report 1998* (Oxford University Press, Oxford, 1998).

Woodin, Mike, *Protecting Our Future – Environment Policy for the European Union*, Green Briefings, European Series 4, (Green Party of England and Wales, London, 1999).

Zinn, Howard, *The Zinn Reader – Writings on Disobedience and Democracy* (Seven Stories Press, New York, 1997).

INDEX

The Grip of Death

A study of modern money, debt slavery and destructive economics

Michael Rowbotham

This lucid and original account of where our money comes from explains why most people, businesses and countries are so heavily in debt. It concerns subjects very close to home: mortgages, building societies and banks, food and farming, transport, worldwide poverty, and what's on the supermarket shelf.

It explains —

• why virtually all the money in the world economy has been created as a debt; why only 3% of UK money exists as 'legal tender'; and why in a world reliant upon money created as debt, we are kept perpetually short of money.

• how and why mortgages are responsible for almost two-thirds of the total money stock in the UK, and 80% in the US.

• why business and corporate debt is at its highest level ever.

• why debts mean that a small farm can be *productively* very efficient, but *financially* not 'viable'.

• why national debts can never be paid off — without monetary reform.

• how debt fuels the 'need to grow', revolutionising national and global transport strategies, destroying local markets and producers and increasing waste, pollution and resource consumption.

• how 'Third World debt' is a mechanism used by the developed nations to inject ever-increasing amounts of money into their own economies, and why debtor nations can never repay the debts.

• why politicians who rely on the banks for money can't fund public services.

• why 'debt-money' is undemocratic and a threat to human rights.

The author proposes a new mechanism for the supply of money, creating a supportive financial environment and a decreasing reliance on debt.

Michael Rowbotham is a teacher and writer.

£15 pbk 352pp 1 897766 40 8

Second printing, 2000

Goodbye America!

Globalisation, debt and the dollar empire

Michael Rowbotham

This penetrating analysis of globalisation looks to a future where Third World debt, corporate power, the US dollar and the 'Washington consensus' no longer dominate global economic policy.

The book analyses globalisation and the international debt crisis as aspects of modern economic imperialism. The history of Third World debt, its origin in unjust trade and its monetary structure are explored; this confirms that developing nations do not carry true 'international' debts. In fact their debts reflect the failure of such institutions as the IMF and World Bank and the inadequacy of trade accountancy and financial systems.

To secure IMF and World Bank loans the developing nations have, for years, been obliged to submit to the demands of free-market deregulatory economic policies. This blatantly corporate-friendly agenda – the 'Washington consensus' – has exposed the entire developing world to the commercial aspirations of powerful multinationals, imposing the 'hard' currency of the US dollar.

Michael Rowbotham argues that the developing nations should be released from debts that lack both economic and moral validity. The options for full debt cancellation are discussed, and the generally positive impact of this throughout the global economy is stressed. Cancellation would enable developing nations to regain control over their economic policy, focus attention on their domestic needs and pursue more stable pathways to social progress. This would allow a new, more distributed balance of power to emerge at the international level and encourage more localised, resource-efficient commerce.

The book also explores a range of reforms, including new systems of trade accountancy, a new 'financial architecture' covering investment and lending, and a new development model for the emerging nations.

£11 paperback   216pp   1 897766 56 4

REVIEWS OF *THE GRIP OF DEATH*

A powerful exploration of a complex and important issue and deserves to be read widely.
Times Literary Supplement

A work to be cherished... stands out not only for the quality of the research and the writing, but for the compelling vision that it unfolds.   *Economic Reform.*

Places him on a par with the social reforming economists E. F. Schumacher and Henry George. *The Ecologist*

A radical, shocking and eye-opening exposé of how our monetary system really works.
New Internationalist
